In the so-called "concessions" of the treaty ports Tientsin and Shanghai, foreigners live off the fat of the land. They are exempt from Chinese taxes, they stand above Chinese law. And all quite above board, their garrisons and police are there in force to protect their special status. To third generation settlers this world of privilege is the only world they know, so all the greater the shock when the unequal treaties are abrogated and they find themselves outsiders, held as contemptible as their grandparents against whom the Boxers rose in such bloody revolt.

D1547538

吃麵不擱鹵
炮打交民巷
吃麵不擱滷
炮打英國府
吃麵不擱醋
炮打西什庫

Battle cry of the Boxers, China's Freedom Fighters of 1900

Never mind soya for our noodles,
We're going to smash the Legation Quarter.
Never mind gravy for our noodles,
We're going to smash the British Embassy.
Never mind vinegar for our noodles,
We're going to smash the West Arsenal.

(The ringing rhyme is lost in translation, but not the message.)

i

LITTLE FOREIGN DEVIL

Desmond Power

Pangli Imprint

Second printing December 1996

Canadian Cataloguing in Publication Data

Power, Desmond,   1923–
  Little foreign devil

    ISBN   0–9694122–1–5

  1. Power, Desmond, 1923- 2. World War, 1939-1945--
Personal narratives, British. 3. World War, 1939-1945--
Prisons and prisoners, Japanese. 4. World War, 1939-1945--
China--Tientsin. 5. Prisoners of war--Great Britain--
Biography. 6. Prisoners of war--China--Tientsin--Biography.
7. Tientsin (China)--Biography. 8. China--History--Republic,
1912-1949. I. Title.
D805.C5P68 1996   940.53'175114'092   C95-911002-X

Scanning and film work by:

        North Shore Imagesetting Ltd., North Vancouver, BC.

        Point Blank Communications Ltd., Vancouver, BC.

Printed and bound in Canada by:

        Hignell Printing Ltd., Winnipeg, Manitoba.

Published by:

        Pangli Imprint,
        Suite 212 - 1489 Marine Drive,
        West Vancouver, B C.   Fax/Phone: (604) 925 1508
        Canada.   V7T 1B8   E-mail: pangli@bookwright.com

Author's Comments

The events described in this book are for the most part drawn from memory. But a half-century has lapsed, and it is only natural that some details, such as players' names, have become hazy, if not lost altogether. So I apologize to any who might recognize themselves but not the names I've invented for them, just as I regret giving scant mention or even none at all to those who indeed were very much present.

Then there's the business of spelling Chinese words in English. It seems common practice nowadays to refer to the capital of China as "Beijing," which is how it is pronounced in Mandarin and written out according to the Pinyin method of transcription. And more and more you hear people, who would never dream of calling Paris "Paree," bravely attempting "Tianjin" for Tientsin and "Guangzhou" for Canton. It's quite on the cards then that come 1997, good old "Hong Kong" will give way to the impossible tongue-twister – "Xiang-gang." All a bit much, I would suspect, for Old China Hands. So in deference to the relics of that fast disappearing breed I'll stick with the old way of transcribing the names of persons and places; hence Pootung, Lunghua, Weihsien, and so on.

From ancient times Tientsin's official designation:
"The Bastion at the Heavenly Ford."

CONTENTS

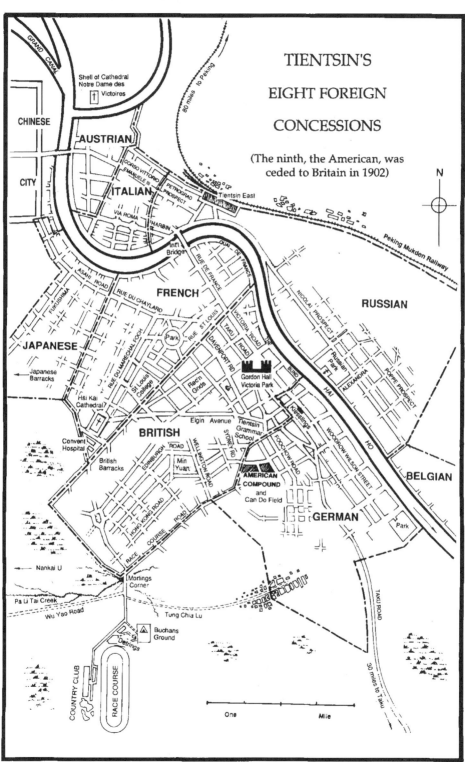

TIENTSIN'S

EIGHT FOREIGN

CONCESSIONS

(The ninth, the American, was
ceded to Britain in 1902)

N

GRAND CANAL

Shell of Cathedral
Notre Dame des
Victoires

CHINESE

CITY

AUSTRIAN

80 miles to Peking

CORSO VITTORIO
EMANUELE III

PETROGRAD PROSPECT

ITALIAN

Tientsin East

VIA ROMA

HARBIN

Int'l
Bridge

RUE DE FRANCE

QUAI DE FRANCE

Peking Mukden Railway

ASAHI ROAD

RUE DU CHAYLARD

FRENCH

NICOLAI PROSPECT

RUSSIAN

FUKUSHIMA

Park

RUE ST LOUIS

VICTORIA ROAD

TAKU ROAD

Russian
Park

JAPANESE

RUE DU MARECHAL FOCH

DAVENPORT RD

BUND

POPPE PROSPECT

Japanese
Barracks

St Louis
College

Racn
Grds

Gordon Hall
Victoria Park

ALEXANDRA

HAI

Hsi Kai
Cathedral

Elgin Avenue

Tientsin
Grammar
School

Kiesslings

WOODROW WILSON STREET

HO

Convent
Hospital

BRITISH

WELLINGTON ROAD

SYDNEY RD

FOOCHOW ROAD

BELGIAN

British
Barracks

EDINBURGH
ROAD

Min
Yuan

AMERICAN
COMPOUND

and
Can Do Field

HONG KONG ROAD

ROAD

GERMAN

Park

RACE COURSE ROAD

Nankai U

Morlings
Corner

TAKU ROAD

Pa Li Tai Creek

Wu Yao Road

Tung Chia Lu

Buchans
Ground

Detrings

30 miles to Taku

COUNTRY CLUB

RACE COURSE

One   Mile

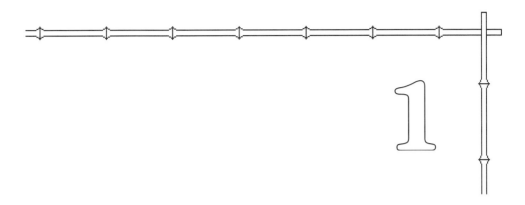

TAI-TAI'S WORD IS LAW

"RUN, MAN, RUN FOR IT," Murat hollers, Igor hollers, they all holler.

For me it's now or never. In one bound I'm out of my amah's reach, and as I race away, ringing volleys of her Cantonese – absurd guttural to a Mandarin-trained ear – throw me into a fit of giggles.

Most of the gang are already there in the *tingzi*, the summer pavilion, Victoria Park's centerpiece, when I bound up the shallow steps two at a time.

"Kick-the-can."

"Bobbies-and-thieves."

"Catchers."

"Kick-the-can."

"Kick-the-can it is."

"No hiding near amahs' corner," proclaims Jim Paisley, who knows his amah will have him by the ear if he ventures within reach. His words are aimed at Igor and Kolya and those others without amahs who forever take unfair advantage, sneaking behind the benches where those chattering harridans congregate.

"No fair hiding in Gordon Hall," Igor Kapoostin snaps back, and with good reason; Jim has the run of the place. The ground floor of that castle-like building is the British Municipal Council's central police station, and Chief Inspector Paisley of the BMC Police happens to be Jim's father. Besides, there is an aura of a shrine about the Gordon Hall, which only thirty years back served as the last-ditch defense when the settlement came so perilously

1

close to being overrun by the Boxer horde.

"Okay, who's *it*?"

"Stone – paper – scissors."

"Right. Alioshka, you and Igor start."

"Hurry, running out of time."

Alioshka is *it* and we're off. I slip through a hedge and run smack into "Tiger." Unlike other Chinese who come daily to the park to perform their grotesque slow-motion shadow-boxing exercises or meditate over their caged song birds, this strange eccentric wanders the gravel paths singing to himself in a tinny falsetto. "Eccentric" is perhaps too generous a term for someone who swallows live grasshoppers and praying mantises. Not only is he quite mad, he tries to involve us in his madness. Without warning, he'll burst into our midst holding out a wriggling insect for us to try. And that's enough to send us shrieking for our lives. But we know how to get even. We creep up from behind and yell, "Tiger! Tiger!" His eyes pop with terror, and he bolts for the gate, taunted all the way by our jeers and catcalls.

But on this particular afternoon he has me cold. He trumpets into my ear: "Devil! Little Foreign Devil! I'm going to cut your heart out and feed it to the crows." In a frenzy I catapult from his grasp and dart for the man-made hillock where I know his ankle-length gown will slow him to a standstill. Even so, I lie low among the ants and spiders till the danger has passed. First thing I see when the coast is clear is Aliosha combing the benches along the Victoria Road perimeter. His three prisoners, Kolya, Achmet and Marcel, are pacing the pavilion. And there, naked on the gravel walkway, begging to be kicked, is the can. I don't make my move. I wait breathlessly for Aliosha to draw farther away. He does. I'm just about to spring to my feet when Dwight Anderson, drat the fellow, emerges from behind the cenotaph, crying: "Pax! Pax! Gettin' late, gotta go." Others come out of hiding. It's all over. Time to face the amahs, that flock of magpies, still squawking their heads off over our decampment.

We go our different ways, Murat and Achmet to their lane off Cousins Road, Igor and Kolya to the Bund where a penny sampan will take them across to the Russian side, Karl to the German Concession, Marcel to the French, Dwight to the American Compound. While Jim Paisley's amah is giving him what for, I tag along behind Yi-jie. And

Gordon Hall towers over the tingzi in Victoria Park

I do so because Tai-tai has given the word, and Tai-tai's word is law. No good pleading that at seven I'm too old for an amah. If I want to go to the park, I go with Yi-jie, and nothing more to be said. But there is more, surely there is. I can say to myself, can't I, that Yi-jie is not really her name, it's her title, a glorified title standing for "Number One Elder Sister." Some sister! She's as ancient as the hills. And testy too. She could teach the Empress Dowager a thing or two. Just look at her now staging a tantrum as she maneuvers the pram containing two-year-old Tony through the sidewalk's jostling mass. At the curb on Taku Road her claw-like hand snatches hold of mine and pinions it to the pram's push bar. And thus we stand waiting for a break in the bedlam of cars, rickshaws, bicycles, and produce carts hauled by mules, by coolies, by combined teams of both. When at last a break does occur, she launches us across with a shrieking "*zou-zou-zou.*" Though she can only waddle on shriveled hooves (her feet have been bound since infancy), we cross safely, her fiery Cantonese threats keeping at bay even the boldest of the coolies, barrow boys, muleteers.

Into Meadows Road, comparative peace and quiet, for this is the start of the concession's residential area – suburban Hampstead transplanted onto the salt flats of northeastern Hopei. As we progress past the hallowed stonework entrance of All Saints Church, a brace of beggar boys who've had no luck with a kilted swell of the Royal Scots Regiment turn their attention on us. A shrill

3

Ageless Yi-jie

blast from Yi-jie sends them scurrying for their lives. After that, except for the occasional street hawker and plodding rickshaw, nothing to impede us all the way to the front gate of our three-storied, red-brick house on Edinburgh Road. But that's as far as we get. Standing there, blocking the entrance, is next door neighbor's Number Three Son Frankie Butterworth.

"*Huijia, huijia* – Go home, go home," Yi-jie yells at him. Then she rounds on me. "No running away, or you'll get what's coming to you."

Though a few months younger than I, Frankie is taller, heavier. I never know how to take him. Sometimes he'll make me an offering of a cigarette card still fragrant with Virginia navy cut. Sometimes he'll pick a fight over nothing.

Today he has adventure in mind. Ignoring Yi-jie's outburst, he says to me: "Let's go Min Yuan throw spears." And for added enticement he brandishes one of those sawn-off javelins the Russian groundsmen stick into the hard-packed earth to mark the cricket pitch boundary.

I switch my gaze from the enticing spear to the enticing grounds of Min Yuan Athletic Park situated right across the road from where we are standing.

"Well, what about it?" Frankie challenges.

"Yi-jie won't let me."

"Tell her to go suck eggs. Come on, you have first go."

"I can?"

"You bet." He presents the spear. "Go on, take it."

With one hand I grip the shaft. With the other I touch the steel point. It's a real spear all right, a lance. I snap to attention pressing the shaft hard against the hollow of my shoulder. I advance a step, couching the weapon as they do in the cavalry. I am a lancer. I am Captain Desmond Fitzdesmond VC of the Third Bengal Lancers . . .

Frankie suddenly lets out an electrifying call: "Charge of the Light Brigade!"

"Charge! Charge!" the lancers' battle cry bursts from my lips.

We are across the street. We are squeezing ourselves sideways through the perimeter railing into the grounds when a harsh voice, harsher than a ship's siren, blasts the air: "Flankee, you no gotta ear! All leddy soon dark outside. You no come, my callee Jimmy give you big stick!"

In a flash Frankie and precious spear are gone. His

4

mother is the one living person in the world he holds in dread. And no wonder – a fiery native of Swatow, when she cuts loose the crows flap away in great flocks.

How different his father, a reed thin Englishman with watery blue eyes and peeled almond head. On the rare occasion that I've heard him speak, he sounds just like the voice on that record: *Sahm, Sahm, pick up thar moosket*. He is a Customs man – outside staff – as once was my own father, Stephen Power. Though of tender age, I am already used to the idea that Customs people rank low in the community, just as I am aware that regard for our family is diminished because Tai-tai works for a living.

The Customs connection isn't the only thing we have in common with the Butterworths. They, like us, are five boys and a girl; though it must be said that we're not all Powers. Father died in 1924 when I was only one. Three years later Tai-tai married James Henry Lambert (pure coincidence that *Lambert* was her father's middle name), an NCO in the Loyals who bought himself out of the army while serving in Tientsin. In time my half-brother Tony came along, then Betty, so while there are six Butterworths, we are really four Powers and two Lamberts.

But never mind, we Powers and Lamberts get on pretty

5

well together. There is never the friction one hears about when a step-parent enters the family scene. Yet we Power boys can never bring ourselves to call Mr Lambert "Dad." He is "*Doong Ji*" to us, a mispronunciation of *Dongjia* – Master of the House, the term given him by the servants.

But back to the "Swatow" dragon. The tongue-lashing she is giving Frankie is getting fiercer by the minute. It's bound to alert Tai-tai, put her on the warpath. I'd be safer indoors facing the end-of-day scrimmage with my three older brothers, Pat, Brian, Jocelyn, in the common room we call "Madison Square Garden."

Pat is holding forth on his day's main event: "I saw Joe Grandon land a giant catfish on the Bund this afternoon," and he stretches out his hands as wide as they can go.

And Jocelyn, not to be outdone: "On Rue Pasteur I was nearly trampled by a company of Annamites marching at the double with fixed bayonets."

"Who swiped *All Quiet on the Western Front*?"

Dead silence.

"Who threw darts at Benjamin Colling's banjo? I'll kill him."

"Not me."

"Don't look at me."

"*Kai fan! Kai fan!*" Our Number Two Boy, Kui Hsiang, storms in with our dinner – bowls of rice topped with mince and greens and bean sauce.

We gather around the table. We eat coolie fashion, bowls to lips, chopsticks working like shovels.

Afterwards, each to his own thing: a tattered story book, a scratchy crystal set, a phalanx of lead soldiers. Then all too soon, Yi-jie, shuffling in like a lame Zouave, threatens and cajoles. Jocelyn and I are obliged to mount the stairs to our bedroom on the third floor.

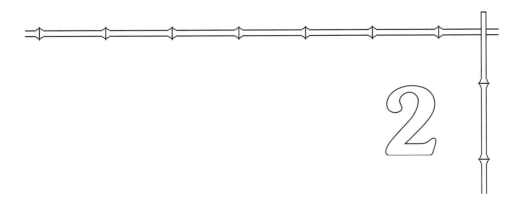

NO PLACE LIKE HOME

R IGHT AFTER TIFFIN, at one in the afternoon, I am tiptoeing out of the backyard when an ear-piercing shriek shatters the siesta stillness. I should have known that Jie-jie, Yi-jie's busy-body of a daughter-in-law, would be standing watch. And now as if on signal, like a treeful of summer cicadas, they all join in – Yi-jie, her son Ah Chin, her granddaughter Ah Kwun, and surely half the servant population of Edinburgh Road. Talk about Cantonese opera, and me center stage! Not a hope in Hades I can escape the ordeal of tea at Dicky Marsh's.

"Why me? Why must it always be me? Why not send Joss?" I plead with Tai-tai.

"Count yourself lucky, Desmond, that of all the boys in the concession *you* are the one Mrs Marsh has singled out to be Dicky's companion. Do I need to keep reminding you that Mr Marsh is taipan of ICI? Like it or not, you're going to the Marsh's today. And I don't want you looking like a ragamuffin. Pull up your socks. Haven't you got garters? And you'd better remember your manners. Always refuse a second helping. Always say 'thank you' when you leave."

Why did *I* have to thank *them* when I was the one making the sacrifice? Every second of my freedom was precious to me. Besides, Dicky wasn't one of us. He spoke a different form of English. Even if he hadn't that lisp, I would have found him hard to follow. And what an alien world his home! Though the Marshes must have employed servants, I never set eyes on a single one. It was always Mrs Marsh who received me at the door. Sure of one thing, 7

though, Dicky had no amah. His mother was his amah – strange! She was the one who served tea, and tea in the Marsh household wasn't just bread and margarine and jam; it was a full blown meal – fish and potatoes and pudding, the sort of thing you ate with knife and fork. What's more, they put a glass of milk in front of you. Milk! Ugh! With my Chinese palate I had to force myself to drink it. Why wouldn't the Marshes know that dairy products of any kind are abhorred across the length and breadth of China?

After tea, more often than not, Dicky would get out his working model steam engine and set about amazing me with his grown-up's knowledge of the thing. He not only knew the name of each individual component, he knew its function. He could make the engine puff and blow and pump at eye-boggling speed, even induce it to sound off its whistle. Sometimes he'd call his father to show him some new thing he'd got the engine to do, and the two would put their heads together in man-to-man talk.

When it came time to go – poor Dicky had to prepare himself for bed while it was still light outside – his mother would escort me to the door. And when, under Tai-tai's strict reminder, I asked if Dicky could come to our place for chow, she would look the other way and mumble something about Dicky having to accompany Mr Marsh to the Country Club, or that he had to be at All Saints Church for his confirmation instruction, or something of the kind.

On the road home, dribbling a pebble along the curb, I breathed with relief, for who at Madison Square Garden would do the honors as Mrs Marsh unfailingly did: read aloud a story from *Chums* or *Tiger Tim* or tell about such wondrous things as the chimps' tea party at London Zoo? And thank heavens Dicky wouldn't be joining us at the table. How could I ever forget the look of disgust on Bobby Janson's face when Kui Hsiang came marching triumphantly in with the tureen of steaming *jiaozi*, native dumplings? "Do you really eat that stuff?" Bobby (he was an American officer's son) asked. And it was obvious from the way he asked that he had never ever done so. Come to think of it, I'd never seen him, nor, for that matter, any other of our American acquaintances, enjoying a street snack. How tragic never to have savored *tang-gwer*, toffee apples on a stick – honey sweet yet tart enough to prickle your nose; or *jianbing guozi*, aromatic fritters, wrapped in wafer thin crepes, served sizzling straight off a portable griddle!

But then they were not cheap those fritters – twenty cents big money! *Big* money? Yes, big money, the collective name for the ten-, twenty-five-, and fifty-cent notes in use. We always knew where we stood with big money. Ten ten-cent notes were always worth one dollar. Not so with *small* money, the copper and silver coins, whose value constantly changed. The *jianbing guozi* you bought for twenty cents big money might cost anywhere between nineteen and twenty-three cents small money. We never knew why that was; we simply accepted it as a fact of life. It was only in later years that we understood the reason for the fluctuation: small money was tied directly to the price of copper and silver on the volatile bullion markets.

But back to the early years and Dicky. When he, ever inquisitive, ever persistent, demanded to know why we needed two kinds of money, I parried with the first thing that came to mind: small money was handy to have down in the pants pocket, big money was safer up in the shirt pocket.

I was on firmer ground when he asked what the words meant of my rendition of *Huo Jia*, a common back alley jingle. He'd sung for me the first verse of *The Miller of Dee;* it was only fair that I should respond.

In the Huo household there is a plump baby,
Who daily refuses his rice,
And daily refuses his tea,
Madame says, 'Don't blame me
If he insists on suckling at the breast'.

Dicky turned red. But how much redder if I'd given him one of those others from my repertoire, especially that rhyming one popular with kitchen scullions:

Master, Master, what's for today?
Fried eggs? Or steak perhaps?
Or what about croquettes,
Shaped like my whopping great THING?

We picked up those naughty rhymes long before we knew their meaning. We called each other Warlord Fling Schit Hai and Hu Flung Dung only half-suspecting why it drew such ribald laughter from the older boys. No wonder Dicky wasn't allowed to mix with the gang. No wonder he could never join us on our dragonfly hunts, exhilarating moments in the fields stalking those shimmering masters of flight – spectacular reds, vivid golden-browns, brilliant blue-greens. And he was never around when we went after cicadas perched high up in the treetops. Waste of time, way out of reach, a lot of people would tell us. But then they knew nothing of that cunning Chinese device – a lump of gummy sap (sap from cherry trees worked best) fixed to the tip of a bamboo pole which could be inched right up to where those singing marvels of nature thought themselves safe. And what about our own little trick of touching a certain spot on a cicada's midriff to start it screeching into song? Better not touch the wrong spot or it would pee that white stuff all over your fingers, giving you warts for sure.

And crickets! Would Dicky ever know that three-tailers were female, which, like flat heads and pale skins, were useless in the ring; that it was only the two-tailers, the males, especially the shiny black ones with round heads, that were game for a fight? But even those had to be sufficiently riled. The secret was to place two in a clay pot, then proceed to tickle their tails with the fibrous strand left on a blade of grass after stripping it from its stem. Only one variety of grass would do, mind you, only *it* produced a strand as springy as a cricket's antenna. Boy, how those gladiators resented their backsides tickled! They'd circle the pot chirping in outrage until they came face to face. No stopping them after that. They'd rise on their hind legs and gouge away with their powerful mandibles until one conceded leaving the other chirping in triumph.

Naturally, we all dreamed of capturing a super cricket,

one we could bring to the alley where the big stakes were wagered. No law against dreaming wild dreams of champion crickets and giant dragonflies and far away places across wide oceans. Bobby Janson needed only mention that he was off "home" to New York, where, before the summer was out, he'd be up in the bleachers watching Babe Ruth in action, and we'd be transported with him to Yankee Stadium. And just to hear Charlie Hislop boast that once "home" he was going to be taken to the changing of the guard at Buckingham Palace, why, we'd be there alongside him gaping in wonder at those legendary bear-skins and redcoats.

Curiously enough, it wasn't just the Dicky Marshes and Bobby Jansons and Charlie Hislops of this world who referred to the land of their fathers' as "home." We all did, never mind that for most of us third generation colonials all ties with the old country had long been severed.

The day Dicky and I said our final good-byes – he was going *home* to school – must have happened during Chung Yang Kite Festival, for there we were in the Min Yuan with our "butterflies" and "hawks" and "goldfish" and "fighters" strung out in a row sixty to eighty feet above our heads. We were relaxed yet vigilant for there was always some thoroughgoing rogue who had ground glass glued to the top few feet of his line, which, if he could cross it with yours, good-bye kite! Not the end of the world, because with their simple construction – rice paper glued to split bamboo frames – kites were cheap to replace. But there was always the bother of learning a new one's quirks, of getting it nicely balanced, so that by merely presenting it to a breeze it would go straight up.

I recognized them right away, Mr Marsh and Dicky, entering the grounds lugging one of those great big cumbersome European box kites. Were they thinking of flying the thing? Apparently so. Dicky stood holding the contraption upright while his dad, drawing the line taught from about twenty yards away, shouted "one-two-three – let go," then off he sprinted like a wild man. The unwieldy box went up about two feet before ploughing into the ground. On the next go all it did was skid along the cinder track. For about half an hour they persevered, then the unbelievable – they actually got the thing airborne. Twenty feet up it arced wildly to the right, to the left, then spiraled into a nose-dive. Crash-bang!

I turned to Murat. "Hang on to my line. That's Dicky Marsh. I'm going to say hello."

From close up I was even more amazed that they expected the thing to fly. Its framework was of solid doweling, thick as my finger; its covering, a coarse canvas-like material.

Dicky greeted me with a smile then turned to his father. "Daddy, you remember Desmond. He comes to tea at our house."

The gentleman stared at me with burning eyes.

"Glad to see you, Desmond." He offered his hand. I blushed crimson. I didn't know which hand to hold out.

"Excuse me laddie while I fix this beastly frame. It's cracked, you know." He went on with his whipping, winding the cord in perfect rings, just as illustrated in *Scouting for Boys*. Beautifully mended, he tested the piece against his knee. Crack!

"Confound it!"

"Can't it be fixed, Daddy?"

" 'Fraid not. Going to complain to Harvey & Dodds. Write them soon as I get to the office. Raise the very dickens. Come on, we'd better be on our way."

"Good-bye Desmond," Dicky lisped. "I'm going to school in England. Bedford Prep. I'm going to hate it there."

"No, you're not," his father snapped. "You're going to like it very much." Then he switched his attention on me. "What about you, laddie? Your parents are not by any chance sending you to Bedford, are they?"

I gulped in astonishment. "No sir. Going to St Louis College, sir."

"And where is that, may I ask?"

"In the French Concession, sir."

"In the French Concession? Here in Tientsin?" His mustache bristled, and his nostrils pinched as if they'd taken in a most disagreeable smell.

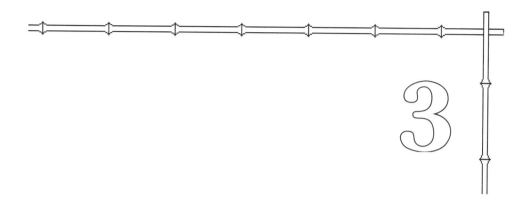

DEAR OLD GOLDEN RULE DAYS

SCHOOL! Say good-bye to freedom. Try not to think of the long trudge down Wellington Road to Seymour Road to the French Concession where at the junction of Rue de Passe and Rue St Louis stands that prison of prisons, St Louis College, policed by black-robed Marists, lay teachers from France, Spain, Germany, Ireland.

Stern, perhaps, but how dedicated those Marist Brothers, how formidable their challenge! For whereas the school's curriculum is in English, only a hapless few of the ragtag student body can claim English as their mother tongue; the rest, a mixed bag of Russians, Tartars, French, Chinese, Portuguese, Annamites – full bloods, half-bloods, quadroons – whose second language, if they have one at all, is that quaint, lilting, bastardized sub-branch of English that inevitably takes hold wherever foreigners settle on the China coast.

The day begins with a white-bearded Brother clanging the playground bell, summoning the damned to their doom, which in the case of Seventh Class, the entrance class, my class, after the hurried rumble of Hail Marys, kicks off invariably with that mindless repetition, that water torture of the brain, the times tables done in Gregorian chant:

> *Two trees are seex,*
> *Tree trees are ny-ya-un,*
> *Four trees are twalf . . .*

Ferrer, Lucien
  Catholic
Kennedy, Alex Gordon
  Protestant
Dobroukin Nicolai
  Orthodox
Ullmann, Gerard
  Israelite
Haenko, V.
  Orthodox
Napoloff, Alexis
  Orthodox
Mansuroff, I. Talat
  Mohammedan
Power, Desmond
  Catholic
Voyajis, Dimitrius
  Orthodox
Zagorsky, Nicolai
  Gr. Cath.
Liu, Tommy
  Pagan

I survive only because nature has shown me an escape. While parroting the words, I let myself be magically transported to the *Kai Wa*, that network of ponds and creeks at the Hai Kuan Ssu end of the British Concession, where at the water's edge, if I keep absolutely still, I'll spot a mud turtle breaking the surface, or a water snake winding through the bulrushes, the frog in its mouth soon to be swallowed whole. And what tingling suspense when I cast my line into dark water at the mouth of the feeder creek where lurk those monster yellow-tailed carp! A thousand pities that that feeder creek will soon be no more, obliging me to search farther afield for good water. How often have I heard Patrick curse the British Municipal Council for putting an end to fishing, so bent is it on reclaiming every inch of the low-lying marshland deeded to it as part of the Boxer Indemnity . . . ?

". . . Attention! Slava! You are dreaming. Tell the class of what you have been dreaming . . ."

Slava Koslovsky, the burly lout from Krasnoyarsk, stares blankly at Brother Sebastian who is approaching him with ruler poised to strike. Instantly, I force my mind to concentrate on the columns of numbers displayed on the yellowed oilcloth scroll. Try to stick it out. Only half an hour till playtime.

Playtime? Freedom, glorious freedom! And tiffin time (lunch time) too. Out in the dusty quadrangle it might be marbles season, every yard of space occupied by boys staking their precious agates and oniks and steelies. Then one day, quite out of the blue, marbles is over. Some mysterious authority has deemed it to be opening day for *bitka*, and soon everyone is pitching *bitkas* – the rubber heel of a shoe – at cigarette cards piled inch high on the ground. Since the thrower gets to keep any cards his *bitka* scatters, you avoid the crack shots. You hate to lose your movie stars, sports celebrities, famous trains, prehistoric animals, which come one to a pack of cigarettes. You maintain vigilance, and especially so when the playground bell sounds, for that's when you snatch up your cards before some bully makes a grab for them. At least you have your treasure safely deposited in your pants pocket while you endure the unendurable confinement of the classroom. Will it never end, this cruel confinement under the cruel black-gowned yoke?

Miracle of miracles, it does end. We Powers are with-

St. Louis College where The awesome but kindly Marist Brothers offered a fine education to rich and poor alike

drawn from St Louis, all four of us, and the exit every bit as hair-raising as the scariest scene of a Lon Chaney movie. Under orders from our supreme authority, Tai-tai, we rendezvous late in the evening at the side gate on Rue de Passe. A hushed word of command, and we steal into our classrooms. Eerie rows of empty desks. Crypt-like silence. "Hurry, stuff your books in the knapsack. Break for it!" Wild dash for the gate. In the flagship rickshaw sits Tai-tai, as composed as Old Buddha on her throne in the Forbidden City, while we in the flotilla following in line astern are kicking the air and babbling incoherently.

What was it all about, that sudden departure from SLC? The older ones in the know kept mum, but it took no time for Jocelyn and me to ferret out the details. Patrick, talented caricaturist and student of great promise (if he could but only control his bent for mischief), had whipped up a pen-and-ink masterpiece of one of the good Christian Brothers engaging in an indecent act. It was the guffaws of his Harbin deskmate that gave Patrick away. A lightning snatch from an alert Brother, a look of Gallic horror, a cry of Gallic anguish, the march to Brother Director's office, the storm of outrage, the harshest sentence in the book – expulsion.

When the venerable Brother Director appeared unprecedentedly at our front door, I was sent out to play. But then how could I refrain from sneaking in through the

15

The proud SLC emblem

back way and up the kitchen staircase and through the pantry and into the dining room where, with an ear glued to the keyhole, I could hear every word of the fate that was being decided for us?

"Madame, you must realize you will fall from grace if you send Brian and Jocelyn and Desmond to that Protestant school . . ."

"On the contrary, it is *you* who are committing mortal sin. It is *you* who are delivering my boys into the hands of Satan."

"Something can be worked out."

"Nothing can be worked out. There is no other choice. I cannot accept the shame and humiliation of Patrick's expulsion. By expelling one boy you have expelled all four, thereby exposing their unblemished Catholic souls to everlasting damnation. . . ."

We were never more filled with trepidation than when we strode the six blocks of Cambridge Road to our Calvary. Tai-tai had read us the riot act. "Tientsin Grammar School," she sounded off, "is the most genteel school east of Suez. You'd better be on your best behavior," she eyed Pat and me, "or you'll wish you were never born."

Yes, TGS was indeed genteel. You have to know that the BMC, as its trustee, took the greatest pains in assuring that the masters and mistresses ferried over from Albion's sacred institutions of learning understood well their mandate to instill into the minds of their charges the very purest of thoughts and manners as per *Highroads of Literature*, *Piers Ploughman History*, and the *Book of Common Prayer*.

"Look, for gosh sakes – GIRLS!" That was Jocelyn sounding the alarm. While I guardedly eyed the pesky pink-kneed Lower School missies hopping about their hopscotch squares, Pat had his analytical eye on those Upper School ones whose tunics and pinafores did little to disguise their blossoming womanhood.

No bell ringing, no rapid-fire Hail Marys to start off the day; rather the whole school assembled, girls to the right, boys to the left, in a high-vaulted, richly-paneled hall pleasantly scented with furniture wax. The Headmaster pronounced a brief prayer in St James's version of English, then led the scrubbed and starched assemblage in a rousing selection from *Hymns Ancient & Modern*. At the *Amen*, prefects flung the doors wide, whereupon in alternating rows, the now spiritually cleansed girls and boys marched out with military precision to their forms.

Forms? Yes – *forms*, the very first new word I learned at TGS. I was assigned to Form Three, not Class Three. Miss Clarke, the roly-poly apple-cheeked form teacher, gave my hand little mothering squeezes as she announced to the twenty-four pairs of inquisitive eyes: "Boys and girls, this is Desmond. He has fallen behind because he missed spring term. So we'll help him, all of us, shan't we?"

The equally proud TGS emblem

"Yesssss, Miss Clarke."

The boys gloating over my bony knees, the girls snickering at my burning cheeks, forced my eyes to the floor as I took my place at an empty desk. It was only when all attention was back on Miss Clarke that I felt it safe enough to glance around. Sons of guns! My immediate neighbors, why, they were none other than Igor Kapoostin and Ura Shirokoff, Russian friends of old. In fact, I was soon to discover that the class was preponderantly Russian, strange for so English a school.

More surprises in store. At playtime, clutches of boys pitching *bitkas* and shouting that familiar *bitka* argot: "*Tak!* . . . *Nitak!* . . . *Konvisvoya!*" And even when they resorted to English, it was that same old sing-song English of the China coast. Why had this school put such fear of God into me? The place wasn't at all sinister. On the contrary, I began warming up to the idea that confinement at TGS was going to be a lot easier to take than at SLC. Certainly, I was less pressured, less restricted. It even looked as though I might be allowed to think for myself, do my own thing.

Pipe dream! I was rudely brought back to reality one writing lesson when Miss Clarke was making the rounds, pausing behind each pupil laboring with J-nib over the sentence she had chalked on the board: *The Quick Brown Fox Jumps Over The Lazy Dog.* Her prolonged pause behind me shot prickles to the back of my neck. Though my defenses were up, I was not prepared for the shrillness of her attack. "No, no, not like that. Who taught you to write in that silly way?" I gazed down at what I thought was graceful cursive script so painstakingly developed under the discriminating eye of Brother Sebastian. "Look up at the board, Desmond. Observe how the letters are formed. That is the proper way, the *only* way, to write."

The words chalked on the board were of a style not

17

much different from printing; the unnatural lines joining the letters being the only pretense to longhand.

"Desmond, my good boy, you copy those words exactly as you see them. Do you hear me? Now let me see you write the word *Quick.*"

I picked up my pen with my left hand, my ablest hand for sketching, and began to form the oval for the capital Q. I got no further. My eardrums took a blast as if from a ship's siren: "Stop what you are doing! Why have you changed hands? With which hand do you normally write?"

I peered at both hands. I showed her the right.

"Then why are you using your left?"

It all came out. Though the good Brothers had detected my left-handedness, they obliged me to use my right. That slowed me at first, but I soon developed a pleasing hand, probably because I was blessed with some measure of my maternal grandfather's artistic talent, the lion's share of which going to my brother Patrick – the lucky devil.

Miss Clark consulted with Mrs Laidlaw (Mistress of Form Five Lower School) and Mrs Kelly (in charge of Kindergarten) and Miss Court and Mrs MacDonald. They brought the matter to the attention of Mr Yeates, the reigning Headmaster. It was determined that to stave off the mental instability that was sure to accrue to the poor hard-done-by Desmond, he must never again be allowed to hold a pen in his right hand.

So it was back to square one, learning to form the shapes of letters as laid down by English schools of the day. For a while I attained no better marks than three out of ten for writing (or should I say printing), and not because I failed to follow the prescribed style of lettering; it was all those smudges I made. (A left-hander's hand pushes across the word he or she is forming, while a right-hander draws the pen away from a freshly inked word.) As further frustration, my remedy, which was to swivel the exercise book at ninety degrees so that I was writing up to down as do the Chinese, proved to be a strict no-no.

Alex Micoutine with Des.

"What are you doing, Desmond. Straighten your work. Do you want to become cross-eyed?"

"No, Miss Clarke."

"Then turn your book straight."

"Yes, Miss Clarke."

No point bucking the system. I could always position the work the way I wanted when she wasn't looking. I would follow the example of Igor and Sarah, always top of the class. They and those other children of the steppes never bucked the system. They conformed to a T, even those who could not shake off their throaty Slavic accents. How those educators from the *green and pleasant land* must have winced at Carapet Kulchasian giving the names and dates of the Plantagenet kings, at Murat Apakaieff describing Henry the VIII's stand-off with the Pope, at Vladimir Tolstipiatoff reciting from Richard II:

". . . *dis ozor-eedont, deemee-paradeece . . .*"

Better not laugh. Corporal punishment at TGS could be brutish. Where at SLC the Brothers took swipes at your open palm with an ebony ruler, here the English Headmaster's rangoon cane and its preferred target, the upturned backside, was infinitely more devastating, as I was personally to affirm on far too many occasions.

And as for infractions not warranting the cane, TGS had a host of lesser punishments of which *detention* was the most feared since it meant being booked, and the book was kept in the Headmaster's office. Booked twice in a week and you got the cane. And woe betide those late for school; the Head made a public spectacle of them, corralling them at the entrance way to the assembly hall so that at the march past every eye could feast on them squirming in their pre-sentencing discomfiture.

The first occasion I was held in the corral wasn't because I'd risen late or that I'd dawdled at breakfast. Quite the opposite, I had set off from home in good time

19

and was keeping up with Patrick's long-legged stride when the sound of a marching band broke through the din of the street. The drums weren't the thundering drums of the Queens Regiment, nor the brass the crashing Sousa of the 15th US Infantry, nor the bugles the blaring staccato of the *16ème Régiment d'Infantrie Coloniale*. No sir, only one sort of band could play such havoc with *Glory Glory Hallelujah* – a funeral band. And, by golly, if it was some great mandarin's funeral we were in for a treat, a blend of the awesome and bizarre, outdoing Barnum & Bailey at their best.

First to come by was the band itself, every member fancifully decked out in the plumes and gold braid of Napoleon's Old Guard; then in sprawling procession: white-garlanded youths with white paper-made ferns held aloft to sweep the Western sky; Ching Dynasty warriors on clip-clopping Mongol ponies; saffron-robed lamas beating tom-toms and discharging bloodcurdling blasts on their thirteen-foot-long alpenhorns; parasol bearers dazzling the eye with the vivid tapestry of their Imperial parasols; Taoist monks intoning chants, clashing cymbals, and blowing panpipes; a pair of towering demons, the scarlet-faced one grimacing hideously, the ghostly pale one frozen in a benign smile; next an open convertible displaying a framed portrait of the deceased, his gaze fixed on the shuffling mourners all head to toe in white sackcloth (you could easily pick out the hired ones by their wailing and breast-beating and hair-pulling); then the procession's high point, a huge vermilion catafalque borne by multitudinous pall bearers (officially sixty-four) in green jackets with red pompoms, chanting in unison to ease the mighty load; and finally, bringing up the rear, a succession of make-believe papier-mâché limousines, horse carts, palanquins, houses, pets, concubines, and coin – silver-paper coin – basket after basket of it; the whole blinking lot to be set alight at the graveside, the flames converting it into the real thing for the personal use of the departed when he reached his abode in the Western sky. . . .

"Good grief!" Pat yelled. "It's ten-to-ten. We'll be shot!"

We weren't murdered, of course, nor could our sentence have amounted to much, for it left no impression on me. And not surprisingly, for barring the savagery of the cane, I have no clear recollection of the penalties exacted on me for my innumerable transgressions. What I can never forget though is the steady fare of arithmetic and grammar and verse and Latin and French I was obliged to digest. By the time I had gone through Lower School and reached Upper Third, tedium had once again become my biggest enemy.

Apart from the sheer heaven of weekends, Wednesday was the day I most relished, for on Wednesdays the afternoon was given over to sports in the truest English tradition.

During the cold months it was soccer, the ground frozen too hard for rugby, otherwise we surely would have been obliged to participate in that bruising madness. In summer it was cricket. Now cricket might look namby-pamby to the uninitiated, but just try to catch that rock-hard ball with bare hands, and, when at bat, face a missile that zipps treacherously off the pitch so that you never know its course until the very last instant. And no yelping when struck. We had to keep a stiff upper lip. We were gentlemen, after all, engaging in a gentleman's game.

For half the afternoon one team would be at bat, and since only two batsmen could be at the wicket at any one time, and they might stay there for hours, the rest of the eleven sat idly in the pavilion. That was when the tattered remnants of a comics sheet would go the rounds. You treated them with reverence, those comics, especially the American kind. *Who* did not relish the escapades of Hans and Fritz and der Captain and der Inspector and Mama, or the Toonerville Folks, or Popeye, or Maggie and Jiggs? And what about Flash Gordon or Tarzan whose breathtaking exploits came out in serial form? A missing issue? It tore your heart out. Nowhere could you buy it. Comics were not for sale, not in the shops, not even in the American barracks. How they ever got to China in the first place was, at least to us, one of planet earth's great unsolved mysteries.

Plonking myself beside Dick McVeigh on one of those lazy cricketing afternoons, I happened to glance at the page of comics he was reading, and I just about jumped out of my skin. Hell's bells! It was a missing *Flash Gordon.*

"Wow, Dick, wherever did you get that?"

"From Konsty. And he's got a lot more, mint condition, tradin' them for marbles. Look, he's at it now."

And there he was, the one and only Konstantin

Ovchinnikoff, a strapping White Russian with a sheaf of comics on his lap, lording it over the boys gathered around.

I sauntered over.

"No, I don't have *Tarzan and the Sacred Scarab*," he was saying. "That was the April 17th issue. But I can get it. It'll cost you five English reds."

"Five English reds! Where would I find five English reds?" Pain showed all over the third former's face.

"Okay, three reds and two steelies."

"What about six German oniks?"

"Three reds and two steelies or forget it."

"Two reds and an agate."

"Okay. But it's a steal. I'll go get *Sacred Scarab* after cricket. I'll bring it to school tomorrow. Don't you forget the marbles."

Murat Apakaieff nudged me: "Did you hear that? Let's follow him."

No trouble keeping out of sight of the tall blond Russian pedaling in front of us. Whenever he slowed, we wheeled behind a rickshaw or mule cart. And thus we proceeded on our friend's tail all the way down Wellington Road and Recreation Road to the French Concession. When he finally dismounted and chained his bike to a lamp post outside the market on busy Rue Gabriel Deveria, we did likewise. But that's when we lost him. We lost him in that great emporium with its hurly-burly of humanity milling around suspended animal carcasses and basins of mouth-frothing crabs and tubs of shoulder-to-shoulder carp and wicker coops solid with hens, pigeons, ducks, geese. Brought to a standstill, all I could do was pinch my nostrils to ward off the stench. I wanted to call it quits. Not Murat. He pushed and shoved as hard as he got from the press of bodies. Suddenly, he cried out: "Konsty, look, Konsty." We elbowed our way through the mass, and sure enough, there was our quarry, large as life, conversing with a vendor, a well-to-do one judging by the red button on his black skull cap. Next thing, the two were heading for a side exit. We got there too late; they'd vamoosed into the tumult of the street. Damnation! But back at the vendor's booth we knew we were on the right track; the place was heaped with packing stuff: hemp cord, gunny sacks, and old newspapers – *American newspapers*!

"Red Button" holds the secret to our mother lode

Twenty minutes later, Red Button was back at the booth – alone.

Murat approached him. "Excuse me honorable proprietor, sir, do you happen to sell the colored picture sheets which come with those newspapers?"

Red Button looked us up and down. "I've none left here, but I have a supply at my residence where I've just taken one of you little foreign devils. What a nuisance you are! Come back tomorrow."

Murat jingled the coins in his pocket. "Our humble apologies, honorable sir, putting you to such trouble." And he jingled his coins again.

It did the trick. "All right, follow me."

And out we went, across the bustling street and through a maze of alleys to a narrow wooden doorway.

"Please to enter."

On each side of the family's brick sleeping platform in the bedroom that doubled as a storeroom was our mother lode – neat stacks of uncreased, unread newspapers.

"Pick out what you want, but don't take all day."

Several generations of the man's family, from gnarled oldsters to young toddlers, gathered to stare goggle-eyed as we breathlessly thumbed our way through three-month-old editions of the *Los Angeles Times*, *San Francisco Chronicle*, *Seattle Post and Intelligencer*.

"Murat, here's your missing *Tarzan*."

"Look at this new *Popeye*."

"Boy-oh-boy-oh-boy!"

Red Button deposited our selection on an ancient set of scales, his forehead furrowing in concentration as he

23

tinkered with the weights to obtain perfect equilibrium.
Nimbly he clacked the beads of an abacus. Solemnly he
announced the price. "Forty cents big money – forty-two
cents small money!"

"What? Forty cents? So cheap? Can't be!"

But it was.

As I pass Murat at assembly next morning, the message
in his black-brown eyes is unmistakable: "Don't tell a
living soul."

"I certainly won't," mine reply.

And now our eyes join the four hundred pairs fixed on
Headmaster John E. Woodall striding down the center
aisle, the tassel of his mortar board dancing a jig, the tails
of his black silk billowing.

"Good morning girls."

"Good morning sir."

"Good morning boys."

"Good morning sir."

"Hymn number twenty-three. *There is a Green Hill Far
Away.* Verses one to four."

Catchy tune, easy pitch. I have long discovered that
partaking in a heretical hymn does not bring an instant
thunderbolt from heaven. As I freely give of my Romish
voice, I spy Konsty in the row ahead, singing his head off,
blissfully unaware of the collapse of his monopoly. My
gaze wanders to Milton Chang (related somehow to the
renowned warlord Chang Hsueh Liang), standing with
eyes closed, emitting reedy chirps – a proper Peiling lark.
And over to the right there's Bal Mundkur, the skeletal
Bengali, more skeletal than his impossibly skeletal father

24

(official tailor to the Queens Regiment), literally screeching out the words: ". . . without a city wall . . ."

"Why is green hill such big deal?" Urik Komoroff mutters. "Lodda green hills round Peitaiho and Shanhaikuan, and who sings about them? Who cares?"

Somebody cares. The boy next to me, Leo Olshevsky, he cares. Look at him, grim-faced as a bonze. A Russian, his family took the same route through Siberia as Vladimir's and Igor's and Ura's in their escape from the Reds. But he's different. He's no Orthodox. He's of the Jewish faith. And he's not the only one who can claim ancient Hebrew lineage. In the next row stand four others, side by side – Mark Meyer, Adolph Shapiro, Isaac Malkin, Isidore Kitzis – and not one of them singing. Understandable, if you believe Leo's stories about the things the British army is doing in Palestine to prevent the Jews from creating a homeland for themselves. That's given them a cause, a fervent cause, fervent enough to inspire Shura Shihwarg, poet laureate of Form Four, to immortalize it in an epic, a modern-day Greek tragedy, in which the protagonist, a kibbutz hero, gunned down by the foe, croaks out his youthful defiance as his entrails ooze onto the blood-soaked Sinai sand . . .

And boy oh boy, you should see Leo shoot sparks when we give all we've got to William Blake's *Jerusalem*: "Till we have built Jerusalem in England's green and pleasant land . . ."!

Why would the English ever want to do that? For the life of me I don't see the sense of it. Anyway, Leo won't even sing *Abide With Me*, General Gordon's favorite. Maybe he doesn't know it was the General's favorite. In fact, so few know, I can count them on one hand. *I* know because that's what Scoutmaster Wallis Watkins told the audience at the rally the other night. Leo wasn't there. Come to think of it, neither was Isidore, nor any of his brethren. Curious, they in the Trumpeldors and we in the Scouts. Well, maybe not so curious. Can't imagine Leo & Co being that interested in committing to memory all that guff about Scotland uniting with England in AD 1606, and Ireland following suit in 1818, and the Union Jack resulting from someone's bright idea of superimposing the crosses of St Andrew and St Patrick onto that of St George. All very well for Leo to turn his back on the glorious annals of the United Kingdom, we have to have it down pat if we

25

are to pass our Tenderfoot, and if we can't manage that, we are nothing, absolutely nothing . . .

"O dearly dearly has he loved . . ."

I come to with a jolt. It's the last verse and here am I still musing over Leo's stubborn reserve.

"And trust in His redeeming blood and try His works to do . . ."

It never fails but that the crescendo of the last verse fades into a tabernacle of silence. And if you happen to sneak a glance at the rostrum, you'll catch the Headmaster basking in the silence, his mortar board inclined, his fleshy proboscis, impervious to the teasing strands of the tassel, pointing down at his boots. The suspense might last a long minute, perhaps two, before his specially modulated assembly voice, now supplicating, now cajoling, launches into the psalm of the day.

That's when I can officially detach myself from the proceedings, because, in accordance with the agreement reached between Tai-tai and the school authorities, we Powers are excused from the teachings of the Old Testament. And for good reason. Are not certain passages as pernicious as any work listed in the Vatican Index? At SLC we were given *Bible History*, a watered-down version of the scriptures, which, to make up for the removal of the juicy bits, was amply illustrated with Dürer etchings of good angels battling bad, of Lucifer pitch-forking sinners into the eternal flame . . .

I give a start . . . *green* hill . . . *green* and pleasant land . . . *green* this *green* that . . . Of course! My *Green* and Yellow Cords! Thank heavens for the reminder. This very night I am to sit for my Pathfinder's badge. If I get it, I am well on my way to earning scoutdom's prized Green and Yellow Cords. I simply have to have the cords for Siege Day, and Siege Day is only weeks away. But first, I must be a Pathfinder. And to be one I have to know Tientsin's streets like the back of my hand. I have to be able to direct anyone anywhere in the concessions. And that includes the German Concession. Frankie Butterworth got thumbs down for not knowing the nearest turn-off on Woodrow Wilson Street, which takes you to German Park . . .

A fanfare at the piano. And the instant Mr Foxlee bangs out the opening chords of *Our Father*, the lovely foliage of German Park vanishes from the screen of my mind.

They sing *which* art in heaven, and I sing *who* art in

heaven. And I never sing that last bit, that redundant bit, addended by Act of Parliament to pep up Jesus' words: "*For thine is the kingdom, the power and the glory.*" But why bring that up now? Let them sing what they like, I'm going to go over the street map of Tientsin. I'm going to see if I can recite page 3 of the Peiyang Tourist Guide. Now, how does it go? Oh yes . . . "*Woodrow Wilson Street runs for eleven blocks in the German Concession before it becomes Victoria Road . . . then after the seven blocks, from Cousins Road to Bristow Road, its name changes to Rue de France . . . and Rue de France it remains all the way to the International Bridge . . . then for the short leg it traverses Russian Concession below Tientsin East, it is called Lapteff Prospect . . . after which it finally ends up as Via Roma in the Italian Concession . . .*"

The pounding notes of *Marche Militaire* snap me back to the assembly's final ritual – the march past. One by one, starting with Lower School, the well-drilled lines step smartly from the hall.

There goes Kontsy. Look at him leading his line, proud captain of the Muscovsky Guards. Wait till he discovers that his secret is out . . . I must remember what the Chinese call Wellington Road: *Si-shi-si hao lu* – Road Number Forty-four. Gordon Road is Road Number Thirteen. Tipperary Road is . . . What the devil is Tipperary Road? It's Sixty something or other . . .

It's eyes front when we tramp past the prefects holding open the great mahogany doors. And it's eyes right when we draw alongside the anxious faces in the corral, soon to feel the Head's wrath.

Golly! There's Wilbur Wotsizname. He was late yesterday. And wasn't he also late on Monday? He'll be pretty lucky to escape the cane.

Another school day is about to begin. . . .

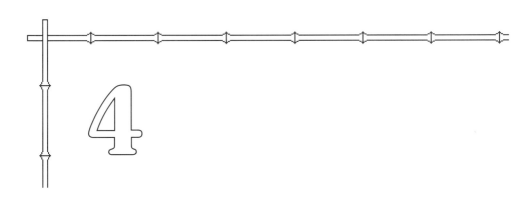

FREEDOM FIGHTERS, OR WHAT YOU WILL

S IEGE DAY AT LAST. Second Tientsin Troop is drawn up two deep outside Canton Road Cemetery. Stripes, ribbons, insignia adorn our service khaki. And no skimping on spit and polish – the copper woggles securing our green neck-scarves glint in the June-day sun as do the emblems on our wide-brimmed hats of the South African Constabulary. Our shoulder patch is a yellow pagoda on a blue background with the inscription: *North China* embroidered in yellow thread. Oh, if only I had my Green and Yellow Cords, what joy! what glory! Those rotters, they never told me I had to be a King's Scout first, and I'm short two merit badges for that. Never mind, sure as kingdom come, I'll have my cords next year. I'll show 'em. I'll show Scoutmaster Watkins. I'll show Scoutmaster Capstick of First Troop. I'll show the Lord High Commissioner of Scouts himself, Howard Payne, Esq.

I cast a sidelong glance at First Troop, British boys the lot, very pukka with their red scarves and white lanyards. Then eyes front, and my gaze rigidly fixed on the line facing us. Stalwarts of the Volunteer Defense Corps, they are in their summer KDs – light khaki tunics, light khaki shorts down to the knees, green-khaki webbing, green-khaki puttees. I scan the front row. I don't see Patrick, but I recognize several of his cohorts: Vladimiroff, Tuleneff, Solovieff, Zamiatin. There are as many Russians in the Corps as there are English. And they serve the Corps well. Everyone knows No. 2 Platoon, the Russian platoon, wins the infantry drill contest year in and year out.

The expectation in the air sparks to 10,000 volts when drums of the British regiment suddenly reverberate up and down Canton Road. With bugles blaring and boots crashing in perfect unison, the guard of honor marches past. I tingle all over, for aren't these men drawn from the bravest of the brave – Lancashire Fusiliers, XXth the Foot, heroes of Minden, Ladysmith, Gallipoli? Now their color party passes ours. Their standard bears the red rose of Lancaster, ours the tri-pointed arrowhead of scouting. We snap to attention and come to the salute, three fingers of the left hand extended horizontally across the stave which is locked rigidly, achingly against the collar bone.

A proud moment. And why not indeed! Are we not part of this grand parade, the drums, the bugles, the hoarse commands, the tramp of boots? Did we not join the Scouts for this? Never mind the good deed for the day, the smiling and whistling under all difficulties. No sir! This is it! Won't we in a few years advance to the ranks of the Volunteers? Won't we be exchanging our staves for Lee Enfield rifles and shining bayonets?

Now comes the electrifying band, the American band – great big sousaphones and saxophones and horns and cornets and clarinets and flutes, even a guy tinkling a glockenspiel. You should hear them crash out Bagley's *National Emblem March*: "Oh the monkey wrapped his tail around the flagpole . . ." But now they're playing *Stars and Stripes Forever*. They are the 15th US Infantry, the *Can Do* boys. Everything about them is *Can Do*. They have their *Can Do* barracks, their *Can Do* ballfield, their *Can Do* skating rink. Even under their regimental emblem – a Chinese dragon on a blue and white shield – is the inscription: *Can Do*!

The French next, the *16ème Régiment d'Infantrie Coloniale*, blue kepis, brown tunics, brown pantaloons. And they have with them today a detachment of scowling Annamites – gnome-like mercenaries – their conical brass helmets bobbing up and down like corks on choppy water. They can never march in step.

And now, dwarfing the Annamites, the cream of Italian manhood, the Royal Italian Marines, handsome six-foot Goliaths, whose carbines seem like toys on their brawny shoulders.

Finally, the Japanese. They always send the smallest contingent, a reduced platoon of unkempt men. And look

at their officers, so unmilitary-like. Just look at their horn-rimmed spectacles. Are they all short-sighted because of the seaweed they eat?

What the devil are we waiting for? Five tormenting minutes have gone by since the Volunteers sloped arms and marched through the cemetery gate. The parade must have already formed inside. They've gone and forgotten us, the blighters.

At last! "Second Tientsin Troop . . . tennnn-shun . . . leffft-turn . . . kweeek-march."

A Roman Catholic dignitary in full regalia – gotta be a bishop at least – is mumbling away in French. Lesser priests sprinkle holy water on some sacred monument. The band sounds an introductory chord then launches into the traditional hymn of remembrance: *O God Our Help in Ages Past.* There's a pageful of verses, and we sing every one. An Anglican padre consoles the dead. He assures them they will not be wearied by age nor condemned by the years. A British bugler sounds the lingering, poignant notes of the *Last Post.* The two minutes of heart-tugging silence for the fallen is a time also for reassuring oneself that it is good to be among the living, good to be breathing the sultry summer air perfumed by massed puff balls of pink mimosa. And thus we remain, saddened yet solaced, until American sousaphones and euphoniums start rumbling the somber strains of Chopin's *Funeral March.* While the band is playing we stand easy, shifting feet, clearing throats, whispering even, but only until Mr Watkins gives the command to pile staves and follow the Wolf Cubs to the corner of the cemetery where the flowers are stacked. With a pot of carnations apiece we proceed solemnly to the lines of graves. Alioshka lays his pot on the grave of a Welch Fusilier, Dwight on a that of French marine. I lay mine at the foot of a Gothic cross inscribed with the words:

Otto Vogt
1878 – 1900
Freiwilliges Verteidigungs Korps

I steal away to stand at the graveside of my maternal grandfather George Lambert D'Arc. Though I don't remember a thing about him (he died when I was a babe in arms), so palpably do I feel his presence, I can scarcely draw a breath. (Tai-tai always said that superstition ran deeper in our family than any other she knew.) Back in line I keep my head bowed lest anyone in Fox Patrol notices my distress.

We were last into the cemetery, and now we are the last out. Crowds of Chinese have gathered on both sides of the street. Though they make no sound, and their faces are devoid of expression, I am stung by a nagging disquiet. Are we Western Ocean Devils not marching shoulder to shoulder with the Eastern Ocean Devils, the subjugators of Manchuria? I keep my eyes glued to the sweat-blackened khaki shirt in front of me as we march to the Canton Road entrance of Recreation Grounds. Thank heavens we don't have far to go. Our den is only a stone's throw from the cemetery. Second Troop has one of the larger rooms of Anderson Pavilion, which is situated on the western edge of the grounds.

Inside the den, Mr Watkins commends us on our bearing. "Jolly good show Hawks, Beavers, Foxes. Well done Patrol Leaders and Seconds. Next meeting, Friday, 6 p.m. sharp. Troop, dismiss!"

With three fingers glued together and pointed upwards at shoulder height, we make a snappy right turn. Mr Watkins keeps a straight face, but he cannot disguise his glow of pride.

"Who's for an orange squash?" Ravil Tahir asks.

"I'll have a coke."

"Lemonade."

"*Vishniak*," I shout out. To me the taste and fizz of that Russian cherry drink is unequaled.

We saunter into the pavilion's refreshment lounge, and with the nonchalance of grown-ups we each grab a wicker chair. The "boy" arrives to take orders.

"That sure was a fine parade," Dwight Anderson opens.

"Better than last year's."

"Last year, do you remember, an English soldier fainted from the heat and Shurupkin broke ranks to go to his aid?"

"He got into trouble for it."

"Serves him right. Shurupkin is always the big hero."

"Where is he? I haven't seen him for months."

"His family moved to Shanghai."

"Des, I saw you at your grandfather's grave. Was he one of those killed in the siege?"

"The Society for Justice and Harmony", one of the official titles of the Boxer Movement

31

American medics
tend Japanese
wounded near
Tientsin—July 1900

"No, he died afterwards, from sickness."

"But he was in the siege, wasn't he?"

"He was. He served with the Frontier Rifles, the old name for the Volunteers."

Alioshka, the excitable Russian, clutches my arm. "My uncle was in the Siberian Rifles. He told me that had it not been for us Russians, the Boxers would have finished off everyone. The Russians were the bravest. They saved you all."

"What about the Germans, the Austrians, the Americans, the Japanese, didn't they also fight bravely?"

"And the Volunteers too. Don't forget the Volunteer Corps. A lot of them got killed."

"If it hadn't been for the Russians," Alioshka presses on, "the Boxers would have butchered every last soul."

"Who told you that?"

"You can read it in any history book you like. The 12th East Siberian Regiment arrived just in time to launch a bayonet charge, which routed the horde of Manchu Bannermen who'd broken through the American lines."

"Never on your life!" Dwight Anderson pounds the table. "Our defenses held. Don't you know who was in charge of them? Huh? Hoover! Herbert Hoover, the brilliant engineer who was to become thirty-first President of the United States. And who do you think were the first to fight their way to Tientsin from Taku? Why, the 9th US Infantry, of course!"

"Don't gimme that. Everyone knows that when the Allied fleet attacked the forts at Taku, the one and only American ship present refused to take part. The captain said he hadn't received orders. The Russians and British and French had to take the forts by storm. They suffered terrible casualties."

"The 9th US Infantry broke the siege of Tientsin."

"The 12th East Siberians."

"I thought it was the Royal Welch Fusiliers."

"It certainly wasn't you Yankees."

"You're nuts! Don't you know that Liscum Road is named after the Civil War hero Colonel Liscum who was killed leading a bayonet charge against the Boxers? If it wasn't for him none of us would be here."

"And what about Linievitch Road? General Linievitch led his troops around the back of East Arsenal to capture the city from behind. And when you Angliskis finally reached Peking and were stopped by the mighty Tartar Wall, who arrived to storm the wall? Who captured Tung Pien Gate? Linievitch and his Cossacks, that's who. Why do you think the gate's been renamed Linievitch Gate?"

"The American General Chaffee was first into Tientsin and first into Peking. It was he who saved the legations."

"Nonsense. Linievitch and Vassilievsky got into Peking first."

"What's the use," I say to myself. "What's the use of arguing with these guys. It was the 7th Rajputs who broke the siege. That came straight from my grandmother Agnes D'Arc, and she ought to know, she was there in person. How many times over the years did Tai-tai recount for us Agnes's ordeal, the fifty-five days and fifty-five nights when death stared her in the face, and then at her moment of deliverance, when the 7th Rajputs came through the sluice gate, how she and other ladies present had to rush to fetch them water, because, in the hundred-and-ten degree temperature, they were croaking 'Panee-panee' and dropping like flies . . ."

Agnes, survivor of the Boxer siege, with young Gracie, our future Tai-tai.

"Say what you like, my friends," Vittorio Carlotto, the taciturn Italian, speaks up for the first time. "We were all

33

NEW VICTORIA HOTEL,
No. 9, Queen's Road Central.
...ger & Farmer
PROPRIETORS.

Hongkong, October 27th 1900.

Dear Mr. Lanning,

Your letter of the 16th just received, and I am glad to inform you that I have heard indirectly about Mr. Mrs. George D'Arc, and they are both of them all right, although they have been through a fearful amount of worry, suspense and anxiety.

The first news we heard about them was from an article published in one of the Shanghai newspapers, about three weeks after the Europeans in Pekin had been besieged. It described the arrival in Tientsin of a Chinese messenger bearing news of the besieged, and concealed in the sole of his boot, was a short letter from Mr. D'Arc to the French Admiral, asking him to send up relief at once, as they could not last out much longer.

George all the time was in Tientsin, half mad with anxiety about his wife, and we heard he went off with Admiral Seymour's unsuccessful expedition to the relief of Pekin. He was also with the troops that entered Pekin some six weeks later on, and have no doubt was one of the first to enter the besieged legation where his wife was supposed to have — tortured perhaps.

Of course, I am only telling you what I have heard from Warren's friend, people who were in Tientsin during the bombardment, and who spoke personally with George D'Arc.

I have not heard a word from them since the relief of Pekin, but feel convinced they are both all right, for if anything had happened to Mr. D'Arc, I am sure to have heard of it, as all news travels apace.

Will let you know any further news my father ...

Sincerely Yours
Wm Farmer

in it together. During the siege we showed how it was possible to be brothers. If only we could be brothers now, if only we could obey the Fourth Scout's Law – *A friend to all and a brother to every other Scout* – we wouldn't be getting into silly arguments. Thirty-seven years ago, Italians, French, British, Americans, Russians, Germans, Austrians, Japanese fought side by side. Seven hundred and fifty gave their lives, sacrificed themselves, so that we might live . . ."

"Hi you guys! Still in uniform?" Jefferson Wu calls out as he and Lincoln Liang, both two classes above me in school, come bounding up the pavilion steps. They are in sparkling whites. Their Spalding tennis rackets are enclosed in fancy zippered covers. They lack for nothing. They are very much spoiled. They along with others from wealthy Chinese families are being groomed for university in the States. America has long converted its share of the Boxer Indemnity into an education fund for Chinese – Chinese of good standing, naturally. And it is common for those who take advantage of the plan to affect such names as Jefferson, Washington, Franklin, Lincoln.

"Hi Lincoln, howarya?"

"Fine."

"Why are you all dressed to the nines?" Jefferson Wu asks.

"Big parade. Siege Day. Dincha know? You should'a bin there."

"Been there! You guys crazy?"

"Not so crazy," snaps Dwight Anderson. "The ceremony was held to commemorate the defeat of the Boxers, that vicious lot of savages who murdered innocent women and children, foreigners and Chinese alike. They had to be stopped. So we stopped them and saved your skins."

"They were a bunch of cutthroats," someone adds.

"Cutthroats? They were freedom fighters, heroes, martyrs. Your own leader, Sir Robert Hart, said so. He knew they were trying to save China from foreign take-over."

"Foreign take-over? You're crazy, Jefferson. If it were not for us foreigners you'd have no civilization, no schools, no hospitals." Purple in the face, Dwight has difficulty getting his words out. "You now have a taste of our American way of life. You have American democracy, American freedom . . ."

"American freedom! If you could just put yourself in our

35

shoes for once, you wouldn't be using that term so freely. Try to imagine, if you can, your America, your sweet land of liberty, as it stood in the 1860's, racked by civil war, coffers empty, cities destroyed, the masses destitute. Picture the Administration, uncertain, nervous, desperate to find some way of putting the pieces together, when into Boston harbor sails a Japanese man-o-war, bristling with cannon. Its landing party pressures the city elders into permitting Japanese merchants to set up shop in the finest waterfront real estate. A little later, a Burmese vessel, armed to the teeth, arrives in Puget Sound. The captain demands audience with the Governor of the State of Washington. With a pistol to his head, what else can the Governor do but agree to the Burmese demand for a trading post in downtown Seattle.

"When news of the Japanese landing at Boston reaches the White House, the President, his cabinet, his staff, even the messenger boys are sickened with disgust. What decent household would allow a snapping street cur into its parlor? Do not those unwashed, unsanitary Orientals smell to high heaven? Are they not totally ignorant of the most rudimentary rules of propriety? And yet they have the utter gall to discuss trade, offering worthless trinkets for the hemisphere's finest grade Sea Island cotton.

"A senator is despatched posthaste to Boston with orders to advise the Japanese firmly but politely that their presence is unwelcome, that there is little likelihood of commerce, and last but not least, that their proposition to barter heroin for cotton is unthinkable. Don't they know that the possession of narcotics is a criminal offense in each and every state of the union. The obdurate Japanese prolong negotiations. More of their ships arrive loaded to the gunwales with opium and heroin. American drug pushers are not difficult to recruit. Trade is brisk until internal revenuers, coming on the scene, seize and destroy a large consignment of the vile narcotic. And what is the Japanese response? They despatch a fleet of ultra-modern propeller-driven ironsides that easily smash the feeble resistance offered by the primitive American brigs. To compensate for the revenuers' insolence, America must fork out a huge indemnity in silver bullion. But that's not all. Long Island is ceded to Japan in perpetuity.

"Burma and Siam, aghast at the gains of the pesky Japanese, insist on their fair share. New York, Miami, Los

Angeles, and Seattle are opened to them and their soldiery. Back in Washington the President searches vainly
for some way to convince the intruders to leave. American
freedom fighters find a way. They grab hold of two Japanese and two Burmese and hang them by their necks in
the nearest village square. Right away Japan and Burma
marshal a huge fighting force of soldiers and marines and
rush them to Chesapeake Bay. At first the naval forts at
Annapolis offer stout resistance, but they cannot withstand the frightful fireballs that the invading warships
spit out in great streams. After the defenders die to the last
man, the invaders sail on to Baltimore, which they
overwhelm within hours. Marching overland they come
face to face with the urgently assembled Army of the
Union. The despicable foreign devils take unfair advantage, their soldiers run at the crouch instead of facing the
foe upright and with banners flying and drums beating.
Helpless before such devious conduct, the Americans
throw down their arms. They can only watch with horror
as the fiendish Orientals in an appalling act of infamy put
to torch the Academy of Sciences, the Library of Congress,
the National Museum, the National Art Gallery, the very
Capitol itself.

"The President, willing to make any sacrifice to rid the
sacred capital of the Yellow horde, urges Congress to enter
into a humiliating treaty, one which permits the opening
of foreign legations within earshot of the Oval Office. And
that's not all. Enclaves are to be opened up in New York,
Boston, Baltimore, Philadelphia, Galveston, Portland,
Seattle wherein foreign nationals can enforce their own
laws, station their own police, garrison their own soldiers,
collect their own taxes, and trade in whatever merchan-
dise their hearts desire. To add a touch of legitimacy to the
enclaves, they are given the term 'Concessions.'

"These Concessions are, however, mere appetizers – the
main course is yet to come. Mexico annexes Louisiana
and takes control of all trade and communication links in
the neighboring state of Texas. Rude cabaleros pour into
New Orleans and give it a new Spanish-sounding name
that translates as 'The Lord of the South.' Cuba now
enters the scene for the first time. It declares war on the
United States and easily wins the first and only battle of
that war. As reparations it is given Hawaii, Rhode Island,
and a piece of Texas. Burma decides it's time to take over

37

JEFFERSON WU'S AMERICA UNDER FOREIGN YOKE

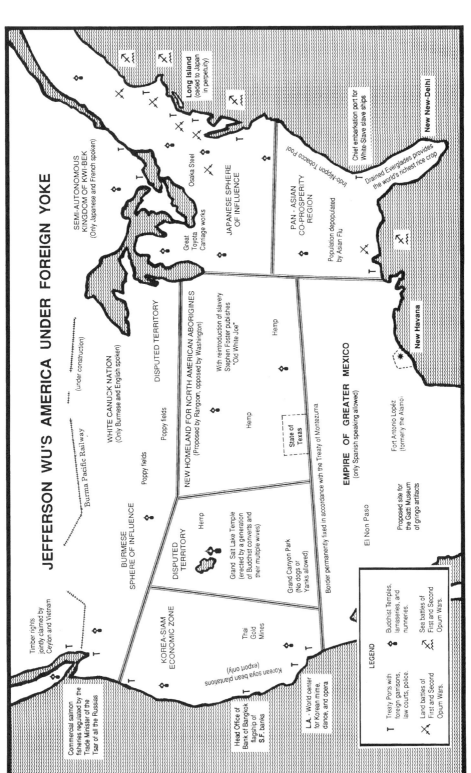

Commercial salmon fisheries regulated by the Trade Minister of the Tsar of all the Russias

Timber rights jointly claimed by Ceylon and Vietnam

Burma Pacific Railway

(under construction)

WHITE CANUCK NATION
(Only Burmese and English spoken)

DISPUTED TERRITORY

Poppy fields

SEMI-AUTONOMOUS KINGDOM OF KWI-BEK
(Only Japanese and French spoken)

Long Island
(ceded to Japan in perpetuity)

BURMESE SPHERE OF INFLUENCE

Poppy fields

Great Toyota Carriage works

Osaka Steel

JAPANESE SPHERE OF INFLUENCE

NEW HOMELAND FOR NORTH AMERICAN ABORIGINES
(Proposed by Rangoon, opposed by Washington)

With reintroduction of slavery Stephen Foster publishes "Old White Joe"

Hemp

Indo-Nippon Tobacco Pool

Chief embarkation port for White Slave ships

New New-Delhi

Drained Everglades provides the world's richest rice crop

PAN-ASIAN CO-PROSPERITY REGION

Population depopulated by Asian Flu

Head Office of Bank of Bangkok flagship of S.F. banks

KOREA-SIAM ECONOMIC ZONE

Korean soya bean plantations (export only)

DISPUTED TERRITORY

Hemp

Thai Gold Mines

Grand Salt Lake Temple (erected by a generation of Buddhist converts and their multiple wives)

Grand Canyon Park (No dogs or Yanks allowed)

Border permanently fixed in accordance with the Treaty of Montezuma

Hemp

State of Texas

L.A. - World center for Korean mime, dance, and opera

El Non Paso

EMPIRE OF GREATER MEXICO
(only Spanish speaking allowed)

Proposed site for the Gatti Museum of gringo artifacts

Fort Antonio López (formerly the Alamo)

New Havana

LEGEND

T — Treaty Ports with foreign garrisons, law courts, police.

◆ — Buddhist Temples, lamaseries, and nunneries.

✕ — Land battles of First and Second Opium Wars.

✕ — Sea battles of First and Second Opium Wars.

Ontario, a traditional American dependency. India occupies Florida, turning Miami into a powerful naval fortress. Malaya and Ceylon come to snatch what little is left.

"And all the while this great land grab is going on, the United States of China, dedicated to the proposition that all men are created equal, complains loudly and bitterly from the sidelines about the perfidious behavior of the nations involved in the despoilment. Its Secretary of State, Hei-tze (Americans with their silly system of spelling, spell it Hays), presses the other powers into agreeing to an 'Open Door' policy, one which gives everyone the right to trade in each other's sphere of influence. Therefore, the great liberty loving republic, without occupying an inch of land, without dirtying its fingers, gains privileges as piratical as those of the worst offender.

"From the very beginning the foreigners introduce religious commissars: monks, preachers, medicine men, for the purpose of converting the 'heathen' Americans to the true faith of Buddhism. The most ardent of these commissars hail from the lamaseries of China. They stop at nothing in their resolve to convince Americans to abandon their ancient belief that God in one of his three mystical manifestations visited the world in the guise of a Hebrew carpenter's male child – a child born out of wedlock, the Lamaists are keen to point out. At first, native Americans treat the missionaries as harmless crackpots, but when they begin constructing monasteries and temples and schools and are successful in converting a number of gullible inhabitants – handing out free bread as enticement – it's no longer a laughing matter. To the President it is the last straw. He bars further entry of pagan proselytizers. 'What!' say the Chinese, 'that's intolerable interference with our God-given rights. Send in the marines! Shoot a dozen senators!' Washington relents. Free entry is granted to all religious men. The zealots from China can now spread to any province they please, convert whomever they wish. They fatten and multiply. Their only constraint is their own internal division. The Hinayana sect expounds individual austerity while the Mahayanas teach faith and good works. Each faction calls the other heretical, and each pleads with the native Americans to shut their ears to the offending blasphemy of its rival . . ."

"Holy Moses!" Dwight Anderson has to shout to be

heard. "What the heck was all that about? I've lost track of all that Hyana-Myana monkey talk. Anyway, what's it got to do with American freedom?"

"American freedom, my dear Dwight, insofar as it concerns China, is empty talk. We Chinese have our own ideas of freedom. We had them a thousand years before America was ever thought of. And you'd better know that nothing in the world is going to prevent us regaining that freedom. Time is on our side. The day is fast coming when you'll all be gone. Today's proud parade is proof positive of that. Three of its original cast are no longer to be seen saluting at the gravesides. I am referring to the Russians, the Germans, the Austro-Hungarians. And who will be next? The Japanese? The Italians? Surely you must know they're on the carpet at the League of Nations over Manchuria and Abyssinia. Mark my words, Siege Day will soon be a thing of the past, its remaining participants gone with the wind. And when you are back in your own homelands it may begin to dawn on you that the only reason why your families came here in the first place was to exploit the Chinese . . ."

"Not us."

"No sir."

Jefferson sticks out his chest. "Then pray tell me why they ever came here. . . ."

NOTICE.

TIENTSIN PIGGERY AND HAM SUPPLY,

East Arsenal, & Victoria Road, American Concession.

The Undersigned begs to notify Hotel Managers, Clubs, Messes and Private residents, that he has this day opened a Retail Store and solicits their patronage.

M. GEISMAR.

f23 5 04

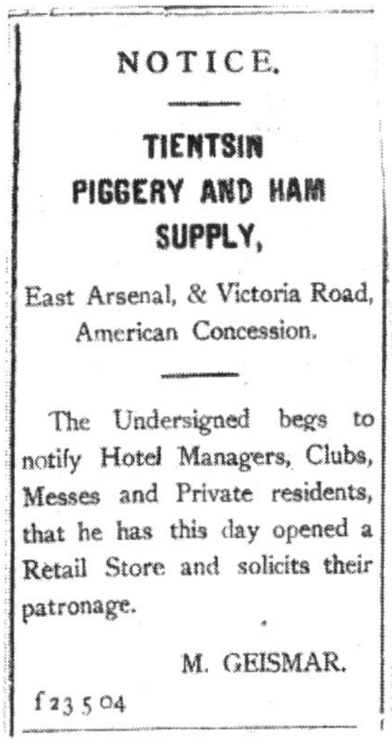

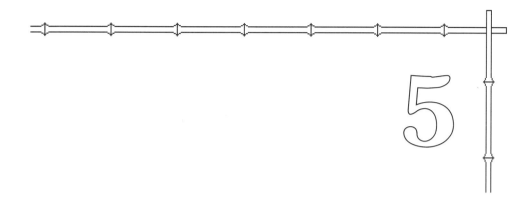

EARLY ARRIVALS

WHY HAD OUR FAMILY COME OUT TO CHINA? Even in my younger days I lost count of the number of times that question was put to me. And no quick answer as in the case of Igor Kapoostin and Alex Micoutine and Yasha Coblenz whose families had come down from Siberia to escape Bolshevik terror. As for Joe Pascual and Fatty Sparks, they were in China because their fathers happened to be serving with the 15th US Infantry, stationed in Tientsin. I was sometimes tempted to say that my own father, like Dick and Joe Hall's and Sandy Kennedy's and Frankie Butterworth's, having been recruited overseas by the Chinese Maritime Customs, was invited to China by the Chinese. But then most people knew that the Chinese Customs service wasn't really Chinese; it was foreign-controlled; its top wallah, the Inspector General, more often than not a Briton as were most of the internal staff.

Tariffs, rules and regulations, in fact all official documents were in English first. English was the rule. Inevitably, in the English way, there were the somebodies and the nobodies. High and mighty management stood a world apart from the tidewaiters, examiners, appraisers, so many of them drawn from the flotsam and jetsam of the Western world. Advancement from the lower ranks was discouraged. You might hear of appraiser so-and-so working his way up to an inside position, but he was the rare exception. For the mainstream, the only escape from the lower decks was to serve out the employment contract then sign on with some local firm. My father, Stephen Power, was one who took that step.

He was the twelfth of fifteen brought into this world by Thomas and Margaret Power in the tiny hamlet of Querrin, County Clare. A brood of fifteen! All too common in fiercely Papist Ireland, the constant threat of famine notwithstanding. His farm income inadequate for so many mouths, Thomas took to bootmaking to augment his living, but even so two of his brood died in infancy. For the thirteen survivors it was a question of reducing their number or suffer the same fate. Only three stuck it out on the old sod. Five emigrated to America, three to England, and two to China. China! Heathen Cathay! Incredible, you might think, for rural folk whose horizon stretched no farther than Kilkenny or Kilkee. But not really so incredible. Word of job openings paying 70 taels (ten English pounds) a month at Chinese Maritime Customs simply channeled up the Shannon in the ordinary everyday way to Kerry, to Limerick, to Clare. Hardly surprising then all those O'Sheas and O'Learys and Gallaghers lighting up the China coast from Taku to Ningpo Mo Fah every March 17th.

Jack, Thomas Power's fourth born, signed up with "Customs." A probationary tidewaiter, posted to the treaty port of Tientsin, he was astounded by the macadamized streets and modern buildings of the foreign concessions. In no time he was enjoying a standard of living unimagined in rural Ireland. He despatched letter after letter urging his younger brother Stephen, unemployed since graduating from the Christian Brothers' College, Kilrush, to put in an application. Stephen did so, was accepted, and set sail in the summer of 1912. As with Jack, he had the good fortune to be stationed in Tientsin and not in some backwater post where there was not another foreigner within a hundred miles. By 1915 he was firmly enough on his feet to be courting Grace, the daughter of a well-established Tientsin couple, George and Agnes D'Arc. He won Grace's favor, but not her parents'. They, with better prospects in mind for their daughter than a Customs man from the ranks, and a drinker to boot, withheld their blessing. Normally, in an Edwardian family, that would have been that; a daughter was not supposed to have a mind of her own. Eighteen-year-old Grace, our future Tai-tai, proved the exception by flying the coop and marrying her Stephen before the year was out.

The two brothers
from Clare:
Stephen (left)
and Jack.
Tientsin, 1913.

The few bare-bone facts concerning Stephen's family background, his reason for being in China, his elopement, and his early death, came from my brother Pat. Tai-tai told me next to nothing. When I was old enough to ask, she (by then remarried) would simply say that *he* was with the angels in heaven and that it behooved me to remember him in my prayers. So with no one else to turn to – Uncle Jack having long pulled up stakes and sailed back to Clare – I was obliged to face the cold hard reality of spending the rest of my life knowing that my father would never be anything more to me than a shadowy specter.

Nothing hazy about Tai-tai's side of the family; the D'Arcs featured prominently in her conversation. Moreover, though grandfather George had died the same year as Stephen, and grandmother Agnes was living out her days in England, their name was a household word in the concessions. Any rickshaw coolie could run you to *Da-ke Fandian* – D'Arc's Hotel – a noted Tientsin landmark.

And it wasn't just in Tientsin that the D'Arcs cut a niche for themselves; they had gained public notice before ever coming to China. George's father, Lambert D'Arc, an expert wax modeler who had left his native France to create effigies for Madame Tussaud in England, achieved fame when he branched off on his own to work on moving figures – marionettes. In his article *D'Arc's in Dublin* (Theatre Notebook, vol XLVIII-1), John Phillips, arts historian and specialist in the puppet theater, describes D'Arc's as being one of the leading marionette companies at a time when Britain was pre-eminent in the field.

It was during the 1880s when the reputation of D'Arc's Marionettes was at its peak that Lambert and his two sons, William and George, began touring the show over-

43

seas. At times they set off individually, William covering South Africa and Australia, and George Japan and China. Everywhere they were well received, puppetry's world of make-believe continuing to catch the public's fancy until it gave way to radio and cinema some twenty years later. It was the time of Joseph Conrad and Robert Louis Stevenson, a time when crossing vast oceans and visiting distant lands was imbued with mystique and romance, as George could personally vouch. On his 1894 tour of the Orient, while captivating audiences with his marionette productions of *Blue Beard* and *Murder in the Red Barn*, he himself was captivated – by the show's vocalist, Agnes Maney. They married on their return to London. A year later their only child, Grace, was born.

They left Grace behind with relatives when in the autumn of 1899 they set off for Peking, the eight-week ocean voyage, much of it through the tropics, too precarious for a three-year-old. Moreover, once in Peking, they were going to have enough on their hands, not only with their marionette performances, but with court bureaucracy. George was under commission to create a wax effigy of the Empress Dowager Tzu Chih. And a very good thing Grace was not with them, for, within weeks of their arrival, tens of thousands of fanatical "Boxers" rose up to slaughter every foreigner in the land – man, woman, and child. Panic raced through Peking's legations when missionaries and converts pouring in from the countryside brought word of mutilation and mass beheadings. It seemed certain that they would all face the same ghastly end, the detachments of legation guards too fragmentary to withstand a siege.

44

Before the first shots were fired, George, along with a Frenchman and an Australian, volunteered to entrain for Tientsin to raise men and supplies. At Langfang, halfway to their destination, the Boxers blew the track. Braving fusillades of blunderbuss and musket shot, George's party made a break for it through the sorghum fields. Hiding by day and moving by night, they ran into a patrol of Sikhs at the outskirts of Tientsin before their pursuers could close in on them.

George had hardly time to regain his breath before he was heading back to Peking with Admiral Seymour's hastily assembled relief force. At Langfang – where George's gutted train was still lying on its side – the force was attacked by overwhelming numbers of Kansu warriors. Seventeen hundred of Seymour's original two thousand men managed to claw their way back to Tientsin but only to find the enclave itself under intense bombardment by the Imperial army's rapid-fire Krupps guns. The five-mile perimeter held, but it was a close call; the allied storm troops, fighting their way from the coast, arriving just as the defenses were crumbling. And it was no walk-over for the elite regiments from Europe, America, and Japan; it took acts of extraordinary valor to raise the siege. Colonel Emerson Liscum, a Civil War hero promoted on the field at Gettysburg, fell leading a bayonet attack against a crack Manchu banner brigade. Major Bruce, Commander of the Weihaiwei Regiment, was cut down when he set out to spike a particularly murderous artillery piece. Casualties were indeed so heavy that the advance on Peking had to be put on hold until reinforcements arrived. Six agonizing weeks went by before Commander-in-Chief Gaselee gave the order for the eight-nation force to advance on the capital. Ten days of marching and fighting and fighting and marching, and George, now in the uniform of the Frontier Rifles, stood on the ramparts of the Tartar Wall looking down onto the legation quarter, the point from which he'd set off two months earlier. How he must have fallen on his knees in thanksgiving when he discovered his beloved Agnes among the survivors!

Despite the heat of the moment, Sir Claude MacDonald, British Minister in Peking, found time to praise Agnes and to recommend her for a medal for aiding the wounded while under fire. A fragment of his personal letter to George is shown on the next page:

45

... and Agnes got her medal

After the smoke of battle cleared, a generous UK government offered free passage home to all who survived the siege. Quick on the uptake, George and Agnes boarded the first ship out. One would have thought that having barely escaped with their lives theirs was a one-way ticket. Not so. Whether they had been bitten by the "Call of the East," or were lured by the ready fortune to be made in the flourishing foreign concessions, they were soon heading back to Peking, this time with daughter Grace.

But even more venturesome for a couple in mid-life, they gave up their calling in the entertainment field for a career in the hospitality industry. At first they bought into the Hôtel de Pékin, owned and operated by their close friend and fellow siege veteran Auguste Chamot. But all the action was down in Tientsin, eighty miles to the south. So that's where they moved, and that's where they commissioned the construction of D'Arc's Grand Hotel. Their foresight paid off. The hotel, ideally situated near the downtown end of Race Course Road, enjoyed full occupancy from the start. A fairy-tale ending to their story? Yes, but that would have to wait a few years. After only thirteen months of operation the hotel burned to the ground. A sensational event for Tientsin, at least that's how the papers saw it:

GREAT FIRE IN TiENTSIN,

D'ARC'S HOTEL COMPLETELY GUTTED.

One of those terribly-sudden catastrophes which shake the nerve of the whole town has just occurred, when an institution which appeared to be in full glow of comfort and security one night is no longer in existence the next morning.

D'Arc's Grand Hotel, opened but a little over a year ago, and built specially for the proprietor by the Tientsin Land Investment Company Ltd., was burnt down between midnight and three o'clock yesterday morning. Fortunately no lives were lost.

Fire was first seen coming out of the bed-rooms on the upper floor at the south-west corner of the hotel, at the end of Racecourse Road. In an incredibly short time the whole building was ablaze. The flames, helped by a strong wind that was blowing, ran along and in less than half-an-hour the whole building was hopelessly involved.

A general fire alarm was given over the Settlements, and the Volunteer fire brigade responded to the call with great promptitude. Despite the intense cold the Volunteers worked

47

with perseverance and energy, and it was undoubtedly owing to their efforts that the fire was prevented from spreading. In this work, they were ably assisted by the German Pioneers. The French and Russian firemen also arrived and bore their share of the night's work, the Russians pulling down the verandah and tearing down the highly inflammable woodwork. The Chinese firemen from the City and the Japanese and British detachments also came on the scene. The German brigade had two streams on, pumped from the canal, and deserve great credit for their activity.

At half-past one the entire hotel was a roaring furnace, red hot beams crashing through to the basement and sending up dangerous showers of sparks. It needed the greatest vigilance to cope with this new danger.

Earlier, a pathetic incident was witnessed when young Miss Gracie D'Arc was aroused and after running out on the balcony in the bitterly cold night partly dressed, insisted on going back for her two dogs, which she safely carried out of danger. An amusing incident arose when the hotel's much prized cockatoo was carried out, screaming "Mother, mother!"

Universal sympathy will be felt for Mr George D'Arc, one of the most popular and ever-genial of hosts, who after three years of unremitting labour, assisted by a devoted wife, had by sheer pluck and energy built up a most promising business and won himself the esteem of all. It is to be hoped that this blow will not discourage him and that he will quickly regain that buoyant lightness of heart for which he is so well known.

****

Far from discouraged, George immediately drew up plans for a new D'Arc's Hotel, the one that was to shine as a Tientsin showpiece in the decades ahead.

The "ever-genial host" of the new D'Arc's Hotel continues to serve in the
Frontier Rifles (forerunner of the Volunteer Defense Corps).

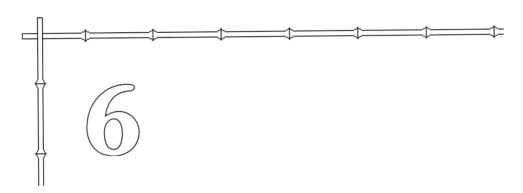

THE FABLED LAND OF PEACH BLOSSOMS

IS IT SATAN'S DOING or simply a trick of fate that disaster will so often strike when all is going well? It happened to George and Agnes D'Arc on the night of January 18, 1904 when fire destroyed their hotel. It happened to Hazel Booth, Denis Fulton, Jimmy Larsen, and scores of others from Chefoo School when on the afternoon of January 5, 1935 their ship was boarded and captured by pirates. It happened to me on Sunday morning February 9, 1936 when our warm and secure (at least to my thirteen-year-old mind) fold came asunder with the departure of Patrick and Jocelyn for England, and Brian soon to follow.

As can be seen opposite, *North China Star* considered Pat a popular enough figure to warrant equal billing with Adolf.

Never mind that the paper had it wrong (Joss, not Pat, was joining the RN), a large crowd of well-wishers gathered at Tientsin East to see the boys off on their seventeen-day journey that was to take them across Siberia, Russia proper, Germany, and France. The sight of Pat waving at the carriage window as the train inched along the platform brought copious tears to the bevy of young maidens present. And no wonder, as a crooner on Tong Fang Radio (*Smoke Gets In Your Eyes*, his theme song), he was quite the heartthrob. Weeping being the most catching of human emotions, the tears on all those faces launched me, despite my manly efforts to contain myself, into my own barrage of sobs.

NORTH CHINA STAR

February 7, 1936

POWER LEAVING NEXT SUNDAY FOR ENGLAND TO JOIN ROYAL NAVY

Mr. Patrick S. Power

Mr. Patrick S. Power, youthful sportsman of Tientsin, is leaving Sunday morning for England via Siberia to join the Royal Navy. He is a Tientsin boy, and was born here 19 years ago.

Young Power is quite an accomplished youth. As a sportsman he has made the local team in the interport ice hockey series against Peiping. A member of the Old Grammarians Club, he represents his old school in ice hockey and football.

During the Summer he plays on the Tientsin Swimming Club's water polo team, and he is also an ardent fisherman.

He has taken a number of prizes for his caricatures, several of which have been reproduced in local papers. He also has appeared in small parts in amateur theatricals, and, as a member of the Air Raiders, has been heard broadcasting every fortnight over the local Station.

Power leaves with his younger brother, Jocelyn, who intends to continue his studies in England.

HITLER OPENS 4TH WINTER OLYMPICS IN PRESENCE OF 80,000

United Press

Garmisch, Feb. 6.—In a howling snowstorm, a crowd of 80,000 sports enthusiasts watched Herr Adolph Hitler open the Fourth Winter Olympics at the Garmisch Ski Stadium, in a ceremony in which the participants paraded in national groups, the Reich Chancellor saluting and a cannon booming with the passing of each flag.

Doctor von Salt, greeting the various competitors, said that he hoped it would be a "tournament of peace, leading to a better understanding among nations," after which Herr Hitler declared the games opened, saying the athletes should compete in spirit of sportsmanship.

With Herr Hitler's words, flames shot forth from the special towers erected in nearby hills, which will burn until the games close on February 16.

Herr Hitler then departed for Munich by automobile amid the waving and cheering of the crowds.

The first competition will be the hockey games. The United States will play Germany and Canada will meet Poland.

Ever since I could remember, Pat had taken me under his wing. How proud I was to be seated by his side at *Friday Night Fights* at the American Barracks! What triumph when he had me appointed mascot of the *Pirates*, that mostly Russian ice-hockey team he played on! And how could I ever forget those occasions when he whispered into my ear at breakfast: "Go dig worms at Weitze Creek. We are going after golden carp." And no need to worry about a written excuse for the teacher next day. He could forge Tai-tai's signature to perfection. One Palm Sunday when everyone thought we were at Mass, we were having marvelous sport with *huang zhuan* – local pike – at their most ravenous following the ice break-up. (Even to this day I can savor the tang of fresh thawing earth that wafted in the air that long-ago spring morning.) On the way home we picked a fern each (no palm trees in Tientsin) from the hedge bordering Min Yuan. Till Easter Sunday those ferns of ours adorned the mantelpiece in the drawing room alongside the ones blessed at High Mass by Monseigneur Jean Baptiste Leclerc, Archbishop of Shantung, Honan, and Hopei.

With Brian's departure to London University (Tai-tai could only afford to give one of us a higher education and he got the nod), I was elevated to the position of elder brother. And one of my first duties as such was to oversee the rickshaw carrying Tony and Betty on the day we moved house. Our hearts couldn't have sunk lower when we said good-bye to our beloved eleven-room home at 20 Edinburgh Road. No more Madison Square Garden, no more chasing across the road to Min Yuan to fly kites, no more training for the Olympics on the cinder running track. Our new much more compact house on Sydney Road (it was years before we could call it home) was hemmed in by the high-walled Liang residence on our right, the Husisian family – Mr and Mrs and Johnnie (Carapet) and Alice (Arousiag) – on our left, and the forbidding Sikh Temple at the rear. The only place for Tony and me to hunt crickets and shoot catapults was the postage stamp of a field standing between our front yard and the side wall of an imposing red-brick building, the residence of the distinguished Canadian missionary, Reverend Hugh MacKenzie. I don't think the reverend or any of his abundant progeny – the names Norman, Findlay, Esther, Florence (Mrs Eric Liddell) spring to mind – gave

FIGHTS!

RECREATION HALL

AMERICAN BARRACKS

To-day   **To-day**

9.00 P.M.

MAIN EVENT
FOR THE WELTERWEIGHT CHAMPIONSHIP OF THE ORIENT

GRAY   vs.   **CREIGHTON**
15th U.S. Inf.   Shanghai

8 ROUNDS 8

SEMI-FINAL
GREEN   vs.   **SEMINOFF**
Peiping Marines   Tientsin

6 ROUNDS 6

SIEGRIST   vs.   **BOTTI**
Peiping Marines   French Army

4 ROUNDS 4

HEMMING   vs.   **VELISOFF**
Worcestershire Regt.   Tientsin

4 ROUNDS 4

WILLIS   vs.   **MEZIEK**
15th U.S., Inf.   Peiping Marines

4 ROUNDS 4

RANDALL   vs.   **KID NICK**
Peiping Marines   Tientsin

4 ROUNDS 4

KID FRISCO   vs.   **ALEXIS**
Tientsin   Harbin

3 ROUNDS 3

Seats Now On Sale

Make Reservations by Chit or Phone 34374, the Athletic and Sentinel Office,
American Barracks.

Dismal Desmond
the popular
stuffed dog
of the day

two hoots about our climbing their wall, it was always the servants who came running out to shoo us away.

I had never experienced a bleaker time. Someone (Doong Ji?) dug up that needling label I thought I had long outlived – *Dismal Desmond*, the popular children's toy of the day, a spotted dog with droopy ears, droopy snout, droopy expression. I had yet to learn that dark clouds really can have silver linings. And for me the silverest of linings came with Tai-tai's announcement that our numbers now depleted we could go to Peitaiho for the whole summer. The *whole* summer, Heavens to Betsy, when we'd never ever stayed longer than a fortnight in that most beguiling spot on planet earth! Beguiling? Yes, for sure. Who could fail to be beguiled by Peitaiho's perfumed air, tranquil bays, verdant hills, which some sage once likened to *Shih Wai Tao Yuan* – the fabled land of peach blossoms beyond the living world?

I still can't believe it's happening, but here we are, only two days after school has broken for the summer, being led by Tai-tai onto the second-class carriage at Tientsin East for the seven-hour journey along the northern coastline of the Gulf of Peichihli. Our excitement reaches fever pitch when with bells clanging and whistles shrilling and the locomotive letting off tremendous blasts of steam, we lurch into motion. Soon we are rounding the great salt pans of Tangku and running alongside ancient junks plying ancient waterways, and all the time drawing closer to the vast range of purple mountains. Pretty hair-raising when the train slows to walking pace as it crosses the shaky Luan Hsien Bridge a hundred feet above the river bed. Tai-tai keeps her eyes shut. Hard to say whether it's a case of nerves or whether she has been lulled by all that rocking and swaying. Not me. Not once do I close my eyes. When there is nothing to look at, I reach up to retrieve my kit bag from the overhead rack to take stock of my treasure: the spool of gut line, the hooks, sinkers, sheath knife, catapult, scout's compass, fifty cents small money.

At Linsi, hawkers crowd the window with trays of *feiluoji* – mouth-watering red-smoked chicken. How can we forego so wondrous a treat? Risking a storm, we rouse Tai-tai. And we do the same at Changli, North China's fruit capital, where cherries grow as large as walnuts, and the apricots are said to be perfumed by the gods. As we munch away, Tai-tai remarks: "I wonder how the poor dears are doing." And by "poor dears" she means, of course, our amah's family, all three generations, back in third class, who, from the moment of departure, have surely been laid low by their old nemesis – motion sickness. Tai-tai has good reason for bringing them. She herself can stay only two days. We are going to be under the amahs until she returns in August for the fortnight's vacation due to her as a secretary in the Hongkong & Shanghai Bank.

But for now she's still boss, and she shows it as we arrive at our hotel (it was Peaceful Hotel that year) by scotching our plan to race for the beach. "Don't you dare. We're all too tired. To supper and to bed. It'll be morning before you know it."

Every few minutes I toss and turn on my creaking camp cot. "Morning before I know it? Doomsday will get here first!"

But the very next thing it *is* morning – brilliant white-yellow morning. I rush through my ablutions. I make a bee-line for our table on the verandah. I attack my breakfast. Jie-jie won't have it. She adjures me with her "*Mahn-mahn, mahn-mahn*" – go slow, go slow. But never mind what she says, I make quick work of the porridge flooded with lukewarm milk of a peculiar taste, of the eggs turned and fried crisp, of the bacon hardly fried at all, of the soft sweetish rolls into which I stuff unrestricted lashings of butter and strawberry jam.

Soon as Tai-tai quits the verandah, Tony and I are off, leaving the amahs howling in our wake. The salt tang and the roar of breakers speed us on, but we're smart enough to keep an eye out for stones, the soles of our bare feet cradle tender. Not so in a fortnight when they'll be thick as cowhide.

Suddenly, we are at West End Beach, that great stretch of golden sand, and there it is, the ocean – immense, sweeping, magnificent. A mad dash to see who's in first. Surprising sting to the eyes. Mouthful of salt. "Youch! Jellyfish!" The small inch-round transparent ones the deadliest. They get into the swimsuit. They sting that most private part of one's private parts. Scamper up the burning beach. Rub sand on the sting. Bask in the dazzling rays. Squint at the endless void of blue.

When Tai-tai arrives, bedecked in her yellow beach

All set for
a morning's
fishing at
Tiger Rocks

kimono, we, that is Tony and Betty and I and our amahs and other people's amahs and fruit vendors and fishermen and the odd passer-by, collect at the hotel's *peng* (straw-matting sun shelter) to hear her hold forth in her aristocratic Mandarin. It's an age before she catches my eye and gives the nod. At once I make my way along the rocky trail that skirts Anchor Bay. I catch sight of a lucky fellow down there on the breakwater, his rod doubled, playing a fish. How my fingers itch for my own rod! But it's too late to head back to the corner of the hotel verandah where I left it. I turn my gaze on that old familiar sight, the fishermen's summer camp – several junks pulled up on the sand, the one nearest the edge of the coarse grass overturned to provide shelter from the sun. I descend to beach level and proceed past the big hotel, Peitaiho Hotel, past the rich muckamucks lounging in the shade of their Taj Mahal of a *peng*. I wade ankle deep in the surf between Baby Beach and Tiger Rocks. Now before my eyes is the curving inlet of American Beach. I know that if I climb the steep promontory at the far end, I'll be gazing down onto English Beach and Legation Point and Temple Bay. Better turn back, it's a long haul to Peaceful Hotel.

The Fleuriets are there on the verandah, all seven of them: Père, Mère, André, Roger, René, Madeleine, and baby Aimée. They've got the bungalow next to ours. They're all jabbering away with Tai-tai who has total command of French, just as she has of German, and of Chinese. René clutches my arm. He wants to come fishing with me in the morning.

At first light we're at Tiger Rocks with rod and tackle, and the handful of sea worms we bought for ten cents from a grizzled fisherman who dug them up at low tide. In no time I locate the swirling blackness of that underwater chasm where Patrick and Leslie McKenzie took those whopping rock bass two years back and where I triumphed with my very first trophy half-pounder last year. Gently, gently, lower the gut line, feel for the bottom, raise the rod which raises the sinker about ten inches. No reel. We fish Japanese style. We depend on the pliability of the rod tip to play the fish.

The first tug. The heart takes off. Thump-thump-thump-thump! How can the rib cage stand such buffeting? Don't strike, not yet. Agonizing wait. Three sharp tugs in rapid succession, and the rod tip ploughs beneath the surface. Strike! Opposing forces gone mad. Breath-stopping thrill. That powerhouse down there surges this way and that – hope it's not a dogfish – give a bit, take a bit, use the next big swell to draw it into the long narrowing tide pool. Furious bout of thrashing, and there it is on its side, gills gaping, eyes angry, dorsal spikes fully extended. It glistens with the luxuriant black-brown-yellow markings of a *hei luzi* – rock bass to us. Watch out! Get spiked, and you'll know about it for the next forty-eight hours.

Have to wait for my fingers to stop their crazy trembling before I can re-bait the hook. Split open the stringy seaweed-matted outer covering to get at the moist or-angey creature inside. Never mind its searching incisors; the worst it can do is give a little nip.

René is fishing some ways off on a large smooth slab. A dry, comfortable place. I know it well. Though it juts a good thirty feet farther out into the sea than where I am standing, there's a sand bank there, the water too shallow for bass. Okay for bream later on in the year. Hope he hasn't seen me get my bass. Don't want company.

Tug-tug-tug-tug, little jerky tugs, Dammit! Eggfish, rascally eggfish. Variegated blue-white-green sprinkled with orangey freckles. Eye-catching for sure, but deadly poisonous. And with their razor-sharp teeth they can cut your line as if it were cotton thread. Even when you manage to land one, its stomach will blow up like a balloon making it devilishly hard to retrieve your hook. Worst of all, once they find you, they never leave you.

I move to a new spot.

Ten o'clock. Can see families arriving on American Beach. The younger kids screech and holler, the brawnier ones swim out to the raft, which is anchored about fifty yards from shore. They're diving off it. Too far to disturb the fish, but the bass have stopped biting anyway. Can get sandfish in shallower water if I want them, but I don't, and it's too early in the season for *bai luzi*, those black-speckled silver beauties. Doesn't matter, the basket's loaded with rock bass and red-finned perch. René wants to head back to the hotel. I want to stay. He hobbles off. He's got a gammy leg. Seems like he's always had one. I clamber over one string of rocks to the next. I stop at the deepest tide pool. Zebra-striped rockfish, spotted sculpin, and blue crab vanish at my approach. Stay perfectly still

and they emerge from underwater caverns concealed in the seaweed jungle. A top-heavy hermit crab begins its tedious trek across a clearing. A stickleback darts out of its private domain. A shoal of minnows flash silver as they scatter. It's a wondrous world within a world. Could stay and watch for hours, but breakers are exploding against the rock faces. The spray stings my face. The tide is encroaching fast. Better get back to the beach before I have to swim for it. There's a long walk ahead, and the late morning sun is already beating down. . . .

"Thought you were never getting back," Tony calls out to me. "Igor Kapoostin came looking for you. He said you could find him tomorrow morning at his family *peng*. It's four *pengs* to the left of ours on West End Beach."

And sure enough, that's where I catch up with him and his pal Ura. They are caulking and painting a flat-bottomed paddle boat, proudly named the *Standadt* after Tsar Nicholas II's royal yacht.

"When the paint's dry we'll go jellyfish hunting," Igor announces.

Jellyfish hunting! How can he have forgotten what happened last year? We had gone out in *Standadt* about a hundred yards from shore and were idling in the gentle swells, peering three feet down for the occasional pastel-hued jellyfish, its top large as a washbasin, its undulating tentacles two feet long at least. Igor wanted one to take back to the fishermen who made them edible by drying them out in the sun after scooping out their soft underbellies. He soon had a monster pink in his landing net. Then a blue. Then a gray-white. Ura and I began lending a hand. We loaded the boat. Crazy thing to do. A sudden movement, and the boat tipped. Next thing we were sloshing around in jellyfish concentrate, not an inch of skin escaping the cruelest stinging imaginable. . . .

I don't mince my words. "You won't ever catch me jellyfish hunting again. Let's go to Lotus Hills."

"Terrific idea," says Igor. "We'll hire donkeys."

"I'll bring Tony."

"Okay."

For sheer adventure, hard to beat an expedition to Lotus Hills, especially when mounted like Buffalo Bill. No sooner do we take our pick from the parade of donkeys and ponies for hire than the triumphant *mafoo* (groom) speeds us onto the quilted saddle and hands us a switch

59

to fend off not only the attacking horseflies, but the disappointed *mafoos* who grab at our feet, swearing to the heavens their steeds are superior in every way.

Igor takes inordinate time over his selection. He even looks into the donkey's mouth, heaven's sakes. The wait is unbearable. We yell at him to get a move on, but his only response is a teasing shrug.

At last we're off, galloping with cowboy exuberance. But do cowboys gallop all the way across the Great Divide? No sir, not even Tom Mix. So we likewise settle into a canter, and pretty soon to a sedate walk; it's a good long way to the ancient Kuan Yin temple at the base of the hills. An hour later, after we have tethered our faithful steeds beside the temple wall, we are breathing air thick with the resinous scent of pine as we snake our way along the footpath through highland forest, through clearings carpeted with bluebell and yellow-petalled lotus, through stands of wild azalea, until at last we stand triumphantly on the lichen-clad outcroppings of the peak.

I point out First River, which from our height is a silver ribbon etched on a green velvet plain.

"Its real name is Tai River," instructs Igor, always in the know. "Peitaiho means north of the Tai River."

"Okay, then what's the real name for that range of mountains that everyone calls 'Queen Victoria On Her Deathbed'?" And there it is, though not as striking as at sunset, but recognizable all the same, the eerie silhouette, formed by distant crags, of the Queen Empress lying in state.

"*Nu Huang Shan* – The Empress Mountain," Igor retorts

with an impish grin.

"What are you saying, Igor? Why would the Chinese even begin to think of naming . . ."

"I can see Anchor Bay," Tony suddenly chimes in, pointing in the opposite direction. "And Tiger Rocks and Lighthouse Point. And over on the left, I think those are the sand dunes."

Yes, that blob of shimmering white is the sand dunes all right, the starting point of the great crescent bay, on whose far side, if it's a clear day, you can discern the shapes of ocean vessels anchored at the coaling port of Chinwangtao.

"Can you see the Great Wall?" Igor asks, sweeping his hand across the vast panorama of mountains, which from time immemorial have been China's northern bulwark.

"No way."

"Can you see it, Ura?"

"Nope."

"But people say they can see the Great Wall from here."

"With a telescope."

"No, with the naked eye."

"Most unlikely when you can't even spot Shanhaikuan, the fortress city where the Wall sweeps down to the sea."

"Look," Tony cries out, excitedly. "There's Eagle Rock."

"Where?"

"There, to the left of East Cliff."

"East Cliff! That's where Leslie McKenzie got a giant rock bass the other day."

"Let's go fishing there tomorrow."

"Terrific, let's go."

And that's how our summer went, action-packed with adventure. How much greater the shock then when Tai-tai and Doong Ji arrived, obliging us to think the unthinkable – it was time to pack. Where had the days gone?

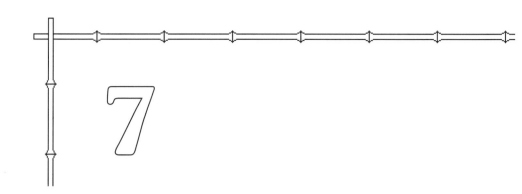

A SKATER'S WALTZ

BACK IN TIENTSIN all seemed strange and unreal. I'd forgotten what it was like, the taste of Gobi dust, the smell of engine exhaust hanging in the air. And the background roar I kept hearing was not the roar of the sea; it was all that motor traffic. Yet in a few days the dust and the fumes and the traffic were the norm, and it was the tranquillity of Peitaiho that was the dream.

Murat Apakaieff, subjected all summer to the retained heat of brick and asphalt, came calling.

There was a whine in his voice. The place was getting him down. He was plumb out of ideas. Could I think of something to do?

"We could always go for a swim at Parkes Road pool."

"I've been suspended."

"Well, we can go to Peining Park, hire a rowboat."

"Crazy! Don't you know how far it is?"

"We've got our bikes."

"And sweat like mad? No thanks."

"Aren't we sweating like mad just sitting here? Come on, let's go."

And so we went. We rode our bikes through the French and Japanese concessions and out past the Chinese City. We might as well have stayed home and played cards, for even an afternoon in a rowboat on a picturesque lake failed to shake my friend out of his doldrums. Afterwards, to keep the peace, I accompanied him to a re-run of Paul Muni's *Scarface*. Next evening it was *G Men*. And then he began badgering me to come with him to the Odeon where his idol Humphrey Bogart was starring in *Black Legion*. I could see now why he had taken to turning up his coat collar and angling the brim of his father's fedora. No more gangster films, I told him, my pocket money didn't stretch that far. Besides, I had other things in mind which he, not being a Scout, wouldn't understand. Two more merit badges – First Aid and Signaler's – and not only was I a King's Scout, I would have my Green and Yellow Cords. Last Siege Day I was in Peitaiho, but what about the coming one? Come hell or high water I was going to cut a dash with my cords at Canton Road Cemetery next June 17th.

Murat the George Raft look-alike with papa's fedora

So nothing for it but to break off with Murat and seize on Patrol Leader Promptoff's offer to stay behind after our Friday meetings to coach me. He knew his stuff did Patrol Leader Victor Promptoff. Through October and November he drilled me so assiduously I could name and locate every major bone and artery in the human body. All that was left to do was ask Scoutmaster Watkins to set a date for the tests. Then winter struck. Never so early in December did Siberian winds whip through Tientsin, frosting all the windows in fern-like designs and freezing the Hai Ho in a solid sheet of ice. For days International Bridge was impassable. Mr Watkins, who lived across the river in the Russian Concession, called off Scout meetings until further notice.

Not everyone minded the premature onset of winter. To skaters it was a godsend. For the first time in its history Tientsin Skating Club opened before Christmas. And what a club, what facilities! Its massive matting structure housed a hockey rink, a beginners rink, a figure skating rink, and an encircling forty-foot-wide track. On the promise that I'd improve on my school marks, Tai-tai got me a season pass. As for skates, I had my pick of the jumble of CCMs, Polars, and Solingens left behind by my brothers.

I was in the rink's changing room lacing on my boots when Murat Apakaieff, of all people, plopped down beside me.

"Say, Deska, you've missed a lot of fun. Where've you been?"

"Nowhere in particular."

"I saw you outside Anderson Pavilion in your pansy Scout's uniform."

63

"You'd better not let George Constable or Pupiesh or Braddy Hovey hear you say that. They'll show you they're no pansies."

"But they get a kick out of tying knots. What a bore."

"You'd be surprised, Murat, how much fun we have in the Scouts."

"I'm talking about real fun. Come, I'll show you."

Stepping off the sawdust walkway onto the ice, we were immediately drawn into the stream of one-way traffic. And such well mannered traffic, everyone keeping sedately in time to the *Merry Widow Waltz*. If that was what Murat meant by "real fun" then he needed his head examined. But then maybe not. Some skaters *were* having fun. As we went by the hockey rink, the yelling and shrieking from a pom-pom-pullaway chase was wild enough to drown out the loudspeakers. I nudged Murat. I jerked my head. He shook his. "Forget it," he said. "Kids' stuff."

Speed skaters, three of them, swooped around us then shot to the outside of the track where they could get up even greater speed. I quickened my pace, so did Murat, but only to block me with his forearm. "Kids' stuff," he muttered.

We drew up to a girl, all in white, her white fur cap showing up the glossy black-brown of her shoulder-length hair.

Murat did the incredible. He called out to her: "Hiya Tura, howya doin'?"

"None of your business."

I was aghast. Not Murat. He cheeked her a second time. "Want ter skate with Deska and me?"

"No thank you."

I slowed. But Murat, the crazy gink, accelerated, tugging me along with him. He caught up with the girl. He took hold of her arm. "Come on, *durak*," he shot at me, "don't be so slow."

He wasn't far mistaken calling me a *durak*, a Russian dolt. Doltishly, I stuck out an elbow; it was the girl who showed me how to link arms. And worse, I'd forgotten how to skate, my balance all wrong, my knees refusing to flex.

"Can't you keep in step?" Murat scolded.

I don't know how I managed it, but I somehow got my skates to swish in unison with theirs. Never before had my arm nestled in the warmth of a girl's arm. Never before had my hip brushed up against a girl's hip. Waves of inexplicable excitement surged through me. Something told me that no matter how exciting, how overpowering that feeling, I mustn't show the slightest sign of it. So while the two carried on with their chitter-chatter, I stayed mute as a tailor's dummy. We were into our third lap when I felt Tura tense. "There's Margit and Vladimir," she tinkled. "I must join them. He always buys hot dogs." Then with an abruptness that was nothing short of being rude, she disengaged her arm from mine and glided over to a girl skating with a smirking beanpole of a fellow dressed in a yellow roll-neck sweater and tweed knickerbockers.

Murat nudged me. "*Nichevor*, never mind, I know that Vladimir guy. He's a sissy. We can easily get rid of him. *We'll* buy the hot dogs. You take over Margit. Look at her. She's not bad."

That's when I had my first real look at the girl he described as being not bad. Not bad? She was absolutely stunning in her natty red beret, black leather jacket, swirling red skirt . . .

"Well, howzabout it?"

I clamped my lips tight.

"Coming?"

I shook my head.

"Well, I'm not going to let Tura get away that easily. Yesterday, when they switched off the lights at closing time, she let me kiss her."

Kiss her! My knees buckled.

Next evening, after tea, after showing Tai-tai my home-work – she laid down the law on that – I sped down Recreation Road to the rink. I couldn't get my skates on fast enough. No sign of Murat, I sallied out alone on the ice. I wove my way around twosomes and threesomes. I chased speedsters on the track's outer edge. I sauntered behind learners. Still no Murat, no Tura. But there, oh my God, was Margit, her poise, her elegance, her grace – sheer magic. And the way she was swinging and swaying so naturally with the waltz coming over the loudspeakers, the piece must surely have been composed with her in mind. As I sped past, I sneaked a sidelong glance. Drat! She was looking the other way. Never mind, race around the track, come up from behind, and not so fast this time. My reward – an expression of aloof majesty radiating from an immaculate oval face. The face turned my way. I instantly averted my gaze and slowed my stride so that I fell back into the anonymous parade of skaters. That didn't do for long. My heart was still kicking in overdrive. "Chase her, go on, chase after her, get up speed," my inner voice commanded. Why not? I took a deep breath and set off. I was going at a fair lick when that voice returned: "And this time you introduce yourself, Mr Desmond Anthony Power" . . . No way! . . . "All right, wait for Murat then. He'll show you how" . . . Now that's being sensible. . . .

I was coasting along under the spell of fairy lights, grand waltze, and swish of skates when some saucy gallant swerved right into my path and hooked arms with a sweet young thing. At once I was struck by the maddening thought: "What if Margit's smirking Mr Knickerbocker shows up?" Instantly, as though with a mind of their own, my legs began working like pistons. No soldier going over the top pushed on with grimmer determination. How many laps did I cover with my swooping stride? Four? Five? And not the slightest sign of her. Where had she gone? I was no fool. I knew where. She was being treated to a hot dog by that dapper ladies' man. Time to call it quits.

I was dawdling along, watching for the changing room exit, when miracle of miracles, there she was before my very eyes, red beret, black jacket, and all, leaning casually against the boards of the figure skating rink. The next thing I was conscious of was the resounding bang I made when I careered into the boards alongside her. I found myself parked so close I could inhale the puffs of vapor she was exhaling. No law against that. I had as much right to be a spectator as she. While my unfocusing eyes were trying to follow a scarecrow of a woman doing a tedious figure eight that relentless voice inside my head kept insisting that I say something, anything, to the goddess at my side... "I will, I will," I pleaded, "but gimme time, I need time." What a lie! Just the thought of uttering a single word, and I turned to stone. But I could still grasp at straws. Maybe another miracle, maybe *she* might say something to *me*. Of course, she didn't. The nightmare lasted a full five minutes before she turned to leave. And when she did and her jacket swept against my sleeve, I swear I saw stars.

All through classes next morning the vision in the black jacket and red beret held complete command of my senses. And even at midday while at home having my tiffin it kept me in thrall. Back at school, just before the afternoon bell, desperate for someone to share my burden, I accosted Murat in the playground.

"Why weren't you at the rink yesterday?" I opened.

"I took Tura to Star Theatre in the French Concession to see *Rose Marie*. She let me keep my arm around her the whole time. She's hot stuff. What about you? Did you pick up Margit?"

"Pick up"! How could he be so crude?

"There goes the bell, Deska, I'll see you at the rink tonight."

"It's Friday. I've got Scouts."

"Too bad. Tura tells me Margit kisses."

Needless to say, I skipped Scouts that evening. With the whole weekend to do my homework, I was early at the rink. Murat was even earlier. And he hadn't wasted time. There he was, a cocky James Cagney, dallying with two molls – his Tura and my Margit. Did I rush out to join them? Nothing of the kind. I fell in with the fast-growing crowd of patrons at the hot-dog stand. What had come over me? Why had I panicked? Why was I hiding? Was it because Murat found out that Margit kissed? Was that it? If I had had the slightest inkling I was going to lose my nerve, I never would have come skating, I never would have subjected myself to the jostling elbows and tiresome babble and attacking fumes of wieners and sauerkraut and English mustard.

I swear to heaven I would still have been there at closing time, singing the blues, had it not been for that smirking ladies' man, Mr Knickerbocker himself, who shouldered his way into the refreshment area, eyes scanning left, scanning right, obviously on the prowl. And his prey – who else but my Margit? He couldn't help but catch up with her, and when he did, wouldn't that double-crossing Murat throw my sweet angel at him just so he could be alone with his Tura? I sprung into action. I clomp-clomped along the walkway hell-bent for the ice. Almost immediately I spotted Murat with our two sweethearts. I swept up to the trio. What I witnessed turned my blood cold. That rogue who called himself my friend had an arm around Margit's waist. All right, I would show them I was above that sort of behavior. I glided past with chin raised – jaunty, proud, indifferent. And when I heard Murat call out my name, as I suspected he would, I put on my best John Barrymore look of nonchalance.

"Hey, Deska, where've you been? How come you so late?"

I kept my lips sealed. I kept my eyes focused on him, only on him.

"Tura, you remember Des?"

Tura said something. I nodded, but I would not meet her gaze.

"Margit, I want to introduce you to my Irish friend, Desmond Power. Desmond, this is Margit Szladek."

Again I nodded. Again I looked away.

"Come on, join us," Murat said.

Though I could feel Margit's burning stare as I took her proffered arm, I forced myself to look over her head. I did a bit of a hoppity-skip to get in step with them. How gauche! And what a sight I must have looked, my eyes glazed, my lips fixed in a weak artificial smile! What wouldn't I give to be the suave Murat! And why couldn't I call the shots as he did? We'd gone only a single lap when he pronounced, bold as all get out: "Isn't it time, ladies, that we stopped for a hot dog?"

"Yes," chirped Tura.

"Yes," chirped my enchantress.

Immediately, my free hand was searching my pocket.

Thank God for the milled edge of a fifty cent piece! More than enough for two hot dogs by any manner of reckoning.

It was while we were waiting for our order and Murat had won the girls' attention with his Humphrey Bogart talk, that I dared glance at Margit's face. How could anyone not be mesmerized by that finely sculptured nose, those rich dark brows, that creamy-white complexion? She caught my gaze. She gave me a divine smile.

I was floating in heaven when Murat announced, quite matter-of-factly: "Too bad, Margit, that we have to say good-bye." Then he addressed me: "Did you know, Deska, that our Margit is leaving Tientsin?"

Impossible. I couldn't be hearing right.

"Yes," she said, turning her incredibly beautiful face fully on me. "My father is being transferred to Swatow. Poor Mama, she loves skating so. It's been in her blood ever since, as a girl, she learned to do figure eights on the Danube. She comes here to practice every day. There's no ice in Swatow. Don't you think it's unfair?"

Unfair? What about me? No person on earth, living or dead, had ever been asked to bear such unbearable anguish. The end of the world couldn't come soon enough.

Glad it didn't! Next skating season Lucy Attree and Mary Hayes were adorning the Country Club's frozen ponds.

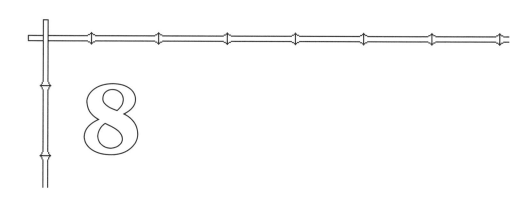

THE TENTH SCOUT LAW

"TROOP, GATHER AROUND, POW-WOW TIME. I want you to pay close attention to what Bunny has to say."

We shuffled forward and squatted in a semi-circle facing Scoutmaster Wallis Watkins and Assistant Scoutmaster Bunny Billoughway. The stern look on Bunny's face told us we were in for a serious talk. Bunny was an Amerasian. He and his Japanese mother had been abandoned by Sergeant Billoughway of the 15th US Infantry when he returned to the States after completing his five-year term of service in Tientsin. According to US law, neither Bunny nor his mother had claim to American citizenship. They went through hard times, the mother barely able to feed and clothe the lad let alone send him to school. Fortunately, the Marist Brothers who ran St Louis College absorbed half his school fee, and the Knights of St Columba chipped in with the rest. He repaid his benefactors in the only way he knew how; by excelling both in class and on the field. As a member of Second Tientsin Troop he earned every merit badge conceived by scoutdom. He had both his Green and Yellow, and Red and White Cords, but more incredibly, he had the fabled Bushman's Thong. It was said he was the only Scout east of Suez to gain that distinction.

Born impervious to the cold, he thought nothing of having us out in the biting wind on a February afternoon flashing our semaphore flags across the frozen rugger pitch at the Union Church end of Recreation Grounds. All feeling would be gone from our fingers and toes before he'd deign to lead us back to our den in Anderson Pavilion. But we had our reward – the brew-up – the traditional outdoorsmen's ritual performed indoors. And just as it would do outdoors, the heavy-duty dixie on the pot stove simmered forever before coming to the boil. At that long awaited moment, the Tenderfoot delegated to the task would proceed to consign half a packet of NAAFI tea into the bubbling turbulence. And only after it turned a rich red-brown would he ladle the brew into our tin camping mugs. Of course, those who couldn't wait for the super-heated mugs to cool paid for it with a good sharp scalding to tongue and lip.

Listen to what Bunny has to say

It was on such an afternoon, after tea was over, and the cleaning up done, that Mr Watkins called us together for our pow-wow. And so there we were, seated cross-legged, bushman style, all ears for what Bunny had to say.

"I want to remind you of one of the most important lessons our founder, Lord Baden Powell, spelled out for us in this the Scouts' bible." Bunny paused, brandishing his yellow-covered copy of *Scouting for Boys*. "Well done if you've read the page I told you to read and can still look each other in the eye. Shame on you if it leaves you hanging your head. That can only mean you've been eating food that's too rich or that you've been sleeping on your back in too warm a bed. Now, speak up anyone who isn't following me."

Not a peep from the troop.

"You can only be a true Scout," continued Bunny, "if you follow the tenth scout law, which is . . . ? which is what, Andrey Ovchinnikoff?"

"A Scout is clean in thought, word, and deed," the curly-headed Tenderfoot from Beaver Patrol rattled off smartly.

Even as Bunny rewarded him with a nod, his eyes were sweeping across the troop. The raspy breathing of Fox Patrol's Arkasha Strigine was the only sound that broke the prison-cell hush.

"Those of you who think it smart telling smutty stories should know that that's the first step on the downward path to what the Chief Scout calls '*Beast-li-ness*'. Now any questions?"

I stole a glance at Hawks Patrol grouped on my right. Some had faces of stone, some had sadness in their eyes. Not Vahab, Urik, or Louis. They were exchanging knowing

71

NORTH CHINA

looks. Ah, yes! Weren't they the ringleaders of the circle that met after meetings in the badminton shed to tell jokes? Wasn't it Urik who just an hour earlier had repeated for me Vahab's latest: "What's the difference between Mae West and a rooster?"

"Surely, one of you has a question?" Bunny went on, coldly persistent.

King's Scout O'Toole raised his hand.

"Yes, what is it Michael?"

"Has all of this to do with thinking about girls, sir?"

Before Bunny Billoughway could gather his thoughts, the golden boy answered for himself: "I never think about girls, sir."

The shouts of wild laughter were instantly silenced by the CLANG-CLANG-CLANG of Scoutmaster Watkins's hiking cane on the cast-iron dixie. Glaring like a ferret, he turned to Bunny. "Carry on if you don't mind, Assistant Scoutmaster."

A recharged Bunny addressed the troop: "Anyone who's not too sure of what I've been getting at, I want him to speak up right here and now."

There was a shifting of positions, creaking of knees, clearing of throats.

"What about you?" He pointed to First Class Scout Francis Phillips. "Do you understand what I've been saying?"

"Yes, sir. That girls are dangerous."

"That's *not* what Bunny's been saying," Mr Watkins shot out.

"Excuse me sir," broke in Michael Tingey of Hawks Patrol. "Did you know that at Phyllis Evans's party they allowed mixed dancing?"

"Boys and girls? Never on your life!"

"But they did. Richard Evans told me himself that he danced the fox trot with Constance Gheradi."

"Under strict supervision, I should hope . . . Now what is it Volodia?"

"Permission to speak, sir."

"Permission granted."

All eyes now on pesky Volodia Perovsky of Fox Patrol.

"In the Sokols, Ataman Yugovich told us that if you think too much about girls before you get married you can develop curvature of the spine."

Arkasha Strigine's pumping shoulders and gurgling

guffaws sent Tenderfoots da Silva and MacAulay into peals of giggles.

"Silence, I say. Stop that silly nonsense at once!"

Before dismissing the troop, Mr Watkins ordered Arkasha to step from the ranks. Under withering looks from both scoutmasters he stood with eyes lowered and head bent, exposing the half-inch of bristle that stood out like a nail brush over his entire scalp. He was a month overdue for his Russian close-crop. And how did he ever manage to wash and dry his face, so pitted was it with acne sores?

You couldn't find anyone more loutish than Arkasha, yet you couldn't help taking to him. And probably so because the grown-ups were always picking on him, always making him the goat. Right now, as we were filing out, several of our patrol whispered words of encouragement. I did better; I gave him a wink and a nudge. Shouldn't have done. I caught Mr Watkins's attention.

"Just a minute, Desmond, just a minute, if you please." The scoutmaster's ferrety eyes had me covered.

"I thought you were going to try for your First Aid badge."

"And your Signaler's," Bunny added.

"I am, sir," I said limply.

"But haven't you missed meetings?"

Snappy thinking, and I came up with the perfect excuse. "I was swotting for my Cambridge prelims, sir."

"There's talk in the troop that you've been at the skating rink mixing with the wrong sort."

Why oh why was I born to blush? Always it was my face that gave me away. Now, they'd never believe another word . . .

". . . If you really want those badges you've got to work for them. Nothing without effort in this life. You know that, don't you?"

"I do, sir."

"Then you are going to work for them."

"Yes, sir."

"Work hard?"

"Yes, sir."

"Good lad. Now I want you to think carefully about what I'm going to say. Patrol Leader Arne Cedervall will shortly be leaving Tientsin. His Second, Ura Abramovitch, is transferring to the Sokols. Hawks Patrol will be in need of both a patrol leader and second. You might fit the bill for

73

leader, but you will have to prove it by putting in a jolly good effort over the next three months. Will you give it a try?"

"Yes, sir. I will, sir. Thank you, sir."

Why didn't I have the guts to speak my mind? Why did I say yes when I was having such a hard time maintaining my keenness for scouting?

Fox Patrol's
Dismal Desmond

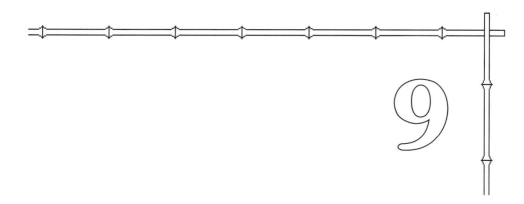

THE SAMURAI CAME DOWN LIKE A WOLF
ON THE FOLD

FOR THE SECOND YEAR RUNNING I missed Siege Day parade. And again Peitaiho came first, but Peitaiho with a difference; no hotel for us, Tai-tai having rented one of the largest houses at the resort – the Quelch residence. Of two-storied solid stone construction, it was a veritable mansion by local standards. The only drawback, it stood at the edge of Tsao Chang Village, a good twenty-minute brisk walk to the sea.

And it wasn't as if we had the house entirely to ourselves. Mr Quelch was retaining two rooms on the upper floor where Tony, Betty, and I were forbidden to venture. But why should we want to when we had so much space for ourselves and the space so richly furnished?

Mr Vernon Quelch was a curiosity, not because he was such a tiny man, and not because he tended an orchard and managed a herd of goats and kept bees, but because he was one of the rare few who stayed in Peitaiho all year round. For ages we'd known him by sight. All of Peitaiho did. You couldn't miss him perched on his donkey, trotting along the dirt track, calling out greetings to all and sundry. Locals would respond with their own salutations and good-natured jibes, addressing him as *Kui Xiansheng* – Mr Kui, or by his sobriquet *Luotuo,* a derivative of the word "camel," a common enough term, and not meant to be demeaning – for hunchbacks. Yes, Mr Quelch was a hunchback. Not so rare in those days. Wasn't Mr Penchly one, and Isidore Rachman, and Solomon Colling, fellow altar boy at the Jesuit church on Race Course

Road? No flies on Solly. Before Mass, when the sacristan wasn't looking, he'd show us how to snaffle a good feed of Communion wafers. Though he might be dwarfish, we didn't trifle with him. He could crack your fingers in his gorilla grip.

But back to Mr Quelch. There he was, greeting us with a warm catching smile at his front gate on that first afternoon of the wonderful long summer that lay ahead.

"Welcome, welcome. Lao Liu and Hsiao Wang will take your bags. Hope you enjoy your stay. Help yourself to all the fruit you want. (We knew all about his fabulous orchard, having raided it for years.) And when you need fresh milk, just ask Liu to milk a goat."

Goat's milk! Ugh! Horrible stench! Ghastly taste!

". . . And watch out for the bees. They're a bit unsettled this year. Swarmed when they shouldn't have. Wear nets if you want to try a comb. Liu will show you where the nets are."

With the orchard to ourselves – cherries and plums already ripening; apples, pears, apricots, peaches, and grapes only a month off – what else could we ask for! The beach, of course, the beach, the ocean!

Next day at first light I was at Tiger Rocks looking down into my secret blue-black chasm. Half an hour and not a bite, but what did I expect with mussels for bait. They were never any good. Then I spied on American Beach the spectral figure of a fisherman wading knee-deep in the surf, his long-bladed spade poised for a sharp thrust into the sand. I lost no time getting over to him. Ten cents was all it cost for a fistful of mat-encased sea worms. The sun was a little too high over the brightening horizon for my liking, nonetheless, before they stopped biting, I had three handsome rock bass strung through the gills in the narrow tide pool.

The roisterous teenagers on American Beach drew me there like a magnet. Would they give me the cold shoulder? Probably. I stole into an empty *peng* – a perfect observation post. The tall, tanned he-men who crossed my line of vision had to be Shanghai city slickers, so brash, so cocksure. But not all the girls were from Shanghai. Two of them I knew from Tientsin Grammar School – Bessie and Lucy Attree. I'd only ever seen them in their school tunics. Now in form-fitting Jantzens they were absolutely stunning. Why couldn't they stay put for

Line of 'pengs'
(Sun shelters)
along
American Beach

a second? Why did they have to stroll off to the far end of the beach? But look, there they were on their way back, graceful as gazelles. And look how proudly they faced up to that much-too-handsome-for-his-own-good Johnny Weissmuller. What a swank, flexing his biceps and sticking out his chest! Before I could think up the worst possible disaster to befall him, he let out a wild Tarzan call and went charging into the surf, and what do you think, the whole shrieking herd of gazelles went stampeding after him. Now they were all doing the American crawl, their powerful overhand strokes taking them into the swells and out of sight. So much for that. Time to go looking for Igor.

At West End Beach the Kapoostin *peng* stood empty, but the family must surely have arrived; for there up on the sand above high water mark was Tsar Nicholas II's royal yacht *Standadt*, freshly caulked and painted. Well, I could always look in at the Kapoostins on my way home; their bungalow less than a stone's throw off Tsao Chang Road. No luck when I got there, only Igor's mother and his little flaxen-haired sister Gali were in. No matter. I could always try tomorrow.

But next day I was back at American Beach. And the day after, and the day after that. With each succeeding day I ventured one *peng* closer to those golden gazelles. Then disaster. Female voices shrilled: "Hey! Who are you?" . . . "What are you doing here?" . . . "Do you belong at this beach?" The two gazelles in form-revealing suits

77

putting me through the third degree were Betty Grable and Dorothy Lamour look-alikes. "How come you're so pinky pale?" . . . "How come you're so skinny?" Before the rest of the herd could arrive to pour on more scorn, I slunk off behind the pengs along the strip of spiky sea grass that led to Anchor Bay.

Rounding the row of junks at the fishermen's camp, I came face to face with Igor. "Sonovagun Deska, I went twice to Quelch's place. Where've you been? Anyway, now that I've got you, Ura and I are thinking of crossing the sand dunes to the 15th US Infantry camp at Chinwangtao. We're going first thing in the morning. Wanna come?"

"How you gonna get there?"

"By bike. Urka and I have ours. Maybe the Quelches have one."

The Quelches did, and Mr Quelch said yes, I could borrow it anytime. So off we pedaled along Main Road, a pretty grandiose name for a stretch of sandy hardpan that sort of paralleled the meandering shoreline. From the *tingzi* – the picture postcard pavilion – which stood on the highest point of East Cliff, our goal, Chinwangtao, looked darned close, not more than a two-three hour ride once we got past the dunes. We reached the dunes easily enough, streaking down the path cut into the steeply descending rock face. After that, heavy going in the soft-soft sand.

We managed to get halfway across the scorching Gobi Desert before we were obliged to call it quits, the sand in our axles and gears more than we'd bargained for. To find our bearings we dismounted and climbed to the peak of the highest dune. Directly ahead, endless desert. A mile to our left, the lush green patchwork of *gaoliang,* maize, and millet. Close by on our right, the bright blue expanse of the gulf. We gazed enviously at the twenty-foot junk moving along at leisurely pace, the native oarsman's brown torso twisting and turning as he worked the fish-tail stern oar, the man at the prow, a Westerner, judging by his white panama, trolling for lunker sea bass. Didn't take much imagination to know what tackle he was using – American, the best that money could buy – steel trolling rod, anti-backlash reel, silk line, Heddon plug. Fishing at its ultimate. Fishing beyond our wildest dreams.

We decided our safest bet was to head for the *gaoliang.* Fatal mistake. We got out of the sand all right, but we hadn't counted on the gullies that remained hidden until we were right on top of them. I went straight down one, landing in a heap. We managed to straighten out Quelch's bike. The front tire had a puncture we could fix, the puncture in my calf we could not. Pierced by a spoke, my leg grew increasingly numb. The left pedal was sticky with blood all the way home.

Despite the amah's daily administration of iodine and Tiger Balm – which burned like billyo up to an hour after application – it was weeks before I could take a step without grimacing. A shut-in at the height of summer? Unthinkable! Fortunately, Mr Quelch had a stack of *National Geographics*. And even more fortunately, a Victrola, a classy smooth-working one that never wound down in the middle of a record. The records were mostly Beethoven, Mozart, Hayden, and the like, but there were some Frank Crumit: *Abdul the Bul Bul Ameer* and *Gay Cabalero*, and some Eddie Cantor: *Makin' Whoopee*, *Barney Google*, and *Yes We Have No Bananas*. I played them over and over again. Poor old Mr Quelch. I must have driven him out of house and home.

When at last I was able to get about with the aid of a stick, I followed a daily regimen of hobbling down to the orchard to pick apricots, then feast on them seated atop the low rock wall on the southern edge of the Quelch property. Every day, without fail, I'd see a farm boy toiling in an adjacent field. He was perhaps a year or two younger than I, but already doing a man's work. Much to my surprise, unlike most village lads, he wasn't at all shy of "foreign devils."

He smiled a greeting. Then, rather cheekily, he asked: "What's your name?"

"Dieh Shi Men." I replied, giving him the closest Chinese sound for *Desmond*. What's yours?"

"Hsiao Szer."

"What are you doing?"

"Turning sweet potato vines."

I watched him slide the tapered end of a pole under a creeper that clung flat to the ground, and then with an upward thrust, flip the creeper over so that the pale undersides of its elongated leaves faced upwards. Then he'd do the same again to the next creeper, then the next, till he finished a row.

"There doesn't seem much point in what you're doing," I called out.

"There is. If we let the sun shine on both surfaces of the leaves, the sweet potatoes will grow faster and bigger."

"Can I have a try?"

He gave a sweet smile, but shook his head.

Next day, more amenable, he did let me have a go. After a few missed shots, I got the hang of it and began tossing creepers over my shoulder in reasonably straight lines. I found the work strangely soothing. After each throw, I'd be drawn to the next creeper, examining the path it had taken, and after loosening any tangles, making a quick thrust to flip it over onto its back. Despite the broiling sun I was reluctant to let go when the lad made a grab for his pole.

The following day he arrived with a pair of poles. We both went to work.

"Do you want to go for a bathe to cool off?" he asked when we stopped for a breather.

"The beach is too far. I have a sore leg."

"Are you a cripple?"

"No. I had an accident. My leg'll get better."

"I didn't mean the sea. That *is* quite a long way. I meant a water hole not far from here."

"As long as it's not far."

He led me across a sorghum field, then another, then into a quarry where a body of still dark water lay walled in on three sides by vertical rock faces. Was the water stagnant? Fast moving Vs made by knife-fish cutting the surface told me it wasn't.

He removed his trousers and tied a knot at each ankle end. Then he swung the open waist into the water, trapping the air inside. Using these crude water wings as support, he dog-paddled in two feet of sun-warmed water close to shore.

I edged my way along the marble-smooth rock to where the water looked black as pitch.

"Don't do it." He called out to me. "Don't go in there. It's very deep. There's no bottom by that ledge. That's where a villager fell in and drowned last month."

I took off my shirt and dived in. Lovely water, cool, caressing, invigorating. I swam across to where he lay wallowing among the tadpoles.

He stared at me goggle-eyed. "I told you it's dangerous. Have you gone mad?"

"It's not a bit dangerous. It's easy. Do you want me to

The donkey winds its endless course

teach you to swim?"

"No thank you. Why would I want to learn to swim?"

"So you won't drown like that villager you just told me about."

"But I have Kuan Yin to protect me. At home we burn joss sticks in her honor." He gazed at me with wide-open innocent eyes. "Do you know who Kuan Yin is?"

"Yes. She's your goddess of mercy. We have one too. Ours is called Mei Li – Mary. She is the mother of God."

"Mother of God? How can that be? If the supreme creator has a mother, he must also have a father. Then the father will be the supreme creator, won't he? . . . won't he?" he demanded.

If I couldn't explain it to myself, how could I explain it to him? I dropped the subject, and though we began seeing a lot more of each other, he never brought it up again. Sometimes Mr Quelch's steward would hire him to clean out the donkey stall or milk a goat or pick fruit. Afterwards I'd walk back with him to Tsao Chang Village where his parents would welcome us with tea, which we drank from thick blue-glazed earthenware bowls. I watched as they hitched a blindfolded donkey to a yoke connected to a millstone. A slap on the rump, and the faithful beast would start on its endless course, a twenty-foot circle worn down to hardpan by untold years of use. While the stone was revolving, one of Hsiao Szer's sisters poured maize into a feeder hole. Nothing was wasted, the girl's nimble fingers retrieving every last grain that spilled. She worked silently as did the rest of the family. On the rare

81

occasion that they did address one another I had to think hard to make sense of their strange country vernacular.

Hsiao Szer announces that tomorrow he has the day off. It's market day at Ta Lü Chuang (Big Donkey Village) and that's where he's heading. I tell him I'm coming too. We hitch a ride on a mule cart. Talk about rough going! The wooden wheels bounce in and out of endless ruts and potholes, pitching us mercilessly about the bare platform. I am bruised all over by the time we get to Ta Lü.

But once in the village square I give not another thought to my aches and pains. I am caught up in the ebullience of the *laobaixing*, the country folk, who fill the air with cries of greeting and shouts of laughter. And there's all that rumpus from over-excited watch dogs barking their heads off at the uncustomary influx of people, cows, goats, donkeys, chickens, ducks.

A stage show is going full swing in the center of the square. Acrobats on stilts perform incredible tricks while attendants crash cymbals and screech in weird falsetto.

Under banners emblazoned with large-scale characters, stall keepers shout their wares. Crowds gather around displays of fruit, grain, bolts of cloth, wickerwork, pots and pans, knick-knacks of every kind.

Seated at a low table, a bespectacled scribe reads out a letter he is in the process of concocting for a client; other clients, awaiting their turn, unashamedly interrupt, offering suggestions of their own.

A storyteller with grossly exaggerated gesticulations chants verses from the *Travels of the Monkey Deity*, a sort of Chinese *Pilgrims' Progress*.

"Tell your fortune!" An ancient with wizened face and stringy beard calls out to Hsiao Szer.

Hsiao Szer shakes his head.

"What about the little foreign devil?"

"No!" I move to escape.

Hsiao Szer stops me. "Why not?"

The crowd immediately thickens. We are hemmed in by a sea of inquisitive faces.

Hsiao Szer plucks at my sleeve. I squat beside him. The crowd presses closer.

"Fifty cents," the ancient mutters.

I place the coins on a paper groundsheet imprinted with

a grid of eight-character diagrams representing the Heavenly Stems and Earthly Branches.

"Under which of the Twelve Earthly Branches were you born?" the soothsayer asks.

"Dog or Pig, I'm not sure. It was Chinese New Year's Eve. The year was 1923 according to the Western calendar."

"Is that so? Tell me then at what hour of the day were you born."

"Right at midnight, according to my amah."

"Did you hear that?" the ancient addresses the crowd. "He was born during the hour of the Rat, at the moment of transition when the Dog gave way to the Boar."

Gasps of astonishment, oohs and ahs. "The little foreign devil is half Dog half Boar."

"Does it matter?" I ask.

" 'Does it matter!' The foreign devil says: 'Does it matter'!"

Screwing up his eyes and uttering incantations, the man rattles the contents of a hollowed-out bamboo container. He points its open end at me. "Pick out four sticks," he commands.

I do as he says.

A hush falls over the audience as he arranges the sticks with their green and red markings face upwards on the grid. He goes into a trance. It seems an age before his rheumy lids part. He peers into my eyes. "You picked the sticks with your left hand?"

"Yes."

"You are left handed?"

"Yes."

"Very unpropitious."

A rumble of voices in the audience. "Left handed . . . he is left handed . . . the poor little foreign devil is left handed . . . most unpropitious . . ."

For a whole minute the ancient is sunk in an expression of beatitude. Then, coming to, he chimes, sing-song fashion: "According to the arrangement of the constellations, this year will be an unlucky one for you, unlucky to sow seed, unlucky to participate in the harvest. The repair of graves will put you at great risk . . ."

Chuckles break all around.

". . . however your granaries will be safe from the ravages of insects . . ."

Ripples of laughter.

There is mystic power in "eight" especially with the eight-character combinations used in divination

"Tell him," a voice sounds from the crowd, "tell him he faces dreadful calamity if he rides a white horse."

Shouts of good-natured laughter.

"Tell the little foreign devil his grain will spoil if he rides a black horse."

Roaring hilariously, the onlookers screw up their faces and slap their thighs. The ancient puts on such a look of sufferance the hilarity ebbs to a few guffaws.

". . . All in all, this will not be a propitious year for you. Whatever you do, you must not presume to lay a foundation stone . . ."

Ignoring the mirthful applause, the old fellow picks up my four sticks, wipes them carefully on his sleeve, and replaces them in the container.

My fortune has been told. The crowd disperses.

At a food stall Hsiao Szer and I share half a watermelon. A rare treat for me, melons strictly forbidden us in Tientsin – cholera! But here in the virgin countryside, how can there be cholera?

We are both dead on our feet when it comes time to leave. A smoother ride back. We loll on sacks of flour that cushion the worst of the shocks. We watch the sun's fiery display as it settles behind the hushed mountains. We gaze at the stars lighting up one by one in the violet sky. We arrive at Tsao Chang long after dark. All the inhabitants, even the easily spooked watchdogs, have retired for the night.

For two consecutive days Hsiao Szer failed to show at the sweet potato patch. Had he gone to work on a neighboring farm? I stood on a grave mound and scoured the surrounding fields. Not a sign of him. Nor for that matter could I see anyone else working the land. Even the magpies ceased their cheeky chattering. The stillness was eerie.

At tiffin time Mr Quelch came to see Jie-jie. I heard only bits and pieces of their conversation, but I caught the flash of anxiety on Jie-jie's face.

". . . Not to worry, the Japanese have by-passed the coastal plain. They are moving down the main line towards Tientsin . . ."

" . . . Can we get back to Tientsin . . . ?"

" . . . No, you'd better stay put until we hear from Missy.

World War I
"four-stacker"
USS Paul Jones
anchored off
Temple Bay

You must tell everyone to stay within the grounds. You'll be safe here . . ."

Next day Igor showed up.

"What do you think of the news?"

"You mean about the Japanese?"

"Yes. They've invaded China. They've attacked Peking. At Tientsin where they thought they would have a walkover, the Pao An Tui, the lightly-armed para-military police, fought them to a standstill. The Japanese had to race an extra division down from Manchuria. Now the main fighting is at Nankao Pass, northwest of Peking."

"What's going to happen here?"

"Father says nothing much. The Japanese invasion troops that swarmed down from Shanhaikuan are busy grabbing all the rail towns on the main Peking-Mukden line. There's a rumor they're burning down the houses and butchering all who stand in their way."

"Do you think they'll come to Peitaiho?"

"Hard to say. Maybe the British and American navies will scare them off. I saw lots of ships this morning. Come down to the beach with me. I'll show you."

Despite the amah's screeching instruction to keep in bounds, I left with Igor. We latched on to a group gathered at the promontory overlooking American Beach. What a sight those naval ships a mile off shore! Were there six, seven, eight? Couldn't be certain. When you scanned the horizon, you'd pick out another gray shape that wasn't there a moment before.

"That's *HMS Kent*," announced someone presumably in the know.

"And there's *HMS Sandwich* and *Lowestoft*."

"I'm sure one of those four-stack destroyers is the *USS Paul Jones*."

"They say the flagship *Augusta* is at Tsingtao. Admiral Yarnell's aboard."

"That's a French cruiser over there."

"No it's not. It's Italian. I was there when its cutter

85

landed at Legation Point yesterday."

Either the warships had scared off the Japanese, or they simply had no interest in Peitaiho; we saw not a sign of them, that is until Tai-tai packed us home. She had arrived on the second train to get through from Tientsin. The normal seven-hour journey had taken her twelve.

At Peitaiho Junction, where Rising Suns flew from every lamp post, we had to pick our way along the platform chock-a-block with men in sweat-stained olive green to reach the Tientsin-bound express. There seemed little hope we could get seats together until Tai-tai let fly with a sharp tongue. When magically a bench seat for four emptied for us, she pointed me to the window while she, like a mothering hen, took the place by the aisle. It wasn't long before she was fussing and fuming. Easy to see why; Japanese officers, oblivious of our presence, were lounging about in their underwear and stomachers, those wide woolen bands wrapped around the middle to ward off chills.

The urgent handbell and even more urgent whistle sounding from somewhere up front drew not the slightest response from our locomotive. We just sat and sat and sat. No two ways about it, we were stuck. And there is nothing more stressful, as any traveler will tell you, than being stuck in a stuck train. Just as Tai-tai began to mutter about giving up and getting off, carriage couplings cannonaded up and down the length of the train, and with a great whining and groaning the wheels began to turn. Slowly we drew past clusters of storm troops in olive-green and past flatcars loaded with roped-down field guns and limbers. Then still at a crawl we came up to a walled village about the size of Ta Lü. My spine chilled at the sight of the flattened huts, charred beams, smashed carts. Not a sign of life, not even a scavenging village cur.

We were making good progress, roaring along, click-clacking over points, when there was an almighty hiss of steam and we shuddered to a halt. The bare rock face looming a few yards from the window told us we were in a cutting, an eerie place bathed in gloom. At first there was some faint shouting way in the distance, then silence, oppressive silence. If there was cause for alarm, the Japanese opposite us gave no sign of it. They sagged against each other, their eyes closed, their heads lolling. I too must have sagged, for when I next looked up, we were in bright sunlight and chugging along at a pretty good lick. At Linsi, no jam of peasants, no hubbub of vendors, just a bare cement platform. At Luan Hsien the big bridge was down. We had to disembark and make our way to a pontoon of anchored sampans over which we crossed in single file to a train waiting on the far bank. Near Tongshan, a locomotive lay dead on its side. And all across the salt flats more smashed huts, more burnt-out rail cars.

That audacious look on Tai-tai's face was enough to bring us through to safety

Arriving at Tientsin East, we drew alongside an armored train. It looked abandoned until a shadowy movement in a gun turret slot caught my eye, and I found myself exchanging looks with a ghostly face. Tai-tai grabbed my arm. "What's the matter with you Desmond? Get a move on, collect your things."

As we filed out of the station, a Japanese sentry bellowed like a maniac. "Ignore him," Tai-tai commanded. "Keep going."

Her audacity paid off. Despite renewed bellowing, we crossed International Bridge unmolested. At Rue de France an officer of the *Infantrie Coloniale* stepped from behind a sandbag redoubt to check us through. While he and Tai-tai were jabbering away in French, I feasted my eyes on the heavy caliber *mitrailleuse* manned by fierce Annamites. They had the gun trained on the Japanese side. We were in safe hands.

News of our return spread quickly. First to come calling were Carapet Kulchasian and Frankie Butterworth.

"Boy oh boy you missed it all!" Frankie trumpeted "You missed the big battle. You shoulda seen the warplanes. Shoulda seen the bombs falling on Nankai University. Giant clouds of smoke. Ear-shattering explosions!"

"That was nothing," Carapet chimed in. "I was at Slafka Savchenko's house in the Russian Concession when the Pao An Tui attacked the Jap airfield. Talk about scary, all those machine guns firing at once."

"What about the British Concession, did any bombs land here?"

"The race course."

"That's outside the concession."

"Well the Italian Concession then. An Italian marine got killed."

"The French came under fire. A French sergeant and some men were wounded."

I tossed and turned for what seemed most of the night. How could I ever get to sleep in that stuffy kennel of a room? Oh for those cool night breezes that swept Mr Quelch's verandah! Should I roll up the mosquito net? In Peitaiho the amahs lit coils of punk to keep mosquitoes at bay. Green Monkey Brand. *Makee Muskeety All No More!* it said on the package. Damn being in Peitaiho! Carapet and Frankie would always have it over me. Imagine seeing bombers in action. Imagine being in the Russian Concession when the Chinese attacked the airfield. With any luck I could have been with Carapet. I could have witnessed the battle. Must have been just like the big one they showed in *All Quiet on the Western Front*... Dammit, I forgot to tell Frankie about the armored train . . . and also that locomotive on its side . . . there could have been dead soldiers lying around it . . . there *were* dead soldiers lying around it . . . all over it in fact . . . must tell Frankie and Carapet . . . .

I woke with a start. My pajamas were soaked with sweat. Though details of the nightmare were fading fast, the stark background scene remained frighteningly vivid – the flattened huts, the smashed carts, the charred remains of a village that could only have been Ta Lü. . . .

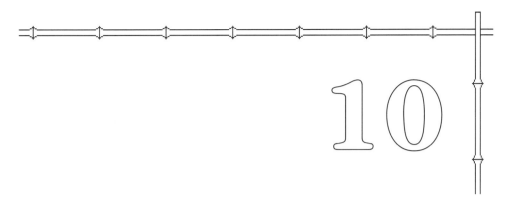

AS CRUEL AS THE HUNS UNDER ATTILA

KUI HSIANG, now promoted to Number One Boy, ushered in Frankie Butterworth while I was still at breakfast. "Hurry man, hurry," Frankie cried out, "Let's go see soldiers at the barricades."

"*Mahn-mahn, mahn-mahn,*" – slow down, slow down – Kui Hsiang exhorted.

Slow down? He might as well tell me to stop breathing. I gulped down my porridge and leapt for the door.

With Frankie in the lead, we sped off on bikes to Morling's Corner at the southwest tip of the British Concession. Lancashire Fusiliers were standing guard, the bayonets fixed to their Lee Enfields were wartime black. A Lewis gun on a wall of sandbags was pointed down the road leading to Tung Chia Village. At the entrance to the village a Rising Sun hung limply from a bamboo pole.

"Be off with you, boys, be off with you," the fusilier officer who shooed us away sounded as if he had a potato stuck in his throat.

We rode down Race Course Road to the American Compound, an area of four city blocks that jutted into the ex-German Concession. The sandbag emplacement on Shensi Road was shoulder high and twice the length of the one at Morling's Corner, and more soldiers manned it. But they were less businesslike than the fusiliers. One of the Can Do infantrymen was squatting on his haunches reading comics. Another was wiping a dismantled Browning which lay in bits and pieces on a groundsheet. A big

heavy-set fellow, comfortably ensconced in a rickshaw, was exchanging banalities with a pack of Chinese youths. One tried out his English on him: "Rickshaw Johnnie! Catchee whiskee soodah Johnnie!" Then another: "Got some choo gum Johnnie!" And the delighted American quipped back in Chinese: "Ting-how, Charlie, ting-how, ting-how!"

"You wouldn't think there was a war on," I said to Frankie.

"Wouldn't you? You wanna see signs of war? Come, I'll show you."

In ten minutes we were at the Bund. The riverside thoroughfare, normally a mêlée of mule carts, wheelbarrows, wharf coolies, was blanketed in the eerie silence of a ghost town. At least that's what I thought until the rear door of a stationary armored car swung open and a head poked out.

"What the heck you doing here, Frankie?"

"Jim, it's you! I'm just showing Des around. You know Desmond, Pat Power's younger brother?"

In the moment it took me to recognize Jim Butterworth – the black tank-corps beret low over his forehead giving his pudding face even more of a pudding look – he acknowledged me with a "Hi kid."

Frankie puffed out his chest. Not many boys could boast of a brother in the Volunteer Corps, and a corporal in the Armored Cars, to boot!

And now this hero figure in battle dress – holy Moses! to think I was once his next door neighbor – eased himself onto the vehicle's rear deck. The webbing holster attached to his webbing belt bulged with a heavy service revolver. He stood nine feet tall.

"You guys better scoot," he ordered. Then, à la Victor McLaglan at his bruising best, he shook his fist at the opposite bank. " 'em Japs over there want to start trouble. If they do, we're gonna show 'em what's what."

At first glance across the river, nothing much changed. There was that ever-pleasing sight – the cupola of the Orthodox church nestled in the foliage of acacias and willows gracing Russian Park, Tientsin's largest park, in what had been Tientsin's largest concession. (We still called it Russian even though the Soviet authorities had long ceded it back to China.) Then I saw Jim Butterworth's Japanese. Must have been a full regiment of them,

Rickshaw delivers sandbags to US outpost

strutting about the shady embankment as if they owned the place, which of course they now did.

"But Jimmy, can I first show something to Des? Then we'll scram for sure."

"Okay, but be quick about it."

I followed Frankie to the edge of the wharf.

"There," Frankie said, pointing with his chin.

A bluish-green thing, inflated like a balloon, was bobbing along in the water. When it suddenly dawned on me that the thing was a human body, my breath froze.

"There's more. Look over there," Frankie said.

The two bodies floating by were bound together with straw rope.

My toes cringed. "Ghastly, Frank. How come two together?"

"Jim says the Japanese bind them, shove them in the river, take pot shots at them. He's seem whole rafts of them go by – men, women, children – some still alive."

"Can't anyone do anything about it? Can't the Japanese be stopped?"

"Nope. No one can stop them. Looks as though they've won the war. Jim told me there's a strong rumor the Chinese 29th Route Army positioned southwest of Peking was beginning to hold its own when its general sold out. That's why Peking and Tientsin fell so easily. And it's the same all over. The Japanese are shouting their *Banzais* all across Inner Mongolia, Hopei, Shansi. Jim says there's absolutely no hope for China."

James Butterworth might be a corporal in the Armored Cars, but that didn't mean he was always right. There certainly *was* hope for China, all kinds of hope.

I hadn't been back in Tientsin a fortnight when I came upon Kui Hsiang in our back alley reading aloud from a newspaper to a gathering of house servants, street hawkers, passers-by: ". . . At Ping Hsing Pass, in Shansi Province, three thousand men of the invader's famed Itagaki Brigade were passing through deep cuttings in the jagged loess terrain when they were suddenly attacked by battle-hardened veterans of Mao Tse Tung's Eighth Route Army. Their front and rear blocked by intense crossfire, the Japanese made a desperate attempt to force their way up the steep banks. The one machine gun crew that did manage to reach the top was immediately wiped out. From high ground Red Army fighters rained grenades onto the frenzied mass. There were no survivors. Hundreds of guns and scores of trucks were taken. . . ."

And more hope emanated every day from Shanghai where a new front had opened. Chiang Kai Shek ordered his divisions not to give a yard, and they staunchly obeyed. It was only after eighty-nine days of battle, with Japan bringing to bear the full might of her modern naval and air power, did the shattered remnants of the heroic Nationalist army withdraw into the interior.

The Chinese and Japanese might be locked in mortal combat, but for foreigners in the sanctuary of their concessions, it was life as usual. In school, the same old morning assembly, the same thumping piano, the same march to the high-vaulted hall, the same formations facing the Headmaster – girls to the right – boys to the left.

"Good morning girls."

"Good morning sir."

"Good morning boys."

"Good morning sir."

"Hymn number one-five-six, *He Who Would Valiant Be.*"

We rang out our solemn declaration to be ever valiant " 'gainst disaster," ever constant "serving the master." We bowed our heads at the sweet Elizabethan words from the Book of Common Prayer. We reflected, sometimes morosely, sometimes smilingly, at the announcements – a change in class schedules – a revised date for the forthcoming exams – an unspeakable infraction perpetrated by a fourth former soon to receive his just deserts.

One morning, an announcement that pricked up our ears. Could a half-holiday be in the offing? "Tomorrow I want every one of you to look your best. School ties obligatory. Prefects, you are to be in your grays . . ."

Who could it be? What renowned dignitary? A year before it had been Commander Seymour, son of the legendary Admiral Seymour, vanquisher of the Boxers at Taku, Tanku, and Tientsin, proud paladin of the Empire, after whom Seymour House, my school house, was named. Then there was Bishop Staunton, the rotund purplish-nosed prelate of the Established Church, whose pontifications were so drawn out, his la-di-da accent so excruciating, the half-holiday was hardly worth the purgatory suffered . . .

". . . it gives me extreme pleasure" – Headmaster Woodall's booming voice jolted me back to the present – "to inform you that we are to be honored by a visit from His Majesty's Ambassador to China, the most distinguished Sir Hugh Knatchbull-Hugessen. . . ."

And next morning, the thin, bird-like, balding man came up to the lectern as the final strains of *Gaudeamus Igitur* died away. In frightfully posh Oxfordese he enjoined us to play the game both on and off the field, to give of our best to King and Empire. I lost him at that point, musing: Whose king? What empire? Our class of twenty-five having only six Brits . . . Would the man never end? All told he launched into seven "in conclusions" before his concluding conclusion we were all anxiously waiting for: "I have requested, and your eminent Headmaster has jolly kindly concurred, that you be granted a half-holiday. . . ."

The Head shot to the lectern to smother the scattering of handclaps before they could gain momentum and sweep the hall. This was *his* day after all.

"Let us show our appreciation to Sir Hugh for giving us so much of his precious time. Three cheers for Sir Hugh Knatchbull-Hugessen. . . Hip-Hip-Hip-Hooray . . . Hip-Hip-Hip-Hooray . . . Hip-Hip-Hip-Hooray . . . Tiger . . . Wheeeeee . . . ." And just as the final wheeeeee died away, Vahab Izgur, our redoubtable Tartar hero – on and off the field – rendered one last acclamation: "Good old Snatchballs!"

"*Poor* old Snatchballs" would have been more like it. Only a week later, that worldly-wise elder of His Britannic Majesty's corps diplomatique made the fateful blunder of having a Union Jack painted on the roof of his limousine before setting off on the Nanking-Shanghai road, a two-hundred-mile stretch now considered by the Empire of Japan to be its own private backyard. Circling low, a Japanese fighter pilot, affronted beyond measure by the sight of the offending emblem, swooped in with all guns firing. Gravely wounded (he was hit by nine machine gun bullets according to the *North China Daily News*), Sir Hugh was rushed to hospital. The surgeons worked miracles. So must have his patron saint. He lived to see another day. (And to go on to even greater distinction as the UK Ambassador in Ankara whose personal valet turned out to be the Nazi master spy "Cicero," so trenchantly played by James Mason in the post-war film of that true life thriller.)

Screaming protests from London, bleating apologies from Tokyo. "Didn't mean to aim at the honorable gentleman. Over-keenness on the part of our fighter ace. Samurai spirit, don't you see? Shan't happen again – promise."

But it did happen again – and almost immediately. This time it was the Yanks who copped it. A formation of fighter-bombers from Japan's 2nd Combined Air Group, coming in low over the Yangtze to ascertain that it really was the Star Spangled Banner they had spied on the stern of the river gunboat at anchor, whooped with gleeful "bombs away," then jubilant "*Banzais*," as the *USS Panay* settled to the silted bottom of the Yangtze.

Where did we hear it all before, the aggrieved party's outcries, the offending party's contrition. "Ever so sorry. We will, in accordance with the spirit of Bushido, consider reasonable compensation. And oh, by the by, His Divine Majesty has requested of the royal chamberlain that a court official of appropriate rank be deputized to offer condolences to the bereaved." The most heart-rending of the scenes flashed by Movietone News was that of very weepy Tokyo maidens, in very English school tunics and very Japanese mouth masks, laying shoulder-high wreaths on the steps of the US Embassy.

June 19, 1927
The Sixth Marines land at the Tientsin Bund

... and they bring their tanks with them.

"America will never stand for it," Tai-tai announces at the dinner table. "They'll send in the marines as they did in '27 when Chiang Kai Shek threatened the concessions."

"I remember the marines landing," says Doong Ji.

"I do too," says Tai-tai. "I especially remember the stir they created with their airplanes and whippet tanks and armored cars and field guns."

Unable to contain myself, I burst out: "I remember all that. I remember seeing the tanks on Meadows Road."

"You couldn't have, you were too young," Doong Ji snaps.

"But I do, I do. We were in the park. We dashed out onto Meadows Road. I remember the amahs going berserk."

"You must be dreaming. You were only four."

I know it's no dream. How can it be, so deeply etched in

95

Pat and Joss with Can Do friends Victoria Park 1927

my memory, that electrifying sight of my very first airplane? I can see myself climbing about the rockery when an immense thunder of engines fills the whole sky. And there sailing majestically over Russian Park is a biplane with red wings and red fuselage, followed moments later by a squadron of perhaps seven in V formation, each a different vivid color. Talk about thrills by the minute! The planes are hardly out of sight when a column of whippet tanks come roaring up from the Bund. The amahs scream their heads off trying to herd us in, but we dash through Meadows Road Gate, yelling like imbeciles : "The Yanks are coming! The Yanks are coming . . . !"

And now, as I relive that once-in-a-lifetime show of shows, Tai-tai and Doong Ji are deciding the fate of Japan: "This time they've gone too far" . . . "It's undeclared war, that's what it is" . . . "Congress will be up in arms" . . . "President Roosevelt will never stand for it" . . . "They'll sound the alarm in Manila" . . . "General MacArthur will cancel all leave" . . . "There'll be a Yankee landing before the month is out. . . ."

But no Yankee landing. Quite the opposite, in fact. The colorful Can Do Regiment, the 15th US Infantry, after twenty-six years in Tientsin, was pulling up stakes, going home.

Frankie Butterworth broke the news.

"You gotta be kidding," I told him.

"I'm not."

"Can't be true."

"My brother Jim heard it straight from Mr Gunther of the National City Bank."

"What about Tab Berry, Stinkee Hoover, Lynn Decker, Dwight Anderson, Joe Pascual?"

"They're all going, the whole lot of them."

That was the hardest part to take – the departure of fine fellows, the severance of warm ties. We taught them English cricket and Russian *lopta*; they taught us American baseball. We went to their homes at Thanksgiving and Halloween when they dressed up in the weirdest costumes and got up to the strangest antics. And there was that incredible celebration at Can Do Field on the Fourth of July – crashing bands – tumultuous baseball – delirious crowds. And boy oh boy, the ice cream, to us the rarest of rare treats except for that one magical day of the year! A burly Can Do soldier would call out: "Hey kid, over here!" And he'd plop three scoops: pink – white – brown into a gigantic cone. Heaven! Sheer heaven!

Generosity came second nature to those Yanks. There was that evening back in '35 – we were still at Edinburgh Road – when the doorbell rang and there stood Bill Kirksey at the front entrance. "We're going home tomorrow, Pop's finished his tour of duty, Mom said for me to give you these." And the "these" turned out to be sleds, three of them, shiny, sleek, with metal runners and steering mechanisms – pictures of beauty. The Kirkseys could never ever begin to imagine what untold joy those sleds gave us winter after winter on the frozen canals and ponds out by Pa Li Tai.

March 2, 1938 must surely be counted as one of Tientsin's most heart-stirring days. Mid-morning, First and Second Troops, in full uniform, staves and all, are formed line abreast along Victoria Road opposite Astor House. And a hand-picked squad of the BMC Police are in position fronting Moyler Powell. North of Gordon Hall, between Hall & Holtz and National City Bank, stand the guard of honor from A Company, First Battalion, the Lancashire Fusiliers. Opposite them are three infantry platoons of the British Volunteer Defense Corps. Lined up along Rue de France is a detachment of the 16th Colonial Infantry Regiment. The FMC Police and Fire Brigade are there too, and the French Boy Scouts. Along the entire route crowds overflow the sidewalk. Seems as though the whole city has come to give the Yanks a rousing send off.

And here they come, the band crashing out *Stars and Stripes Forever.* Then the men, nine hundred strong, marching shoulder to shoulder, grinning sheepishly at the ovation. And a deafening ovation it is with all that shouting and cheering and handclapping and fire-crackers. Women break through our cordon and fling themselves on their departing sweethearts. The last formation draws past. It's all over. A strange feeling of emptiness fills the air. Tientsin will never be the same. No more Friday Night Fights. No more baseball at Can Do Field. No more hockey at Can Do Rink. No more ice cream on the Fourth of July.

The crowd filters away. A breeze disperses the lingering wafts of burnt powder, but it will be hours before the sweepers deal with the litter of spent firecrackers.

Mr Watkins dismisses the troop on the gravel walk in front of the cenotaph a few feet from Victoria Park's main gate.

A tragic scene catches my eye. A great big hippopotamus of a woman lies collapsed on a bench, her mountains of flesh shuddering as she chokes out her heart-breaking lament.

I nudge Rajan Patel. "Take a look at that lady over there. It must be the end of the world for her."

Rajan's Punjabi face wrinkles in a smile. "Hey, Achmet," he calls between chuckles, "Shall we go help that fat Mamichka?"

"No need," Achmet says. "Only Russian playacting, Russian emotion. She'll be okay in no time."

"Vat-hal-you-mean!" snarls Mischka Maltsev. "Vat you talk Roshon playacting, Roshon moshon?" His face is beetroot.

Smartly, Rajan changes the subject. "Hey, look, there's Jefferson Wu!"

"Hi Jefferson, you been to see the Yankees leave?"

"I most certainly have."

"Pretty sad day for all of us."

"Not so. It's a happy day, happy for China, happy for America."

"You don't mean to say you're happy to see them go?"

"Of course. Didn't you hear all those firecrackers? It's a tradition with us. It's our way of celebrating a joyous event. And they'll be celebrating in America too. Bet you anything you like most people over there believe strongly that it was wrong for their soldiers to be used as an occupation army. And as for that other army of occupation, the British, there's going to be an even happier, noisier celebration when they leave."

"But they've been protecting you, the British, the Americans, the French. Are you saying you haven't benefited from their protection?"

"We don't need their protection, never did."

"That's not what Milton Chang says."

"Milton Chang? Why his father is a warlord. His family certainly needs protection. Why do you think they live in the concession?"

Milton Chang and I happen to be buddies. A slender fellow, and though two years my junior, he's in our first eleven. I'm inside left for Seymour House soccer team. He's our speed left winger. Vahab says he has a terrific shot with his left, better than Koreisha's, better than Gutbezal's, better than mine. We all know he is related to the famous warlord, Chang Hsueh Liang, the *Young Marshal*, son of the even more famous Chang Tso Lin, who was done in by the Japanese when they blew up his train during the Manchurian troubles. Milton's branch of the Chang clan resides in a *gong guan* on Rue Pasteur. The Chang *gong guan* like all others is surrounded by a high wall topped with glass shards. Being super wealthy it is only natural for the Changs to protect themselves, though I think they carry it a bit too far. When Milton arrives in a chauffeur-driven car at school each morning, the bodyguard who sees him to the gate always has his hand at the ready on the wooden holster of his German army Mauser.

There are a few others in school like Milton who live in fortified *gong guans*. One such is Washington Pai. Though he has finished school (he and Jocelyn were classmates), he does from time to time invite some of us fifth formers to his place, probably the largest *gong guan* in the British Concession. When we announce through the peephole of the immense iron-studded gate that we are Washington's guests, the guards usher us into a holding area to await his arrival. Though he is there within minutes, he is

99

profuse with apology. And he is still a little red-faced as he leads us under thick canopies of wisteria and honeysuckle and through secluded courts to a moon gate, which opens onto a make-believe world of jagged rockeries and lotus pools inhabited by sluggish carp. There happens to be four separate residences in the complex, each with its own official Mrs Pai. Because Washington is the issue (eleventh son) of the first Mrs Pai, his residence is the largest of the four. As if we are not already overawed, he takes us into a dazzling all-crimson ante room, then through a glittering reception room, a billiard room, an aviary, another reception room, a library, and then finally into a high-ceilinged chamber where on one wall there hangs a larger than life portrait of a figure dressed as an English admiral straight out of *HMS Pinafore*: cocked hat, frock coat, sword, and all. He is Washington's grandfather. He is the Ching Dynasty's penultimate Grand Admiral of the Fleet.

It is common knowledge that Grand Admiral Pai, a close confidante of the Empress Dowager, had been made the dupe in the most colossal swindle that ever a ruler perpetrated on her subjects. When the admiral presented her with the three million ingots of silver, raised by special taxation for modernizing China's navy, the crafty old dragon sank every last ingot into the construction of a single vessel, a super flagship, modeled along the lines of a two-deck Mississippi paddle wheeler. It was an exact replica in every respect but one – its construction material. It can be safely claimed that no other naval architect living or dead had ever dreamed of experimenting with material of such unique durability – clear white marble. Subject to neither rust nor rot, the one-of-its-kind vessel, anchored permanently at the edge of picturesque Kun Ming Lake in the grounds of the Imperial Summer Palace was guaranteed to glisten like new for the next ten thousand years. What other navy, I ask you, could boast of a flagship sumptuous enough for wedding banquets, opera performances, picnics, tea parties, jolly afternoons of mah jongh?

And as for the Grand Admiral, his dream fleet cast in marble, what else could he do but take early retirement. With his gains of imperial office (legitimate payback from sundry arms merchants, naval architects, contractors, and ships' chandlers) salted away in the vaults of Hongkong & Shanghai Banking Corporation's Victoria Road Branch, he took leasehold possession of three city blocks in the heart of Tientsin's well-policed British Concession, then proceeded to call for tenders for the construction of that most fabulous of all *gong guans*, the regally-appointed, multimansioned Pai *gong guan*.

No wonder Jefferson Wu has it in for the likes of Milton Chang and Washington Pai. The Wus are rich all right, but isn't it the rich who suffer most from the pangs of covetousness? Even at this very moment Jefferson has hardly stopped to draw a breath in his slanging of the Pais and the Changs. At Stanford he is going to shine as a debater for sure. Just listen to him letting off steam:

". . . And let me tell you guys there's not going to be a tear shed when those warlords who've taken refuge in the foreign concessions get their due. And believe me, that's going to happen a lot sooner than you think."

"They don't give any trouble."

"You never see or hear from them."

"They're no bother."

"Perhaps, but they must be made to pay for their crimes. You are apparently unaware that most started off as government officials or military officers who, after resorting to every conceivable form of graft to drain the barrel dry, took off for greener pastures. Following each other's example, they formed private armies, recruiting the scum of the earth – bandits, deserters, ex-convicts.

Once in power they levied taxes on villages and towns, not a single penny of which did they remit to the central government. They confiscated granaries. They bled the land dry. The more successful ruled areas as large as Texas. The less successful, when bought off or defeated by a rival, made straight for the haven of the foreign concessions in whose eagerly welcoming banks they salted away their ill-gotten gains."

"They're China's business, not ours."

"By protecting them with your soldiers and police, you've made them *your* business. You don't know how galling it is for us Chinese to see how you side with them."

"We don't side with them."

"Yes you do. You openly sided with them when Chiang Kai Shek marched north to rid them from the land. Never mind, it soon won't matter. Won't be long before you yourselves are ousted."

"You're crazy Jefferson. How can you Chinese push us out when you can't even beat the Japanese?"

"You guys obviously haven't heard of the great Nationalist victory at Taierchwang down in southern Shantung. It was a major battle involving whole divisions. General Li Tsung Jen feinted, fell back, then counter-attacked, trapping an entire Japanese army corps. Sixteen thousand Japanese were slain, and forty tanks and hundreds of armored cars and trucks as well as mountains of small arms taken. Do you need any better proof that we can lick them? And lick them we are certainly going to do. We have to. Someone must put an end to their inhuman barbarity. Photos and diaries found on the Japanese dead at Taierchwang confirmed beyond all doubt the reports of the massacre at Nanking. . . . "

We don't need further proof from Jefferson that it had happened, that appalling atrocity which came to be known as the "Rape of Nanking." *Time* magazine and *The Daily Telegraph* printed eye-witness accounts of the Japanese in their blood-lust, herding prisoners of war and civilians into the fields and then mowing them down with machine-guns; of forcing other defenseless Chinese into trenches, dousing them with gasoline, and setting them alight; of hauling men and women from their homes, trussing them to crosspieces, and using them for bayonet practice. In Red Cross hospitals they shot the doctors, the orderlies, the wounded in their beds. They raped every female they could lay their hands on. And males too. One report told of twenty thousand girls and boys raped and in many cases disemboweled. The holocaust went on for six weeks. The Chinese dead exceeded three hundred thousand.

Frenchy Bodson speaks up for the first time. (We call him "Frenchy" but he's really Belgian. His father is one of the big guns at Banque Belge.) "My dear friend," he says to Jefferson, "we will make zem pay for it. We will join you in your war against zem. We are allies. We are brothers-in-arms."

Jefferson gives him an odd look, then says: "Brothers-in-arms? Brothers respect one another's property, do they not? It wasn't all that long ago when you French and you British went on your own rampage, burning down the Summer Palace, sacking Peking. And not satisfied with terrorizing the populace once, you went about it a second time, aided and abetted by the no less rapacious Americans, Russians, and Germans. Do you know what the Kaiser's orders were to his troops when they embarked for China in 1900, orders that could not have differed much from those issued by the French and English high commands? '*Act with utmost ferocity. Be as cruel as the Huns under Attila. Be so merciless no Chinese will ever dare look askance at a German . . .*' !"

The German monument in Tientsin

103

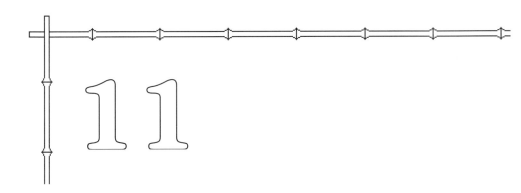

NAKED AS THE DAY THEY WERE BORN

TODAY is just another run-of-the-mill school day so our curiosity is aroused when the Headmaster announces that the hymn to be sung. *O God Our Help in Ages Past*, as any third former can tell you, is usually reserved for Siege Day, Armistice Day, moments of national crisis. And when we hear the somber appeal of the morning prayer: *Give peace in our time, O Lord, because there is none other that fighteth for us,* we know definitely that something is in the wind. And so what an anticlimax, the Head's swelling, quavering declaration: "The world is at the brink of war!" . . . What's he talking about – the *brink* of war? Aren't we already in the thick of war? And doesn't his very next announcement confirm that to be the case? . . . "I have to bring to your attention some harrowing news which will personally touch each and every one of you. You will all remember Wesley Morris, the bright young lad from Form Four Lower School. Tragically, the day before yesterday, while exploring a battlefield on the outskirts of Shanghai, he got hold of a grenade. It blew off his hand. He is in critical condition. But the doctors think he has a chance. . . "

. . . Hand blown off! . . . Wesley Morris! . . . My blood curdles, my toes cringe. Wesley is the spunky kid brother of Railton, our classmate until a year ago when he left with his parents, Salvation Army folk, for Shanghai . . . Poor Wesley!

At recess, still very much ill at ease, I try to keep to myself, but Aliosha Bublikoff comes up to me. "Hey,

Deska," he says, "what do you think of that *Spasoonchik* losing his hand?"

Aliosha can't seem to refer to anyone without assigning him a label. Every Salvation Army kid is a *Spasoonchik* as every Georgian is a *Gruzinski* and every Armenian an *Armiashka*.

But I am in no mood for his waggishness. I say to him: "Let's hope Wesley's going to be all right."

Right then, most opportunely, Vahab Izgur gets Aliosha out of my hair. From his clutch of hangers-on Vahab calls over: "Hey, Alioshka, come tell us about that shooting you saw on Wellington Road."

I cannot shake Wesley from my mind. I keep seeing that impish grin of his at the Christmas party for sons and daughters of Salvation Army officers held in the Children's Hostel on Mersey Road. Why was I invited two years running, me, the only outsider, and smacking of Mass incense to boot? Could Gogs Stranks have told Major Stranks about the poor *Dismal Desmond* who sat directly behind him in class? Or was it Ernie Waller? Or Wilbur Walker, perhaps, mentioning something of the sort to Brigadier Walker? Come to think of it, it must have been Wilbur. Didn't he and I on the occasional Tuesday evening share the misery of detention? Didn't Mr Foxlee book him once for sticking his thumb in the beaker to see what it did to the specific gravity of some substance or other, and me for laughing out loud? Never mind how I came to be invited to those Salvation Army parties, it matters only that I was, that I partook in their sparkling joy, and was for evermore enriched by it.

They were beautiful people, those Australian Wallers and American Dempsters and Swedish Cedervalls and Canadian Sowtons, just to name a few. And they were beautiful in more ways than one. There was that teacher, Miss Stranks, a dark serene Helen of Troy. There was Eleanor Evenden who, even at that tender age, her hair still sporting a bow, was already displaying the radiance that was to turn so many a head in the years to come.

But Wesley, how they must now be praying for Wesley, fighting for his life in a Shanghai hospital. I can see the strained look on Brigadier Walker's face as he pleads with the good Lord to spare the boy. I have seen that look before. I saw it the night he and two other officers came to

our tent at Buchans Ground, shining torch lights in our faces, looking for young James Dempster. Brigadier Walker and Scoutmaster Watkins whispered something to James. He got up, dressed quietly, and was gone. His father, Adjutant Dempster, stationed in the interior, had been shot dead by bandits.

Pyramus
— Shuna Shikwary
Thisbe
— Des Power

It is mid-morning class. We each have our *Midsummer Night's Dream* open before us. We'd better know it well; it is the Shakespeare work prescribed by Cambridge University for this year's English literature exam. And we'd better stay doubly alert while Natalie Shanek is struggling through Titania's solemn affirmation: "*These are the forgeries of jealousy,*" for we've never been able to second-guess our English master Mr May. He doesn't have us reading in rotation. He uses no system. He picks readers at random. I can tell right now by those little twitches of irritation that he's about to make a pick. But before he can do so, there is a sudden, urgent rapping on the door, and in bursts Headmaster Woodall, gown billowing, voice booming: "It's a miracle, Mr May, a miracle. Neville Chamberlain has pulled it off. He's back from Munich with a peace treaty signed by Herr Hitler himself. There's not going to be war." Then he turns to address the class. "Yes, boys and girls, the world is saved. Can you hear me at the back? No war, no shooting, no killing." And with his nose pointed up at the ceiling, he sweeps out as triumphantly as he swept in.

For a second or two, total silence. Then whispers. Then growing rumbles. Mr May is about to bring the class to order when Maxie Rosentool raises his hand. "Excuse me sir," he says, with perfect aplomb, "do you think Premier Stalin is going to accept the piece of paper those so-called statesmen have signed?"

And someone else, just as quick off the mark: "Sir, whose side do you think Mussolini is on?"

While the Gladstones and Disraelis of Form Five Upper School are having their field day, Aliosha Bublikoff jerks his chin to catch my eye. He asks in a gruff semi-whisper: "Why is *Gospodin Vootballski* telling us there is no shooting? Twice last week I nearly got shot. Do you want to know about it?"

"I already know about it. Vahab and Frankie told me."

And what they had told me sounded pretty scary. According to Vahab Izgur, Aliosha was walking past a high-walled *gong guan* on Wellington Road when a single revolver shot went off so close to him it just about shattered his eardrums. While he was standing there stunned, guards burst out of the *gong guan* firing their Mausers at random. With bullets whistling every which way, he flung himself behind a rickshaw. And there he stayed not daring to move a finger till the police arrived. Frankie Butterworth's version – he got it straight from his brother Jim – was that the gunman, ignoring Aliosha and other passers-by, had rung the *gong guan* doorbell then fired point-blank at the face that presented itself at the peephole. And that, according to brother Jim, was standard terrorist procedure for advising the master of the house he was next on the hit list.

Alioshka's second close call came only three days later when he was caught in a shoot-out between gunmen and bodyguards of an eminent Chinese official, slain on the street only twenty yards from his residence. The dead man, Dr T.L. Chao, was not only the most popular of the five Chinese members on the British Municipal Council, he was Principal of Kung Hsueh, Tientsin's most prestigious Chinese high school. *North China Star* pulled no punches in giving the reason for his assassination – he refused to allow Japanese propaganda to be disseminated in Kung Hsueh's classrooms.

Why all this shooting in a foreign concession, a safe island of neutrality in the stormy sea of the Sino-Japanese conflict? Why? Perfectly plain why. The Empire of Japan was flexing its muscles. It was showing by example how the puppet government it had created and installed in Peking must follow suit. They were pretty happy, were the Japanese, with this new creation of theirs. And happier still, knowing they were going to get away with it just as they had got away with their other creation, the vassal state of Manchukuo.

"The Peking government must be recognized by the whole world as the legitimate government of China," they declared.

" 'fraid not," was the British-American-French response. "Chiang Kai Shek's Kuomintang government is the only one we recognize."

"We'll see about that," bristled the Japanese. All they needed to do was give a wee nudge and their Peking bully boys levied a special tax on all imports from the West. And as for exports, they passed a law forbidding goods of any kind to leave Chinese ports without a special permit. In Tientsin these special permits could be obtained only from the East Hopei Trade Bureau located in the Chinese City. So for the first time ever, foreign taipans sent their compradors there, to stand in line, to kow-tow, to grease palms. And what a feeling of power it gave those puppet officials! What giddy heights they attained! Unfortunately for them, up there in the limelight, they were easy marks for freedom fighters. *Freedom fighters?* Well, that's what patriotic Chinese called them; to the Japanese and their collaborators, they were, of course, *terrorists* – pure and simple. Isn't that the same the world over, pot calling the kettle black?

In broad daylight in the Chinese City, *zip*, some high-up would catch it. Next day, *zap*, another would go to join his ancestors. The gunmen were never caught. They simply made their way into the sanctuary of the British or French Concessions.

"As a matter of common courtesy this is to advise you we are sending in our gendarmerie to apprehend those murderers," the Japanese informed the Anglos and Francos.

"Not on your life! Question of British sovereignty," was the proud Anglo response.

And same from the Francos: "*Fous le camp!* Question of French sovereignty."

"Okay, if that's the way you want it, two can play at that game."

So the Japanese infiltrated death squads into the concessions. Any academic or industrialist with pro-Chiang leanings, any spokesman for the Kuomintang, was fair game. Hardly a day went by without some Chicago-style execution, and there was little the British or French police could do about it.

With all that mayhem going on, I was going to be caught up in it sooner or later, and sooner if I stuck with that jinx Alioshka Bublikoff. But who in his right mind would have imagined that it was going to happen on a Saturday afternoon at the Grand, Tientsin's largest movie house? It was after Scouts, most of Fox Patrol, including who else but Alioshka, were up in the rear balcony. The film was *Gunga Din*. Came the big scene, the climax, the three swashbuckling heroes: Cary Grant, Victor McLaglan, Douglas Fairbanks Jr trapped on the roof of a temple, a column of gallant Highlanders marching to the rescue, kilts swirling, bagpipes squeaking, blissfully unaware of the fanatics waiting in ambush. Oh, how we wanted to warn those brave Scots marching to their certain death! But in the nick of time, Gunga Din, Rudyard Kipling's lowly water carrier, put bugle to lip and sounded the alarm. In truest Hollywood tradition the Highlanders wheeled into battle formation. And what a battle, what a din from the muskets, Gatling guns, cannon! But hey! Wait a minute! That last *crack-crack-crack* was too sharp, too ringing to be coming from the screen. And now a muffled shout from the audience, rapid-fire voices, slamming seats, hurrying footsteps. Then the lights came on. Then the mad rush for the exits. In the stalls, a few rows below us and to our left, schoolmate Arthur Li was standing, holding up his wrist, his jacket dark with blood. In the seat directly behind him, a Chinese lady was leaning over a slumped figure. Patrol Leader Promptoff, always the perfect Baden Powell, rushed down to offer his services. Someone – we later heard it was Doctor Heinemann of the German American Hospital – hollered at him to scram. On the landing down the first flight of stairs lay the contorted body of a man. (Next day's *North China Star* stated that he, a Belgian, had gone to fetch his wife's coat – she couldn't stand the film's violence – when by a one-in-a-million chance he stepped in the gunman's way.) Out on the street Achmet rushed over to tell us that Talat had been shot. We learned afterwards that Talat Mansur, North China's breast stroke champion, had felled one of the gunmen with a flying tackle, whereupon the man's accomplice shot Talat in the stomach, then turned and fired point blank at Talat's buddy, Ravil Tahir. Click! Empty chamber. The incredibly courageous and fast-thinking Ravil got Talat to the Jewish Hospital in time to save his life. We also heard that Arthur Li was going to be all right, but the man seated behind him in the stalls had succumbed. He was Dr S.G. Chang, top banker and top Japanese collaborator.

To everyone's astonishment, the British police appre-

Blood 'n Thunder
at the

GRAND

GUNGA DIN

Starring

Cary Grant
D. Fairbanks Jnr
Victor McLaglen

hended the gunmen, all four of them. Right away the Japanese demanded that the four be handed over. "Not on your life," the British responded, cool as all get out.

Was there no limit to Eeengliss arrogance? How velly velly exasperating for the Chrysanthemum Throne! After all, hadn't Dai Nippon gone to all the trouble of establishing a new bank, the Federal Reserve Bank of China? And hadn't the said bank issued paper money so pretty, so arty that it was bound to supplant CNC, China's national currency? And hadn't British and French banks refused to accept the FRB notes as legal tender. And what about all that silver in the French Concession, Chinese government bullion, forty million ounces of it, stashed away deep in the vaults of the Bank of China's Tientsin branch on Rue de Paris?

"Hand over the bullion," the bristling Samurai barked.

"*Va te faire voir*," the gallant Gallic retorted.

Hells bells, how much more could the Samurais take?

Not very much, as it turned out. The very next rebuff was the last straw. The Imperial Japanese High Command put in a polite request to both the British and French authorities for a regiment of the Watanabe Brigade to march down Rue de Takou and Taku Road, that route being a shortcut to the river mouth, where, according to the latest Japanese intelligence, a particularly troublesome band of Chinese terrorists was setting up shop.

And the reply that fell on Japanese ears? "Come-come, gentlemen, you know yourself it's no shortcut. You're only trying to intimidate the concessions' native inhabitants. Request denied."

The morning following this refusal, the morning of June 13, 1939, to be precise, Tientsin's two thousand British and French residents awoke to find themselves hostages in their own concessions. At every entry point steel-helmeted Japanese infantrymen stood guard behind barbed wire barricades. Trucks, cars, rickshaws, and pedestrians were allowed through only after interminable delay. And that was just the prelude. When word spread of what the Japanese were doing at the barricades, a shock wave swept through the community. Their gendarmes were picking out men or women from the queue of people waiting to get through and stripping them bare.

110 Act of war? What else? Surely the time had come for

Britannia, Ruler of the Waves, mightiest of the Conquistadors the world had ever seen, to give Johnny Jap a swift kick in the pants.

Nothing of the kind. The feeble bleats from No. 10 Downing Street hardly reached the milk bottles at No. 11, let alone the War Office. So what better enticement for Tokyo to tighten the screws. And still not a peep from the Land of Hope and Glory. If poor press coverage was at the root of the mother country's indifference, then surely Fleet Street could have borrowed from Tientsin's papers where it was front page stuff every day. They could have picked up any paper, picked up the June 26th edition of the *Peking & Tientsin Times*, for instance, and this is what they would have read:

> *The release after nine days of Mr G. A. Smith, the almost complete stoppage of the milk supply, and a particularly bad case of searching were the features of the 12th day of the blockade yesterday.*

> *Mr and Mrs D. Finlay were victims of the search on Saturday afternoon as the couple were going to the Country Club, of which Mrs Finlay is manageress. Mrs Finlay was taken into an inner hut where a Chinese woman searcher stripped her of everything but her corselet. Mrs Finlay asked the Japanese sentry to leave but he remained throughout the inspection. The woman searcher felt under the*

111

corselet and then, after a most intimate inspection, allowed Mrs Finlay to dress again. The sentry remained there all the time while the door of the hut was wide open, exposing Mrs Finlay to the gaze of many people in the adjoining room. When she left the hut Mrs Finlay found her husband in the open in nothing but a singlet. His clothes strewn all over the ground.

Practically all milk coming in today was stopped. This has hit the British Municipal Hospital, where some patients on a milk diet are in a serious position.

Apologists for Japanese behavior (and there were many of these – and there still are) would say that all one had to do to avoid the embarrassment of public nudity and slapped cheeks was simply to stay put in one's own concession. But then wouldn't that mean saying good-bye to the Country Club, the stables, the camping ground, Peining Park, Russian Park, German Park, and that incomparable gem of a restaurant, Kiessling & Bader? And wouldn't it mean giving a miss to the Race Club's network of canals which, at this time of the year, seethed with surfacing schools of golden carp? Well, not necessarily if you possessed, as I did, that safest of safe-conducts – a slender, made-in-Japan, four-piece rod. For aren't the Japanese, practically the whole race of them, incorrigible Izaac Waltons? And aren't the Izaac Waltons of this world a breed unto themselves: faithful fans of the noble and ancient art of angling, of the tall tale, of brethren anglers? Dismount from my bike? Sure thing. Let the khaki-clad warrior-angler feel the whip of my rod? Why not? He's going to pass me through with a slap on the back. He does so every time.

Though I was never obliged to undo a trouser button, I was sufficiently slowed passing through the checkpoint to have a ringside view of the Nagasaki version of that vulgar sport – "debagging." I saw with my own eyes his nibs, Edgar J. Simpson Esq, taipan of Hopei Cotton, standing out in the open, *naked as the day he was born*. And then there was that acquaintance of Tai-tai's, the director of Belgian Tramways, Monsieur LeClerc, a mountain of pink, shielding his essentials with a Moyler Powell boater. It took the lovable Scottish eccentric, Mad Mac McKenzie, to turn it into a frolic, a chuckling, thigh-slapping frolic. But why should that have surprised anyone? That grand fellow was always good for a laugh. A piano tuner by profession, his work took him to sundry mission stations in the interior where his antics were legend. His Mandarin was pure Peking, but he could revert to harsh Shansi or sing-song Kiangsu when so inclined. And the bawdy pidgin with which he could dress up verses from the Presbyterian Hymnal was remarkable for its inventiveness. What a shock to those straight-laced mission ladies and girl converts when he tested a tuned piano with a verse or two!

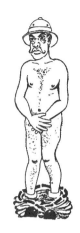

Mad Mac breakfasted at the Country Club every morning. He'd been doing it for donkey's years; no way was he going to let the barricades interfere with his daily ritual. According to the story that went the rounds, the first time they had his pants off, he broke into hilarious giggles when a guard, armed with chopsticks, raised first his left testicle then his right in a mock search for contraband. After that, the show he put on never varied. He'd arrive at the barrier and strip right down to his skin without ever being ordered to do so. And there he'd stand, his clothes bundled under an arm, treating Chinese bystanders to a ribald ditty until the exasperated sentries bustled him through. He wasn't playing fair!

And he wasn't alone, no sir. Others found other ways to tweak Japanese noses.

One day, at our favorite noodles eaterie on Taku Road, Murat Apakaieff grabbed my arm. "Take a look at this FRB dollar. What do you see?"

The green bank note he put in my hand looked no different from any other I'd come across.

"Look carefully."

"I am. But what's there to see?"

"*Durak*, look at what Confucius is doing with his fingers."

"Holy Moses! That's an obscene gesture he's making. And what a mischievous look on his face! What's it all about, Murat?"

"I'll tell you what I know," he said, with a mischievous glint of his own. "The guy who designed this dollar note is a famous Chinese painter who shocked Peking's art world

Naughty Confucius makes an obscene gesture!

when he agreed to go work for the Japanese. And they, of course, lost no time making a big song and dance about him, putting his picture in all the magazines and papers. Well, six months later he disappeared. Not a trace of him in Peking, Tientsin, anywhere. In actual fact all he did was wander into the British Concession and board a Butterfield & Swire ship bound for Hong Kong. By the time the bank authorities noticed that Confucius was giving them the 'up you Charlie' sign, it was too late; millions of the notes were already in circulation. You know how the Japanese hate being laughed at. They must be out of their minds."

"The guy was pretty lucky to get away."

"Not really, it was easy as pie. The Japanese haven't yet been able to interfere with British shipping. You can break the blockade anytime you like. All you have to do is get on a British ship."

And that's how we got to Peitaiho that summer – by B&S coaster.

We were late boarding, so there was hardly time to reconnoiter our cabin before the brave little tub pulled away, gave three toots, and headed down stream. As we passed the Japanese checkpoint on the German Bund, tortured English crackling from a loudspeaker ordered the ship to pull to. The reply, blared through a bull horn, was pure Glaswegian: "Shut yurr durrrty mouth you

114

stupid barrrstarrrd. Can't you see wurrr Brrrutush!" The vessel never faltered in its course, and not another sound from Johnnie Jap. Who dares contend with a surly Jock?

I stayed on deck watching the city skyline recede into the distance. In a little while there was nothing to break the monotony of the barren yellow plain dotted with grave mounds all the way to the horizon. I was gazing haphazardly at the sweep of the bow-wave overflowing the shoreline when a *wonk*, one of those semi-wild native watch dogs, caught my eye. It was feeding on a corpse. The wave snatched the meal from the cur's mouth and sent it into the current. The cur simply plunged in, locked its jaws on a limb, and paddled back to shore.

When the dinner gong sounded, I didn't leave my bunk.

The sleepy port of Chinwangtao where we docked was only one short stop on the PNR line from Peitaiho Junction. And from there a mere twenty-five minutes on the quaint narrow-gauge Emmet train to our beloved Peitaiho Beach.

Our arrival, a bit of a let-down. Where last year we rode donkeys inland to Quelch's place, now nothing so exciting; we took rickshaws to the Rocky Point bungalow Tai-tai had acquired the previous winter from an American missionary. She must have noticed our disappointment; she went all out selling the place. "Look at the lovely cool verandah. Look at that rattan furniture. And just wait till you see the bathroom's all-modern plumbing. You don't know how lucky you are. American Beach is just a stone's throw from our front step. Why don't you go down to the beach right now, all of you?"

The others went, I didn't. I had a pilgrimage to make. I hiked out to the Quelch residence. The caretaker said he hadn't seen Hsiao Szer for ages. Why didn't I try the village. I did but for the life of me I couldn't remember which of the identical mud houses was Hsiao Szer's. Everyone I asked clammed tight. In the end it was Hsiao Wang, Quelch's goatherd, who gave me the news.

"Gone away, whole family, moved to the mountains above Shanhaikuan, father is an Eighth Route Army man."

"Red Army?"

"Yes."

"And Hsiao Szer?"

"He wears the scarf of the Little Red Devils, but he'll

soon be a soldier."

A soldier, Hsiao Szer! I just couldn't imagine him shouldering a rifle, such a scrawny lad with such wide-open innocent eyes.

By the time I retraced my steps to Rocky Point, it was midday. Tony and Betty were back from the beach, which now, under the sun's direct rays, was too scorching for human habitation. The much vaunted Peitaiho sea breezes had given way to a breathless calm. In the surrounding aspens and mimosas, massed cicadas in full screech were telling the world it was siesta time. There was nothing for it but to collapse on a deck chair and wait it out till dusk.

At three-thirty I'd had more than enough of the deck chair. Though it was still hot as Hades outside, I descended the steps carved into the cliff and crossed American Beach to Tiger Rocks. The tide was way in, only the tallest rocks showed above the surface, and they were a good fifty yards out from shore, too hazardous to wade to. Never mind, I could try for sandfish, which at that time of day moved in to feed in the shallows. But what the heck was I going to use for bait? I was about to chuck it in and head for home when I caught sight of the tall, tanned figure making his way towards me, his toes caressing the corrugated sand at the edge of the sweeping surf. It was Leonard Gmirkin, heavens alive! Who else had those twinkling eyes, that catching smile?

"Hi, Des, what you trying to catch?"

"Sandfish, Leoka, sandfish."

"Caught any?"

"No, haven't tried. No bait."

"No bait? I'll get you a mussel." And with that he waded in waist-deep, probing with his feet for submerged rocks. In no time he sank his hand down and came up with a glistening black shellfish. I made a mess of opening the thing. "Here, gimme your knife," he said. Deftly as a surgeon he prised open the clamped valves and gouged out the blob of gray-white flesh which he slid over the hook. Not quite done, he plucked a hair from his head and wound it around the bait. "Stays on longer," he muttered. "But you still gotta be gentle with your cast."

I nodded my thanks. I didn't have the heart to tell him that I'd never had much luck with mussels.

"Try over there," he suggested. "You'll get one there."

He knew his stuff. Right away I felt several sharp tugs,

and when I jerked back my rod, there was that surprisingly strong resistance typical of a bottom feeder making the most of the hollow cone of pelvic fins endowed it by nature to defeat the currents.

"You want to try?" I asked, after I had the twelve-inch yellow-brown sandfish in my basket.

"Sure," he said, giving me one of his wonderful smiles.

I watched him as he waded into deeper, darker water. It was hard for me, slow in emerging from puny adolescence, not to be envious of him, so tall, so deep-chested. And no good pitting my angling skills against his. He was always the more inventive. At Tientsin Country Club while I dangled worms for carp, he stalked *huang zhuan*, those monstrous native pike, teasing them to a frenzy with live frogs.

"Hey, Des, look at this." The gorgeously striped silver bream he landed was flopping about the wet sand.

"That's terrific, Leoka."

"That's nothing. You want to try for swordfish tomorrow?"

"Swordfish!" In my mind's eye was Zane Grey's four hundred pound world-record monster.

He laughed out loud. "I know what you're thinking. The ones I catch are only a foot-and-a-half long, but they're marvelous sport. Wanna come?"

"You bet."

It's mid-morning. Leoka launches his flat-bottomed canoe and is off through the waves. In his kid brother

117

Margie Hale

Vasia's canoe I have to paddle like mad to catch up. He stops about a hundred yards out from English Beach and points down. Faintly discernible ten feet below is a massive submarine rock clad in orangey kelp. I catch my breath when I spot schools of swordfish shooting across it. I watch Leoka lift his slender eight-foot rod upright so that the wind does the work of carrying the fine weightless line out over the churning water. Wham! Strike!

He signals me to have a go. With the sun burning fiercely and the salt spray whipping my face and the powerful swells lifting and lowering the canoe as if it were nothing but a matchbox, I maneuver into position. I raise my rod. The wind takes the line out. Wham! the swordfish strikes with frightening suddenness. The rod doubles in crazy arcs. For sheer excitement there's nothing in the world to beat it.

Or is there? Leoka says to me quite matter-of-factly as we drag our canoes above high water mark: "Want more fun? After you've got your catch in the ice box, why don't you come down to American Beach? I'll introduce you to the gang."

Because I know them from Tientsin, I am able to conquer my shyness when I come face to face with Bessie, Lucy, Mary, Brian, Charlie, Vincy. But those others I meet for the first time – Pat, Rob, Mac, Margie, Cathy, June, vibrant Americans from Shanghai – turn me into a dithering eight-year-old. Because shyness is an emotion totally absent from their make-up, they fail to notice my foolish simpering. They take me as I come.

But I must still prove myself. I do that by throwing and catching the baseball as well as they, and by powering along with the best of them when they swim out to the anchored junk their parents have rented for the summer. They see nothing special in my prowess. They expect it of me just as they expect me to keep pace when they charge back from the water to bask on the sand. Sometimes a curvaceous Lamour stirs up howls of complaint when she pushes her way between bare shoulders and thighs to make room for herself. Sometimes I am the one who has to surrender space. I know I should let out my howl of complaint. But no way. When the firm hip shoves mine, I get such a burst of electricity my lungs are paralyzed.

Afterwards, at dusk, on somebody's verandah, I take my turn winding the Victrola. It's a serious responsibility.

There must not be a moment's delay between Benny Goodman and Harry James. The one in charge simply cannot leave his post. I don't mind. Why should I? It gives me the opportunity to take in the goings on, and I take in a lot. Just look at that pair from Shanghai, so poised, so sophisticated, so completely at ease whether it's a fox trot, tango, or waltz. Look at them gliding, swiveling, cheek to cheek, body to body, molded as one . . . *Tonight I mustn't think of her, Music Maestro, please* . . .

Wow! there's Leoka, cool as Cary Grant, dancing with Margie Hale – gorgeous, statuesque, with cascading ash blonde hair. And sonovagun, Brian Clarke too, another fellow Tientsinner, cheek to cheek with lovely Lucy Attree.

Lucy Attree

I look once, I look twice. It can't be, but it is, and directed right at me, the smile on the face of a girl seated across the verandah. My stomach ties in knots. Let it! Nothing in the world will induce me to budge from the refuge of the Victrola . . .

"What's your name? Desmond you say? What's the matter Desmond? I don't see you dancing? You don't know how to dance? You'll soon learn. Come on." The American parent takes my hand. Though I'm in a blue funk, I force my feet to follow her feet . . .

When the record ends I find safety in the clutch of larking, nudging, giggling twelve- and thirteen-year-olds. But my mind is on the older ones: Brian and Lucy, Leoka and Margie, Pat and Irene. As far as I can determine, not all the girls are spoken for. I sneak a glance at darling freckle-faced Betty-Ann, at vivacious golden-haired June, at sultry dark-haired Constance. Can I summon up the courage? Can I? "*May I have this dance?*" Is that what I have to say? Just the thought of mouthing those words and my heart skips a beat. But I must do it. I must pull myself together. Darn, it's too late. There's only an inch of record left. And anyway, isn't it about time someone changed the needle? And isn't *Little White Lies* a bit on the fast side. Wait for *Penny Serenade.* Wait for *South of the Border* . . .

"Desmond, why are you *not* dancing? Come on, get up on your feet." The persistent parent takes me by the hand. I move like a condemned man on the slow march to the gallows. "Betty-Ann," the parent says, "dance with Desmond."

I'm as rigid as a mechanical toy. I advance three steps.

119

I retreat three steps. I look past the shock of glossy brown hair, but I cannot avoid breathing in wafts of its natural fragrance. When Betty-Ann turns her head to reply to someone's quip, I sneak a quick glance at the heavenly down of her freckled cheek.

She lets me have the next dance, and the next. We hardly say a word. There is no need for words. There is the silent language of the eyes. When a parent announces it's time to quit, we mill about saying our awkward good-byes. Brian will be seeing Lucy home. Pat will escort Irene. Charlie will be with Bessie. Dare I dare ask Betty-Ann? I get the butterflies. But my new-found courage doesn't entirely forsake me. I somehow spill out the words: "May I walk you home, Betty-Ann?" She nods her yes. Lord oh lord, and the night pitch black. A goodnight kiss? The thought of it and I am a quivering jellyfish. Diving into a shark-infested sea holds less terror for me. . . .

Someone said the Gheradis were packing. Someone said the Wallaces. Was Betty-Ann Wallace going? And Margie Hale? How time flashed by that unforgettable summer! The Hales gave a farewell barbecue at Lighthouse Point. Just getting there was pure delight, the flotilla of fishing junks hired for the occasion swishing gently along the dead calm sea. Someone began strumming a guitar. We sang, we held hands, we had not a care in the world. Then on the beach, after barbecued steaks (the first I'd ever tasted) and chocolate cake (as only the Americans can make it), we lolled on the sand, watching the sun paint the sky every shade of red as it sank behind stately *Queen Victoria on her Deathbed.* Two girls dashed into the surf (only girls dared the cool evening water). Phosphorescence turned them into silvery Dianas. The guitar player started singing wistfully: "*Wishing will make it so, just keep on wishing and cares will go . . .*" I joined in with the few words I knew: "*The curtain of night will part, if you are certain within your heart . . .* "

"Hey you guys down there! Hey!"

All eyes turned to the figure on the cliff top. Illuminated by moonlight, he looked vaguely familiar. He started down the dangerous path. Crazy thing to do, but he kept coming. I recognized him unmistakably when he drew close. It was Richard Evans, an American, a class or two

In line astern the
RN flotilla steams
off into the night
(sketched by Lt.Cdr
N.L. Veresmith –
China Station)

below me at TGS.

"Did you guys hear the news? War! England and France have declared war on Germany."

"Where'd you get that?"

"Heard it on the radio. Didn't you see those British warships take off yesterday?"

I remember that morning thinking it strange, Temple Bay empty of ships. Where had they gone: *HMS Kent, USS Paul Jones,* and the sleek *Bartolomeo Colleoni,* flagship of the Italian Eastern Fleet?

My thoughts turned to my brothers: Patrick, in the RAF, stationed at Alor Star in Malaya; Brian, at London University, certain to be called up; Jocelyn, serving in *HMS Shropshire* somewhere in the Med.

In the junk carrying us back to Rocky Point, no bantering, no singing, just serious chatter from the grown-ups, fussing over the possibility of their ship home being rerouted.

It wasn't. In the coming days the Hales, the Ross's, the MacDonalds departed for Shanghai, the McCanns and the Benedicts for Peking, and the Fullers for Hong Kong. We Tientsinners took no part in the exodus. In July our city had suffered a disastrous flood, and though the waters had now receded, there was the immense job of cleaning up. The mass inoculation program underway might control the spread of cholera and typhoid; but there was no safeguard against infantile paralysis.

It was well into October before we arrived home. The Japanese barricades that had been swept away with the first onrush of floodwater were back in place. So we were again hostages, and hostages we remained through the winter and into the summer of 1940. As if that wasn't

dispiriting enough, we were forced to swallow the ever-worsening news from Europe – the debacle in Norway, the blitzkrieg in the low countries, the BEF and French army in headlong retreat, Dunkirk, the fall of France.

Now, any time they liked, the Japanese could breeze into the French Concession, and ours too, for that matter. How could the poor beleaguered mother country give a single thought to her obscure outpost of empire tucked away forty miles inland from the Gulf of Peichihli?

But someone in the Foreign Office must have given it some thought, enough thought to instruct HBM's Ambassador in Tokyo to submit to the humiliating terms laid down by the Chrysanthemum Throne. For the throne's generosity in lifting the blockade, our side agreed to "assist" the French in transferring the Chinese government bullion from the Bank of China on Rue de Paris to the Yokohama Specie Bank on Consular Road. And the British Municipal Council agreed to accept FRB in payment of its utility bills. And our people said yes, the brave Samurai warriors could have their show-of-force march down Taku Road and Elgin Avenue. And they also said yes, the Kempetai could have the four *Gunga Din* gunmen to do with as they pleased.

Saying yes to all those things, how could we ever again face our Chinese friends?

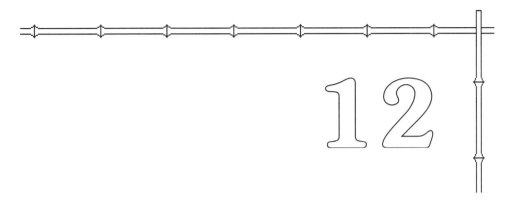

A-SOLDIERING WE WILL GO

" **H**EY YOU GUYS, barricades gone, let's go German Park, haven't been there for heck-of-a-long-time."

"Good idea, let's go," chorused Theodore Mavropolis, Murat Apakaieff, Rajan Patel.

"Crazy. You'll never catch me outside the British Concession. Too dangerous," Alioshka Bublikoff piped up.

"You mean you're gonna let yourself be cooped in here forever?"

"That's right. I'm gonna stay right here."

"Who could blame Aliosha? In recent months things had turned pretty nasty for Russians. Their community had split into factions. And all because of the White Guard and its infamous founder Ataman Grigori Semenov, the renegade Cossack from Trans Baikal, the man who during the Allied intervention in Siberia at the close of the Great War had thrown the whole of eastern Siberia into a state of terror. When his Cossacks, armed and financed by the Japanese, overran a Bolshevik position, they showed no mercy, took no prisoners. And they worked their will upon the populace, Red or White, it didn't matter. In every village that fell to them they slaughtered the men, and raped the women and children. When the Red Army finally swept across the Maritime Province, Semenov slipped over the border into Manchuria. He managed to get to the States, but his reputation followed him, his entry permit was revoked. He then sailed for France where he went to ground in the forlorn world of lost émigrés.

It was not until the mid-30s that he resurfaced, once

123

again in the Far East, once again under Japanese auspices. He soon made his presence felt. In Peking he founded a new anti-Bolshevik paramilitary movement, a revived *White Guard*, which was to spread its tentacles over every Russian community in China and Manchuria. In Tientsin his long-time henchman, Pastukhin, issued an edict from his headquarters in the ex-German Concession, grandiosely designated the *White House*, calling on all local Russians to register. Refuse? Pastukhin learned well from his master. A prominent Russian disappeared from his London Road home. A week later his mutilated corpse was found floating in the creek under the Elgin Avenue bridge.

Incensed at this blatant flouting of British authority, Chief-of-Police Lawless ordered all known White Guard activists in the concession to be rounded up for questioning. Fat lot of good. In just a matter of days a popular TGS student, Victor Promptoff, was kidnapped right from under the noses of the BMC police. And twenty-four hours later it was the turn of another young Russian, though in his case, fortuitously, two off-duty Tommies happening on the scene dashed into the ex-German Concession and set him free. Puppet gendarmes came storming to the perimeter. A detachment from the Durham Light Infantry was rushed to the scene. The confrontation ended in stalemate but not the verbal slanging. The *North China Star* lambasted the White Guard – the *Peking Chronicle* excoriated the English colonial soldiery. And all this hullabaloo at a time when the French were raising a storm over the kidnapping and murder of the brilliant young pianist, Simon Kaspe. Semenov's cutthroats in Harbin had omitted to check Kaspe's citizenship. He might have been Russian born, but he had French papers. From Shanghai, the flamboyant American broadcaster, Carol Alcott, added his voice to the barrage of words: "Jello, Jello, Jello (he always kicked off with this commercial), this is Carol Alcott speaking on Radio XMHA. Criminals in the pay of the Japanese have taken to kidnapping and murdering adolescents . . . "

Too much exposure even for the White House. Victor Promptoff came home to the jubilation of family, friends, and well-wishers.

Pastukhin might be roundly cursed by many, but he was not without his adherents. How could they forget their roots, they who had made the murderous journey a step ahead of the Red menace across Siberia and down through Mongolia and Manchuria to Peking, to Tientsin, to Shanghai? Worse than losing home and livelihood, they had forfeited their self-esteem. Doctors from St Petersburg took work as hospital orderlies. Teachers scrubbed floors. Officers from classic regiments enrolled as NCOs in the British and French police. Disbanded cavalrymen sold themselves as soldiers of fortune to Chinese warlords. Unprotected women went up for sale. Warlord Chang Tsung Chang added twenty Russian maidens to his harem. In the sleazy bar districts of every foreign settlement there was an over-supply of joy girls with blue eyes and flaxen hair.

How those Russian spirits must have soared when a parade of the White Guard came marching by! What memories were stirred when the jackbooted formation burst into the old marching song, *Rasboynichki*! Was this the birth of a new White army that was going to free Holy Mother Russia from Stalin's satanic grip?

It most certainly was, if you listened to Konstantin Maltsev. Absolutely not, according to Serge Vishniakoff who was not afraid to sing out to any who cared to listen that no matter how strong the call, how soul-stirring the message, signing up with the White Guard meant signing up to fight for Japan.

"What then do you propose?" someone asked.

"Get out of China. Get to America, to Australia."

"And how do we do that without papers, without *boomashki*?"

"What are you all talking about?" Konstantin butted in. "Why should we go? We have our rights here. We have more rights here than do the Japanese. We were here a hundred years before the English."

"Nonsense."

Konstantin was ready to blaze away, but no one challenged. And he needed challenge, he thrived on challenge. He rounded on Chuck Collins. "Do you know that two hundred years before your pioneers started their westward trek across America our explorers and hunters and traders had already established colonies in Siberia. Long before you Americans were fighting off your Red Indians we had subdued the Turki and Buriat and Yakut tribes. China was powerful then. The Manchu Emperor, Kang

125

Hsi, blocked our way in the Amur region, but we pressed on, and we eventually reached the Pacific. Probing southwards our traders got to Peking. We got to Tientsin before you Americans ever even heard of the place."

"That's a tall story, Konsty. Everyone knows the Jesuits got here first, then the Portuguese, then the Dutch."

"Look you guys," Konstantin was getting red in the face, "if you don't believe me, next time you're in Peking, go to the northeast section of the city, go to the Russian Orthodox Mission Church, take a good look at the worshippers. They're Chinese, you're gonna say. Let me tell you right now they're not Chinese, they're Russian. Emperor Kang Hsi so admired the fighting skills and courage of the Russian garrison he captured at Albazin that instead of chopping off their heads, as was the custom, he packed them off to Peking and absorbed them as a separate and distinct banner brigade in his imperial army. He deeded to them in perpetuity the northeast corner of the city. Their descendants survive to this day. They are the ones you see in the Orthodox church there. Through generations of intermarriage they might have lost their Russian appearance, their language, but not their Russian religion, their Russian soul. They are a part of China that will be forever Russia."

"Empty words, my dear Konsty, empty words. The Chinese population is so vast it simply swallows up its minorities. You yourself admit that the Albazin Russians have already lost much of their identity. The day will come when, like the Kaifeng Jews before them, they will vanish with hardly a trace." Those were the words of Leo Olshevsky, and he spoke them with a catch in his voice. The disappearance of the once thriving tribe of Hebrews at Kaifeng and the leveling of their synagogue was cause for sorrow among local Jews. Leo was one, an *Ashkenazi.*

"Then you don't believe we have our rights," Konsty shot at him.

"I don't believe we have. I share Sergei's view that we should all get out. I myself am going to try for Palestine. I intend to help in the building of settlements there."

"And I," said Murat Apakaieff, "will go to Turkey."

"America, America is the place."

"Australia."

"Rubbish, wishful thinking. Have any of you got *boomashki*? How can you get there without *boomashki*?"

126

Relics of Peking's Cossacks march in religious procession

"*I* have *boomashki*," Ben Shurupkin retorted. "I have Soviet passport. You too can have Soviet passport. You go USSR Consulate, Number One, Park Road, old Russian Concession. They give you."

"Where can you go with such passport?"

"To Vladivostok, to Moscow, to freedom."

"You'll get shot soon as you cross the border at Manchuli."

"Capitalistic propaganda," Ben Shurupkin snapped. And that was Ben all over; incorrigibly dogmatic, he would cite chapter and verse from Engels or Marx to press home a point. He would tell you it was Jardine, Dent, Russell, and Sassoon who brought opium to China, that it was the Versailles signatories who bestowed upon Japan the confiscated German possession of Tsingtao, that it was Chiang Kai Shek's regulars who brutally suppressed the 1935 student demonstration at Tien-An-Men. He mocked our school's presumption that the history of the British Empire was the history of the world, that the ruling class ruled by divine right. He groaned audibly at assembly when we came to that certain verse of that certain hymn:

> The rich man in his castle,
> The poor man at his gate,
> God made them high or lowly,
> And ordered their estate.

"Shut up Ben, for God's sake. A Soviet passport is not worth a damn. We are talking about proper *boomashki*, real *boomashki*, *boomashki* that will get us to America, to Australia, to Britain."

"Impossible to obtain."

"Yes, yes, absolutely impossible," Ben's supporters sounded in chorus.

Wrong, wrong, wrong as wrong can be. It was *not* impossible. Nick Mihailoff had *boomashki*, the very best *boomashki*, top quality Angliski passport, no less. All he had to do was flip open the stiff cover of royal blue, gilt-embossed with lion and unicorn, and there, plain for all the world to see, was the caveat, in the name of His Majesty King George VI, rendering him the same protection as that enjoyed by any English-born Englishman, even the very Lord Archbishop of Canterbury himself. How did it come about that this Muscovite was able to crack the uncrackable strictures of the Passport Office at Somerset House? Perfectly simple – the scions of Magna Carta in their munificence granted full UK citizenship to all comers, Russians included, who had served five years with the BMC. And not only had Nick and his assistant Leo Vladimiroff more than fulfilled the time requirement with the municipality's electricity department, they were highly regarded by one and all for their competency in running the meter section of said department.

I joined the meter section two months after finishing school, and a month after a friend of a friend of Tai-tai's (who was owed a small favor by Electricity's big cheese Mr Crosby) had put in a good word for me.

"All right, young fellow," Mr Crosby remarked at the end of the three-minute interview in his posh Gordon Hall office, "looks as though you'll do. Call in at Ching Chong's on Taku Road and get yourself measured for a uniform. Go down to Avon Imports and pick yourself out a Hercules."

A Hercules! A brand-spanking new English bike? Wow!

"Yang Fu Tien will teach you all you need to know about *sorchiks*," Nick Mihailoff said to me the day I started. And the first thing Yang taught me was that *dianbiao* was the Chinese term for *sorchik*, which was the Russian term for electric meter. I was lucky; Yang Fu Tien knew his stuff;

Off duty members of BMC Meter section

rear

Kao Shih Ying
Hsiao Li
Nick Mihailoff
Yang Ju Tien

front

Leo Vladimiroff
Des Power
Johnson Sammy

and luckier still, he knew how to put it in clear simple terms. In a week he handed me over to Lao Nien, an old-timer, whose job it was to test all new meters fresh out of packing cases from England. And it was Lao Nien, the taciturn Buddha, who showed me how to compare the dial readings with those of a master meter, and how to speed or slow the RPMs by increasing or reducing the gap between the jaws of a magnet through which the meter's timing disk revolved. I was soon testing meters on my own, the easy ones, the single-phase ones, specified for residential use.

After a meter was deemed to be running at BMC's exact prescribed speed, either Nick or Leo – no one else – would thread a lead blank through the ends of a serrated wire that held down the cover, then with special pliers they would crimp the blank, fusing it permanently to the wire. At every opportunity those two would have me observe that simple procedure, carried out with such religious formality. Then the day came when Nick handed me the pliers and watched breathlessly as I exerted the necessary pressure on the blank to transform it into a seal. My performance must have satisfied him, for right there and then, after a flowery speech affirming that my period of probation had been successfully completed, he presented me with a handsome leather holster in which snugly lay a chrome-plated pair of those precious pliers. "Don't ever let me catch you leaving these lying around. Guard them with your life. Here, let me strap the holster to your belt. Now you can join Yang Fu Tien's installation team."

It took a team of three to install a meter. The apprentice did the joe work, mounting the ladder, clearing a space, and affixing the meter to the wall. The journeyman electrician would then make the power connections. My only role was to seal the meter with the precious chrome-plated pliers entrusted to me.

I didn't take long to catch on that I was extra baggage. Why couldn't they simply give Yang the damned pliers and be done with it? When I asked that of the Chinese staff they laughed good-naturedly. When I asked that of Nick he stared at me aghast. Despite Yang Fu Tien's twenty years of service, despite his unblemished record, a record that even Monseigneur Monet, Bishop of Peitang, would be proud to possess, there was no way that the BMC was going to let him run loose with those pliers.

So I carried on doing what I was supposed to be doing, though I could never really put my heart into the job. Fortunately, it wasn't all testing and installing meters. There was that jolt of excitement whenever the fire alarm went off in Nick's office, and anyone who happened to be on hand would scramble aboard the green ladder-truck before it roared off, screeching tires at every turn. At the scene of the fire we were life-savers, heroes, we could preen as proudly as those firemen in their glistening brass helmets and braided blue jackets.

I was aboard the ladder truck the day it careered down Meadows Road, past All Saints Church, past the grand colonnades of the KMA building, and there, lo and behold, of all places, was that most venerable of institutions, the Tientsin Club – on fire!

It turned out to be a small fire, nothing to write home about, but it let me into that holy of holies for the very first time. I stood by in the foyer as instructed by Nick before he went off with Yang to attend to the main fuse box. It was noon, the club's busiest time of the day. I quickly found that the best way to escape the barrage of penetrating stares was to pretend to be examining the pictures on the wall. Presently, a spindly ginger-haired man with a gingery toothbrush-mustache approached, giving a little cough to draw my attention. He addressed me in the hushed tones of a priest in a confessional: "Excuse me, are you a member?" I shook my head. "Then hadn't you better be off? The fire's out you know." His flexed nostrils said mountains more than his words.

And that was just the beginning of my education. Some weeks later I learned even more sharply that what is sauce for the goose is not necessarily sauce for the gander. It happened after one of our surprise raids on a customer suspected of filching electric power. Yes, electricity could indeed be filched, and in a number of ways: by breaking a meter's seal to get at the points, by tapping into the mains, by hooking up the lighting system to the power line for industrial equipment – the rate for lighting being treble that charged for driving machines.

Acting on a tip, we burst into the very place where I'd been measured for my BMC uniform – Ching Chong the tailor. The whole midnight shift – shop assistants, cutters, seamstresses – tried to block our way. But talk about being caught red-handed! Each and every 500-watt lamp was connected to the shop's industrial power line. Suddenly the owner was on the scene filling the air with shrill invectives. He cursed Nick. He called him *qiong lao Ne* – poverty stricken Russian – the most derogatory epithet for Russians in the Chinese vocabulary. Purple in the face, Nick yelled back in his off-beat Russianized Mandarin. A cutter pointed a pair of shears. An electrician brandished a crowbar. Leo summoned the police.

Next day we were at Gordon Hall to collect our reward, a crisp ten dollar CNC note, which Mr Crosby customarily handed each and every member of the raiding team. We were all smiles. We'd more than earned our ten bucks. We hadn't allowed ourselves to be intimidated.

"How dare you Mihailoff! Have you gone completely out of your mind? Who gave you permission to raid Ching Chong's? Runciman is livid. Don't you know he sponsored Mr Ching for election to council? No reward for your people. I've half a mind to sack the lot of you."

"What got into Mr Crosby?" I asked Leo when we were outside. "Do we always have to clear the raids with him beforehand?"

"No, but we should have used our savvy. Mr Runciman is the most influential member of council. On his say-so the police order their uniforms from Ching Chong's.

131

Kickback, don't you see?"

"Kickback? What's that?"

"Forget it kid, forget what I said."

Back in the shop I asked Yang Fu Tien what he thought of it all. He shrugged his shoulders and uttered that most frustrating catch-phrase in the Chinese tongue: "*Meiyou fazi*" – Nothing can be done.

I asked Kao Shih Ying. "*Meiyou fazi*," he responded. And *meiyou fazi* was what I got from Lao Nien and from the rest of them, even apprentice Hsiao Li to whom ten dollars must have meant a lot. It's *meiyou fazi* when floods inundate the countryside, it's *meiyou fazi* when the annual cholera epidemic hits, it's *meiyou fazi* when the Golden Units, heroes of Chinese soccer, get shellacked five-nil by the Royal Italian Marines!

After cashing my next paycheck at Hongkong & Shanghai Bank, I crossed kitty-corner to the British Consulate. I knew the consular constable, Mr McVeigh, by sight. His son, Dick, was a schoolmate.

"Hello, young Desmond. What can I do for you?"

"I want to join up. Can you tell me please how I go about it?"

"Wait here. I'll see if Mr Bagshaw is free." He was back in minutes.

"Follow me."

I recognized Mr Bagshaw right away. I knew him from cricket, a big affable fellow, bald as a pumpkin, always a wide grin on his face.

"Well, well young man. What are you up to?"

"Desmond wants to enlist, wants to join the Indian Army," Mr McVeigh answered for me.

I caught my breath. It had never entered my mind. Yes, of course, the Indian Army! Billy Laidlaw, Jack Carter, Denis O'Hara, all a class or two ahead of me at school, had already gone to India, had been accepted at Bangalore OCTU, had gone on to receive their commissions . . .

"He's like my Dick. Speaks Chinese like a native," continued Mr McVeigh.

"Champion! We can use all the bright lads we can find. How old are you, Desmond?"

"Seventeen, sir."

"Seventeen? Bit on the young side. Might have to wait six months. Fill out these forms anyway. Mr McVeigh will arrange your medical. Don't look so disappointed. Half a

132

year is neither here nor there. Why don't you join the Volunteers while you're waiting? Get some basic training. Stand you in good stead later."

"How do I join, sir?"

"Easy. Go see Mr Sontag of Peihua Press on Cousins Road. He'll do the necessary."

I biked it down to Cousins Road. I knew exactly where Peihua Press was. My brother Patrick had worked there. Mr Sontag saw me right away.

"Here's a paper to sign."

On the form under the space for "Desired Unit" the words "Armored Cars" had been crossed out.

"I'd like to get into the Armored Cars," I said.

"Everyone does, but they're full. What about No. 1 Platoon?"

I shook my head, and he didn't press the point. We both knew No. 1 was for pukka sahibs, executives with old school ties. And even more out of the question was No. 2 Platoon which every year took the silver challenge cup for ceremonial drill. You had to have Russian blood in your veins to drill with such clockwork precision.

"What about Murray's platoon, No. 3? Lewis guns, just the job for you. All right?"

"All right."

"Go over to Perrin Cooper's on Consular Road. Ask to see Mr Frank Murray. He's the platoon sergeant. I'll tell him on the phone you're on your way."

Mr Frank Murray, managing director of Perrin Cooper, came around the front of his gleaming rosewood desk to gave my hand a squeeze. And such a knuckle-crunching squeeze it was I nearly jumped out of my shoes. When he broke into a smile, his teeth gleamed whiter than white against the sepia of his face. He was an Anglo-Indian-Portuguese from Macao. "Glad to have you young fellow," he opened with a burst of sing-song China-coast English. "Drill tonight . . . O-eight-hundred hours . . . You report to HQ and my goodness gracious, you'll see what a damn fine lot my boys are."

He was already there on the drill square when I arrived. And what a transformation! No more the genial executive in immaculate pinstripes, he was a raging wild man clad in the rough khaki serge of the Somme.

"Snap to it Ozorio," he yelled. "Pick up your clumsy feet you horrible Gobi Desert camel." And to show he meant business he whacked his puttees with vicious swipes of his swagger stick.

I recognized some of the men being put through their paces: Tartars, Greeks, Armenians, Russian Jews, Anglo-Indians, Anglo-Chinese, Anglo-Portuguese.

"Slap that butt, you shriveled up eunuch. Don't baby it!" He snatched the rifle from a skin-and-bones Bengalese, spun it around as if it were a toy pop gun, and struck the wooden stock with such a ferocious blow the crack rang like a pistol shot.

"As you were. Slo . . . ope . . . arms! Pree . . . zent . . . arms! Slo . . . ope . . . arms! Pree . . . zent . . . arms!"

He had me in the corner of his eye when he dismissed the platoon. "Here, you come with me. We'll get you your uniform. I won't have that white-haired whoremonger tossing anything he likes at you."

At the stores he stood by glowering while the grizzled old-time quartermaster put a tape measure to me. I was soon the proud owner of a World War I field service cap, serge tunic, serge trousers, puttees, hose tops, webbing belt, webbing ammo pouches, and boots with inch-thick soles.

"Volunteer Weinberg," snapped Sergeant Murray. "Show this young pup how to get properly dressed. Wait! Hold it! Not you! You won't do! Look at your puttees! Perfect disgrace! You look like a drop-out from Wu Pei Fu's beaten army!

"Hey, you over there, Karachusian. Come help this recruit with his uniform. Look at his buttons and webbing. Horrible! Get him some Brasso and blanco. Volunteer Weinberg, don't you go away. You stay and watch. You might learn something."

Twenty minutes later I was one of them – prickly collar torturing my neck – steel-hard boot leather cramping my toes. Volunteer Weinberg nudged me. "Come along to the mess." I kept in his wake as he forced a channel through the crush of khaki at the bar. I tried not to breathe through my nostrils; whether it was the sour stench of stale beer or the thick, acrid cigarette smoke, my head was spinning, my innards giving off the ghastly warning signals that come with sea-sickness.

Over the nightmarish rumble of voices and eruptions of laughter and rattle of dice shakers, a voice sounded in my ear: "Hey, Desmond, how's Pat doing?"

I SUPPOSE THAT THE NEW ARMORED CAR SECTION WILL BE DRESSED LIKE THIS.

THANK GOD I'M NOT IN THE ARTILLERY.

THERE — THAT FITS, I THINK.

FOOX

THE QUARTER-BLOKE SHOULD MAKE A LOUSY TAILER.

OUR BLUES FIT TO PERFECTION, THE QUARTER-BLOKE'S PERFECTION.

TAKE A LOOK AT OUR OVERALLS.

PAT POWER

AND AS FOR SUMMER WEAR —.

THE QUARTER-BLOKE'S CLOTHES FIT HIM FINE.

The Volunteers' World War I dress as sketched by Pat Power in 1936.

The fair brows, blue eyes, and Hollywood-handsome face looked familiar. I ransacked my brains but couldn't place the fellow.

"Is he playing hockey in England?"

Suddenly it came to me, of course, Tuleneff, Igor Tuleneff, star athlete, terrific skater, Pat's line mate on Tientsin's interport ice hockey team.

"Pat's in the RAF."

"I know, but where is he stationed?"

"In Malaya, in a place called Alor Star."

"Is he okay?"

"Yes, from what I can tell. The censor slices out a good bit of his letters."

"Is that right? Sometimes we forget there is a war on. Give him my best regards when you write, will you?"

"Sure will."

A powerful hand grabbed my shoulder and spun me around.

135

Little Foreign
Devil as a
recruit in the
Volunteer Corps

"You Pat broder? Pat and me same class. I am Sasha Poroshenkoff. I buy you drink." He called out to the Chinese bartender. "Hey Charlie, two beer."

Pushing between us, Volunteer Weinberg shoved a foaming glass in my hand.

"Vad'a hell!" Poroshenkoff snorted at Weinberg. "Dassmont iss *my* fran. *I* buy drink."

"You want a drink, Sasha old chap? Here, take this one, I'll get me another."

Poroshenkoff gave me a big wink. "*N'sdrovia!*"

"*N'sdrovia*," I answered.

"Hey Sasha! Who's this new recruit?" A heavy-set fellow in gray dungarees and black armored-car beret squinted at me with narrowed eyes.

"He iss Dassmont, Pat Power brodder."

"You a Power? I knew Joss best. Are you older or younger?"

"I'm Desmond. Joss is number three. I'm number four."

"Glad to meet you, Desmond. Drink up. Have one on me."

I tingled with elation. They were raising me to their level. They were investing me with the badge of manhood. I could not, I would not, repress the smile that was playing on my lips.

That night I labored long over my letter to Mr Crosby, tearing up one draft after the other – too wordy. I finally ended up with three simple declarations: I was enlisting in the armed forces – I would soon be going overseas – I was obliged to resign from the BMC.

That was pretty close to the truth. I felt sure I'd be on my way to India before the year was out. Meantime, wasn't I a full blown Volunteer? And weren't Volunteers the real thing – almost? Why had we begun drilling three evenings a week? Wasn't it because Mussolini, now in the war on Hitler's side, might nudge the elite battalion of Royal Italian Marines camped at the north end of International Bridge into having a go at us? And what about the Frenchies? Mightn't they throw in their lot with the Eyeties? No one knew for sure. The FMC had officially declared for Petain, but most of our French pals, vehement de Gaulle supporters, had left to join the Free French in Chad. But that was before the Royal Navy bombarded the French fleet at Oran. One thing certain, you didn't hear that popular song any more, the one that was on everyone's lips the previous spring – *Entente Cordiale . . . Vive la France à l'Angleterre . . . .*

And of course last year's other big hit, *We'll Hang out the Washing on the Siegfried Line,* had gone out of fashion soon as the newsreels showed those thatched-topped, bare-chested heroes of the Wehrmacht hanging out their undies on the Maginot Line.

Germans had reason to gloat; but few of them in Tientsin did. And not surprisingly. Hadn't Britons and Germans unstintingly cooperated in the development of each other's concession? Hadn't Herr Gustav Detring served thirteen years as Chairman of the British Municipal Council? Wasn't it he who conceived and engineered the straightening of the Hai Ho so it could be navigated by coastal steamers? Wasn't it he who designed then pushed through the construction of our hallowed Gordon Hall, so it could be completed in time for the fiftieth anniversary of Queen Victoria's reign? And who was it that presided over the inauguration ceremonies on that historic day? Who else but his Germanic Eminence, Herr Gustav Detring!

Tai-tai spoke German without a trace of accent. As young Gracie D'Arc she attended Holy Ghost Convent in the German-fortified naval port of Tsingtao. Indelibly inscribed in our private family scripture was her fairy-tale romance with a lieutenant serving in the cruiser *Emden.* We could all recite verbatim how that romance was

At one time the respected Herr Dello had Tientsin's Studebaker dealership

137

scuppered within days of the outbreak of the Great War when Grandmamam D'Arc traveled down from Tientsin to pluck her daughter from danger. How darling Gracie refused to leave on the grounds that she was affianced to an officer of the Kaiser's fleet. How Governor Meyer-Waldeck lectured her on one's duty to one's fatherland, and how it must always take precedence over personal considerations. And how, when Mademoiselle Grace dug in her heels, the noble Teuton packed her off *tout de suite* with Grandmamam. After a spirited defense lasting two months, Tsingtao fell to a combined Anglo-Japanese assault. But that was not quite the end of the story as the whole world knows. *SMS Emden*, after having slipped through the screen of British, French, and Russian warships just before the start of hostilities, played merry hell with Allied shipping until it met its brave end under the superior guns of *HMAS Sydney* down near the Cocos Islands.

Back in the twenties when it was the fashion on festive occasions for boys to dress up in sailor suits, we Power boys had something extra special to show off. Spelled out in gothic on our silk hatbands was that proudest of names, a name that stood out above all for gallantry and audacity – the name *EMDEN*.

A decade later those sailor suits, salted away in some trunk somewhere, were forgotten, and a good thing too; Germans and Britons were again at each others' throats. It wouldn't do to extol the *Emden* after what happened to the *Royal Oak* at Scapa Flow. Yet how could we bring ourselves to desist from fraternizing with Germans or Austrians as advocated by Mr Walsingham, Chairman of the Royal St George Society? We had no quarrel with Erik Lange or Karl Detter or Charlie or Jimmy Wolter. Was it their fault that Hitler decided to let Chamberlain's ultimatum lapse on September 3, 1939? Anyway, how could one avoid fraternizing at the Country Club whose members (I was now a junior one), irrespective of flag, happily bumped shoulders on the springy hardwood dance floor.

So how should I have responded to Charlie Wolter when he caught up with me on London Road shouting excitedly that Lopez's swing band was playing at the club and that we ought to scoot out there to take in the tea dance? Recalling the warmth of a girl's hand, the suppleness of a girl's back, the fragrance of a girl's hair, my every cell

tingled. But damn, damn, damn, damn, damn, I'd never get back to the drill hall in time.

"Sorry Charlie, have drill tonight. We Volunteers have to learn how to shoot you guys."

He shrieked with laughter. He filled the Tientsin air with Hamburg oaths. He pointed a wagging finger: "You Volunteers couldn't hit the side of a cow!"

On the drill square it took Sergeant Murray less than ten seconds to get the dance floor off my mind. There was something strangely gratifying in mastering the intricate steps of forming fours – forming two-deep – sloping arms – ordering arms, and always remembering to position the thumb in perfect line with the trouser seam, to close the fingers round the rifle stock at the exact precise angle laid down by King's regulations. Yes, sir, in advancing the rifle from ground to shoulder, from shoulder to ground, we gallants of No. 3 Platoon were fast approaching the immaculate synchrony of No. 2. And, by golly, we felt in our bones that we might even reach the sublime heights of the Duke of Marlborough's Very Own Regiment of the Foot, whose superb marching and counter-marching, whose clockwork gymnastics with the musket, gave them the edge, as every schoolboy knows, in their contest with French Louis's legendary *Maison du Roi*. How else, I ask you, plainly and simply, could the Duke's men have pulled off those grand victories at Blenheim and Ramillies?

Sunday mornings, a treat. Not square bashing but a taste of the real thing – target practice with its whiffs of cordite, ringing eardrums, bruised collarbones.

My first shoot, I'm a pack of nerves. And mostly because Sergeant Cooke of Armored Cars is in a foul temper. His words sting. "Prone, you useless wimp, down on all fours." Strong hands take my elbows and plant them apart. "You have to make an equilateral triangle with those skinny elbows and that pigeon chest of yours." Rude hands grab my ankles and pivot my body as though it were a loose sack of potatoes. "And you have to be at sharp angle to the line of fire." He moves on. I revert to my original angle of incidence. Compared with any Daisy or Diana or even Chuck Collins's twenty-two, the Mark III SMLE is a ton weight. If only I could support it on that sandbag! But the sergeant has already snorted *No bloody way* to someone bold enough to ask: I press the butt into my left shoulder. I cushion the stock with my cheek. I peer through the sights.

"What the bleedin-ell you up to? You can't fire from your left."

"But I'm left-handed," is my faint-hearted reply.

"None of your lip . . . Hey, you over there! Isaacs! What do you think you're doing? Yes, you, Isaacs, I'm addressing you. Are you deaf?"

Good! While the sergeant moves on to deal with that other miscreant, my rifle stays pressed hard against my left shoulder.

"Grouping," Sergeant Holden bellows. "Object is to see how close together you can put five shots. Doesn't matter if they're off center. What counts is getting them together. Open fire."

Craaack! I am startled out of my skin by the rifle going off next to me. I have to prepare myself all over again. The front sight wavers. I can't stop it. First pressure, second pressure, Craaack! Not bad. Hit the target. Maybe a little high. Ten o'clock. Resist the temptation to aim at ten o'clock. Take a bead on the bull. Craaack! Ten o'clock again. After five shots my ears are ringing like an alarm bell. Volunteer Herskovitz runs our targets to us.

"Wipe out! No points!" Sergeant Cooke snarls at me.

I gaze at the four holes within a two-inch circle at ten o'clock. One of the holes is oval shaped.

"Two rounds went through there. All five hit," I say.

"Answer me back do you? Right you are. Up on your feet you horrible little squirt. No more shooting for you today."

Funny thing about it, Sergeant Cooke is none other than Donald Cooke, one of the Cooke boys, a near neighbor, who has exchanged Christmas cards with our family since the year dot. Astonishing what three stripes can do to a man. Sergeant Murray's the same. Wild animal. Snaps at everyone. Even his sons.

On Thursdays it's Lewis gun training for our section. Sergeant Murray has all seventeen of us standing in line in the drill hall. Nicely decked out we are in freshly laundered dungarees, blancoed webbing, mirror-polished boots. All eyes are on the solitary Lewis gun parked on the groundsheet. We've had our lecture on the wonders of this World War I weapon, its rate of fire, its rounds per pan, its stoppages – number one stoppage, number two, number three. Lots of reasons why that wonder weapon can fail. Most embarrassing, our sergeant tells us, if it fails in action. That's why, he says, every last one of us is going to learn to take it apart and re-assemble it blindfolded in twenty-eight seconds flat.

Snap-clack-ting! He has four separate parts in his hand. Click-click, he reassembles them in an instant.

He glares at us. "You'd better start shivering in your boots right now if you can't learn to do that. Do I make myself clear?"

Snap-clack! He has a part in his hand. "This here butterfly spring is called the 'ladies' delight'. Volunteer Herskovitz, why do you think this is called 'the ladies' delight'?"

Dead silence.

"Volunteer Herskovitz, I asked a civil question, I expect a civil reply."

No answer.

The sergeant's eyes narrow. His lips quiver. His face distorts. "Volunteer Herskovitz, I will answer for you. It is obvious, with that Fatty Arbuckle gut of yours, you've forgotten what your tiny shriveled-up thing looks like."

Torrents of laughter. Herskovitz blushes crimson. The sergeant smirks. For once he gives us latitude, lets us snigger, lets us wink and nudge, lets us share in his enjoyment of Volunteer Herskovitz's humiliation.

Now he is demon serious again. We know him well

141

enough to freeze. "In three short weeks," he barks at us, "we're going to take this weapon on the range. By that time you will have learned everything there is to learn about it. You're going to learn you don't keep your finger on the trigger like this. Forty-bloody-seven rounds will be gone before you can bloody say Sergeant O'Grady. Butt to your shoulder, steady aim, short bursts like this . . . short bloody bursts. Do you follow me?

"Volunteer Baziuk, you're number one. Volunteer Power, you're number two. Baziuk, when I call the target, you repeat it after me. When I call the number of bursts, you repeat the number after me. When I give the command 'fire', you yell 'fire' before you bloody pull the trigger. Do you understand?"

"Yes, sarzhant."

Urik Baziuk, my Ukrainian number one, grips the stock in the proper prescribed manner. I lie on my right side, remove a pan from the ammo pouch, feel for the center spring, squeeze it with thumb. The instant I snap the pan into place, Baziuk swivels it with a sharp cuff of his palm. He retracts the cocking handle. The first round is in the chamber. We are ready for action.

Sergeant Murray barks: "Target-bottom-right-half-of-green-door-in-front."

The Ukrainian by my side wheezes noisily; he makes no other sound.

"Target, Baziuk, target!" The sergeant bellows.

Stony silence.

"Baziuk! Give me the target."

The Ukrainian has turned to stone.

"What the hell's got into ya Baziuk?"

At last a growly, throaty guttural: "Dargat harf-dor . . . harf-pottom . . . dargat harf-grin . . . harf-front . . . harf-right . . . harf . . . harf . . . !"

Moment of hush, then a riot of uncontrolled laughter. Some hold their sides. Some double up. I roll on to my back in paroxysms. Tears run down my cheeks.

Sergeant Murray is stamping his feet.

Volunteers Baziuk and Power are sweeping the yard when the others go to the bar.

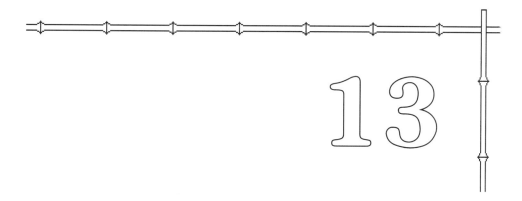

13

TORA - TORA

O N THE MORNING OF August 18, 1940, without
notice, without fanfare, without the roll of a single
drum, the beep of a single fife; the British garrison,
reduced to nothing more than a token detachment from
the East Surrey Regiment, marched stiffly down Victoria
Road and Rue de France and was gone. For the first time
since its inception in 1863, the concession was without
the protection of the Imperial Army.

Couldn't have happened at a worse time! That same
week the entire complement of Chinese constables and
NCO's of the BMC police, three hundred strong, chose to
go out on strike. Damned ticklish situation. Could easily
get out of hand. What an opportunity for the Governor of
Hopei to declare a state of anarchy and send in his
Nippon-trained regiments to take over the concession!

The yellow emergency flag went up the topmast of
Gordon Hall. At every corner of the concession Volunteers
downed tools and hastened to headquarters. A squad
from No. 1 Platoon was assigned to guard the armory at
London Road Police Station. I was seconded to the squad
as interpreter.

In the armory office the atmosphere was tense. Sergeant Bingham and three Volunteers were seated at one
trestle table; two Chinese police sergeants and a corporal
were at another, not three feet away.

"Why are you here? Why don't you leave?" Sergeant
Bingham addressed the Chinese in his limited Mandarin.

"Chief of Police Lawless agreed we could stay," one of

the Chinese replied in perfect English.

"You speak English?"

"I'm a graduate of TACC."

"What's that?"

"Tientsin Anglo Chinese College. Mr Liddell was my teacher."

"Well, well, we don't need an interpreter then."

In the uneasy silence, Sergeant Bingham eyed me as if to say 'what are you doing here?' One of the Volunteers actually said it. "Why doesn't he take a rickshaw home?"

They might be veterans in their twenties, but they didn't have to treat me as though I was still in the care of an amah. Now they were talking among themselves – about girls. Damn their hides! Did they think I knew nothing about girls?

"I took Luba to the Forum last Saturday night," I heard one say.

"Little Club is cosier."

"I agree. I took Vera Somoff there. Say, what do you think of Earl West's band? Isn't it the berries? Did you know that his red hot bass player, Reg Jones, played with Louis Armstrong?"

"Earl West's band is too loud, too brassy. Not enough slow numbers."

"You like it slow so you can cream off on the floor."

"Can I help it when Meg Dunn presses her tits into me?"

"Everyone's had her you know."

"What wouldn't I give to have Marian Delaney?"

"Me too. What a figure!"

"I'm mad about her."

"She's quarter Chinese. Don't you forget that."

"Never mind. I'd give anything to get in there."

"She won't let you anywhere near. I've tried."

"She would if you proposed marriage."

"Even then she'll make you wait until the ring is on her finger."

"How do you know she'd agree to marry you?"

"She knows her betters. She's out to catch one of us."

"I heard she's stuck on that middle-aged Kraut, Hans Beck. He's got money. He's got a car."

"She's not going to win Beck. That old bugger is going out with Clara Michaud. Mitzi de Yong told me he's put her in the family way."

"Never on your life."

"Mitzi should know."

"Wouldn't mind having Mitzi."

"Haven't you? Everyone in town has."

"If she gets knocked up, she'll never know who the father is."

"Like sticking your hand in a hive. You don't know which bee stung you."

The yelps of laughter died down to a few chortles and snickers.

"I like Tish O'Brien."

"Bloody American nun."

"Even so."

"How about Olga Sevchenko?"

"Now you're talking. Russians are hot stuff. Never had one who didn't bite me."

"Luba Chumakoff!"

"Yessir!"

"Chew-my-cock!"

"Ha Ha Ha Ha!"

A period of musing silence, then one of them called over to me: "I say, Power, ask the Chink where the toilet is."

"It's out that door, first on the right," the English-speaking Chinese sergeant answered for me.

There was another period of silence, a much longer one. The First Platooners had exhausted their one and only topic of conversation. They stared at one another, bleary-eyed.

It must have been shortly before midnight when Sergeant Fuchs and a mess boy arrived with paliasses, coarse blankets, a thermos of coffee.

"When we being relieved?"

"You're not. You're staying the night."

I got my turn on a paliasse. I loosened my collar, belt, boot laces, otherwise I stayed fully dressed. My head throbbed, my ears rang. Though immensely fatigued, my thoughts raced wildly. Sleep? Not a hope. I could do without for one night, but what would the others think? They'd know this was my very first emergency. Well then, I could always close my eyes and feign sleep. Before I knew it, I *was* asleep. I had sunk into a deep sleep, progressing from a total void to the inevitable chaos of dreams. I saw myself with Konsty and Ravil and two very attractive Russian damsels in a brown-walled cubicle at Pei An Li Restaurant on Rue du Baron Gros. Beaming that charming smile of his, Ravil kept repeating: "More, eat more," as he pushed this dish, that dish my way. "Come on, don't be shy, try this *lazi-ji*, it's a specialty of the house." The aroma of red chili and green pepper and chives and hot-hot-hot chicken was sheer heaven. Then, damn it to hell and gone, the scene went blank before I had a chance to reach out with my chopsticks . . . .

I am lying wide awake on the lumpy paliasse, putting together pieces of the dream so that I can forge out an agreeable ending. I am having a hard time recalling the names of Ravil's and Konsty's lovely companions. I am trying to picture all those delectable dishes Ravil ordered. *Lazi-ji* was certainly one of them. I can almost taste the peppers and chives. Even now the wondrous aroma suffuses the armory office. But how can that be? I dreamt it in a dream. It's only when I hear slurping as only such ardent gourmands as the Chinese can slurp that I raise my head and look around. At their table the Chinese police sergeants are bent over a steaming canister.

"Help yourself to the dumplings," one of them says.

"I'll stick to noodles, thanks."

"The dumplings are really good. Pork and chives."

"No thanks."

"Are you a Hui Hui then?"

"Yes, I am."

Good natured chuckles from the two others. I smile to myself. Over the entrance of Achmet's and Murat's favorite eaterie on Taku Road there is a great big sign covered in squiggly Arabic script. I know of three other eateries, two in the French Concession, one in the German, that have the same Arabic signs. And there must be at least a dozen more in the Chinese City. None of them serve pork dumplings. They cater to the Hui Hui. The Hui Hui are Islamic Chinese. Achmet's father says there are four million Hui Huis in northern China.

"I'm a Christian," says the TACC sergeant.

"Protestant or Catholic?"

"Neither. I suppose you can say I'm a follower of Tai Ping Tian Kuo."

"Tai Ping Tian Kuo? Never heard of it."

"I have," I say to myself. Lincoln Liang made sure of that. It was going to be the topic of his thesis at university

– "The Foreign Involvement in the Tai Ping Uprising." He would remind us at every opportunity of the discreditable role played by England in quelling the Tai Pings. He said that when the Manchu court pleaded for outside intervention, the British government seconded to them their most promising field officer, Charles Gordon, better known later as General Gordon – "Chinese" Gordon . . . .

". . . my family home was in Tung Hsiang County, Chekiang Province," the TACC-educated sergeant continues. "My paternal grandfather was chief magistrate of Tung Hsiang before he adopted the Tai Ping faith. In seeking a new life he took the entire family to Nanking after the Tai Pings had declared it the nation's capital. Ten years later when the Manchus recaptured the city it took a miracle for the family to escape the wanton slaughter. Together with a small band of the faithful they fled north into Hopei where vestiges of the movement survive to this day."

"Weren't the Tai Pings sponsored by the foreign devils?"

"On the contrary, the foreigners opposed them, despite, ironically, having sowed the seeds of their uprising. The indemnities the foreign governments imposed on China following the Opium Wars were so huge, the burden on the masses so oppressive, that commerce was stifled and unemployment swept the land. The great prophet and messiah, Hung Hsiu Chuan, came upon the scene at about that time. He walked among the down-trodden masses, he preached Christian love, he proclaimed the coming of Tai Ping Tian Kuo – the Heavenly Kingdom of Great Peace – which would bring with it the re-distribution of land and total prohibition of infanticide, opium smok-

ing, gambling, footbinding, and concubinage.

"The movement caught fire. Soldiers, peasants, artisans, and scholars rushed to join the cause. The Tai Ping army with its elite female battle units proved invincible. They ousted the Manchus from Nanking. From there Hung Hsiu ruled China for eleven years. And in those eleven years he restored the nation's pride.

"If it were only the Manchus he had to contend with, then all of China would have been liberated. But alas, disunity developed amongst his generals. And worse, the foreign devils intervened. They knew that with the Tai Pings in power their grip on China would be forever lost. An American came forward to help re-organize the Manchu army. He was cut down in battle. The English Queen sent her best general to train and lead a new Manchu army, one equipped with modern Western firearms. Terrible battles ensued. The nation was drenched in blood. The Manchus and their foreign-devil backers came out victorious. They took their revenge on the population, slaughtering them in the hundreds of thousands . . ."

"Wakey! Wakey!"

Sergeant Bingham's looming face gives me an almighty start.

"Snap to it! You're on for the next two hours. There's some coffee left in the flask. It's lukewarm warm but better than nothing."

My clammy undershirt sends shivers down my back. At the table I sit miserably on my own. At the other table one of the Chinese is missing. The remaining two are asleep, heads down on folded arms. I turn open a dog-eared *Look* magazine. I try to read, but the words swim off the page. Time drags agonizingly. I step over to the window. I think I can see shadowy figures in police overcoats moving about the parade ground.

Sergeant "TACC" calls out to me as he comes through the doorway: "The strike's over."

I go over to Sergeant Bingham and give him a shake.

With the police back on duty, life quickly reverted to normal, but only for a week. Again that yellow flag was flying atop the Gordon Hall. At Volunteer Headquarters our CO, Major Walter Ridler, announced starkly that a mob gathering on the Russian Bund was threatening to storm into the concession. He didn't mince words. He laid the blame squarely on the puppet Governor of Hopei who had for weeks been inciting peasants in the surrounding countryside to rise against foreigners.

Speech over, the usual standing about, the uncertainty in the air, the meaningless small talk – until we got our orders: "No. 3 Platoon fall in . . . "

In the rush for the quadrangle, I was struck by a chilling premonition that this was going to be my last hour. Clambering aboard our armored truck *Suzie,* I forced a sickly smile on my face to show my brothers-in-arms I was not in a blue funk. There was a lot of bantering and shouts of bravado as *Suzie* sped down Elgin Avenue and Cousins Road to the Bund. I was too stricken to join in.

As we drew up alongside the Butterfield & Swire wharf, we could hear the bloodcurdling chants sounding from the demented mob on the far bank: "*Yang gui . . . Yang gui . . . Yang gui . . .*" (Foreign Devils . . . Foreign Devils . . . Foreign Devils) . . ."*Wo-men yao da dao Ying Mei . . .*" (We want to overthrow the English and Americans) . . ."*Wo-men yao qu xiao tu fei . . .*" (We want to wipe out the thieving bandits). . . .

For the mile-and-a-half of the Bund we were given to patrol, our thirty-seven member platoon was pathetically inadequate. I was number one gunner clinging to the Lewis gun bipod clamped on *Suzie's* cab roof. The gun couldn't be swiveled. It could fire only in the direction the truck was pointed, and the truck was pointed sideways to the mob. In the end it didn't matter. Not a round was fired. The mob dispersed. According to next day's *North China Star*, the peasants ambled happily home to their villages soon as the puppet officials had paid them off in copper cash.

Curious how the term *Yang gui* had come back into fashion. One evening, returning from the firing range in one of the armored cars, I stuck my head out just as we were passing a densely populated Chinese area; my topee blew off. A cursing Sergeant Cooke ordered the driver to pull up. I dashed back the twenty yards to where the topee had landed. A group of Chinese blocked my way. Hate showed in their eyes. "*Sha Yang guizi*" (Kill the Foreign Devil). I scuttled back bareheaded.

Sgt. Murray keeps his knees apart for "Suzie". Konsty, in tin helmet, is on his left, Ranil is below Konsty and Des above.

"The CO wants to see you."

"What for?"

Sergeant Murray was in no mood for a chat. "How should I know? Shake a leg. He's at the bar."

What did he want with me, this Major Ridler, this ex-artillery officer with the "fraghtfully" English accent, this gaunt, lantern-jawed patrician who, someone said, had served as Winston Churchill's secretary after being decorated in the field during the Great War.

"Drink?"

"No thank you, sir," I stammered.

He emasculated me with his penetrating gaze. Then he said: "What are you doing with yourself these days?"

I gulped twice before I could give a reply. "Waiting for the next draft to India, sir."

"Jolly good show. Try for the Gurkhas. Stout chaps. When are you leaving?"

"Vice Consul Ogden said next spring."

"What are you going to do in the meantime?"

"Don't know, sir. Haven't really thought about it, sir."

"You really ought to be thinking about your future. The war has to end some time. Have you ever considered making a career in business?"

"Business"? I never really understood what that word

meant, so how could I reply?

"Would you like to come and work in my office? I'm a stockbroker."

I froze. What was a stockbroker?

"Well?"

Simply to get away from him I said what I thought he wanted me to say. "Yes sir, I'll give it a try, sir."

"Champion! Be at 59 Victoria Road tomorrow. Be there sharp at o-nine-hundred hours."

"Damn it, " I cursed as I pedaled home. "He trapped me. He trapped me cold!"

Next morning I presented myself at the offices of Doney & Company, foreign exchange and share brokers. Major Ridler introduced me to his partner, Mr Sam Gilmore, an Irish gentleman in his sixties, a veteran of the Boxer siege. His huge paw took mine in an iron grip, his clear blue eyes held mine in a steady gaze. "Welcome to Doney & Company," he said in the soft cadence of the Irish. "I remember well your grandparents, George and Agnes D'Arc. I was one of the volunteer firemen who tried to save the original D'Arcs Hotel when it burned down in 1904. I knew your mother when she was a school girl . . ."

Major Ridler broke in. "We'll pay you four hundred dollars a month plus one percent commission. You can start right now."

Four hundred dollars! And I thought I was well paid at BMC with two-fifty!

And the work so undemanding! All I had to do was collect the white buy-slips and pink sell-slips for the day and enter the information in a heavy bound ledger. In another ledger I kept track of the transfer deeds, recording the names (mostly Chinese) of the buyers and sellers. During my first week there was a flood of white slips. I had to go at the double to keep up. Seemed as though everyone and his brother was buying Ewos, Wheelocks, Shanghai Dockyards. The following week the mad rush to unload them brought a flood of pink slips. When I totted up my commission at the end of the month, I swallowed hard. My one percent yielded $603.12! Salary plus commission came to $1,063.12 – an absolute fortune!

In the second month my earnings down a bit, but then things heated up, and the running total I kept reached eleven hundred dollars, and there were still another three days to go!

151

"Market getting lively again," Mr Gilmore said to me. "Today it's a bull market, tomorrow the devils will be selling off like mad."

"Isn't it a funny way to do things, sir? Doesn't seem to be any rhyme or reason for it."

"Oh yes there is me lad, by all the saints in heaven there is. I've been in the game nigh on forty years, and I can tell you the Chinee use the stock exchange for nothing else but gambling. They're inveterate gamblers, the whole lot of them. We're not always sure they've got the stock they sell. Have to watch the beggars closely or they'll break themselves and us in the bargain."

I noticed that Mr Gilmore and Mr Ridler rarely went to the reception room where the Chinese clients congregated. Doney & Company, as with so many of the other "hongs" (trading houses) up and down the China coast, operated under the "comprador" system whereby the foreign traders provided the financing and facilities while their Chinese representatives, the compradors, dealt with the Chinese clients.

At mid-morning when the cables started arriving from Shanghai with the latest share prices, I'd chalk them up on a green board which covered an entire wall of the reception room. Sometimes what I chalked brought cheers, sometimes groans. Lively lot, those clients, and friendly too. Wasn't long before I was taking tea with them. Comprador Chang encouraged my presence. Neither he nor his clients knew a word of English. I could prove useful as a go-between.

"Kindly ask Jih Ta Pan (Mr Gilmore), if he thinks the sale of Taku Tug & Lighter will affect the value of Hai Ho Conservancy shares?" . . . "Does he think Chartered Bank will continue to support Hong Wo Export Corporation after its third fire in two years? . . ."

The firm did have an official interpreter. Liu Ying Chen, an office clerk, had pretty good English, but the clients seemed to prefer using me. More than that, they extended a deference towards me that was entirely unwarranted.

"Let me pour you a bowl of tea," a rich merchant would say. "Now tell me, should I sell those 100,000 Shanghai Dockyards, or should I hang on to them a little longer?"

"Judas Priest!" I said to myself. "Why ask me? Surely he must know I haven't the foggiest idea!"

The first time I wandered into the back office where the clerks and chit coolies worked, they all rose to their feet.

"No need to stand. I'm a local like you," I told them. It took them about a month to accept me, to cease acting with rigid formality when I ate my sesame cakes and deep-fried fritters at their lunch table. Hua Wen Chih, the comprador's typist, asked shyly if I'd coach him in English. "Sure," I said. "Be glad to."

Didn't know how tough that task was going to be. Poor fellow, he found it impossible to pronounce even the simplest English word. I hadn't realized till then how outlandish to the uninitiated are so many sounds of the English language; how complex the interaction of throat, tongue, palate, and voice-box to produce those sounds. Hardest for the learner is that tricky roll of the tongue for the "thr" sound in such common words as "throw" and "through". The best Hua could manage for "three" was "tzilly."

He might never master English, but what an ingenious typist! He'd sit before an array of lead slugs, maybe three thousand in all, each the reverse image of a Chinese character. He'd scan the array for the one he wanted, extract it with a pair of tweezers, fit it into the type hammer, depress the solitary key, and zap, word typed!

"What happens when you want to type something in a hurry?" I asked.

"Doesn't take long. Besides, who's ever in a hurry? We've always got tomorrow."

"What if Comprador Chang Pao Lai wants it in a rush?"

"He never does."

"We could always buy one of those new machines from Germany," Liu the clerk chipped in. "They speed up typing no end. A mechanical finger automatically picks up the type slug you've selected. Very expensive though, Jih Ta Pan would never agree to spending the money."

After six months with Doney & Co I found myself feeling quite at home working in a "business." I would even go so

153

far as to say that some aspects of office life, such as the easy-going atmosphere among staff and clients, were pretty agreeable. Might be an interesting career after all.

"Can I have a word with you," Mr Ridler said to me when he handed me my pay check, "Sam and I are pleased with your progress. We're especially pleased with the way you get on with the Chinese clients. Keep up your contact with them, that's very important. We are both, however, wondering about one thing, and that is the time you spend in the back office. If you want my advice, young man, keep away from that place. Maintain a distance from the clerks and coolies, otherwise you'll lose their respect. Don't get us wrong, we don't disdain the Chinese. Sam and I both have Chinese friends. What I have to say has nothing to do with prejudice. It has to do with maintaining respect, upholding authority. In England, you know, managers would never dream of mixing with underlings let alone take lunch with them."

His words were kindly spoken. His eyes, though, had a sting of reproach that was unmistakeable. I was unable to stop the girlish blush that rose to my cheeks.

"Now about another matter. You can take the afternoon off to attend the meeting at TGS. You're interested, of course, in hearing the Consul's announcement?"

"I am sir," I said, though I didn't have the foggiest idea of what he was talking about. I soon found out. It was on the front page of the day's *Peking & Tientsin Times*.

NOTICE TO BRITISH RESIDENTS
A MEETING WILL BE HELD IN THE ASSEMBLY HALL
OF TIENTSIN GRAMMAR SCHOOL AT 2 PM THURSDAY
TO HEAR AN IMPORTANT ANNOUNCEMENT BY HBM
CONSUL GENERAL

When I arrived at the familiar school hall, the rows of theater seats, brought in only on rare occasions such as Speech Day, were nearly all occupied. There were the usual sounds of an impatient audience – rumble of conversation, clearing of throats, coughing. At twenty minutes past two, Mr Osgoode, Consul General, stepped up to the podium. He spoke in measured officialese. "The war in Europe is stretching Britain to the limit . . . His Majesty's Government can no longer safeguard its interests in China . . . The safety and well-being of British

154

residents in Tientsin is of paramount concern . . . The Government has decided to provide shipping for the evacuation of women and children, the aged and the sick . . . The U boat menace has put the United Kingdom out of reach . . . Ships will therefore sail for Australia, New Zealand, Canada . . . Able-bodied men are requested to stay behind to protect Britain's assets. . . ."

The audience was getting restive. I could hear moans, groans, snorts of disapproval; then, ignoring the all-male agenda, a female voice shot out in full fortissimo: "I should like to address the meeting."

"Who's that?" my neighbor asked her neighbor.

"Don't know."

But I did. She was a childhood friend of Tai-tai's. She was Mrs Tupper, doyenne of the British community,

The surprised Consul General turned to an aide. Their heads came together in whispered conversation. Then the aide announced: "You may put your question to me. Kindly keep it brief."

Mrs Tupper's high heels click-clacked all the way to the podium. She ignored the aide, she ignored the Consul General. She faced the audience. Her words rang with bell-like clarity.

"Dear friends, I speak from my heart. I am Tientsin born and bred. My parents settled here a decade before the Boxer Uprising. This emergency is nothing new. We've been through it all before. There were the Boxers, the warlords, the Nationalists, the Japanese, the barricades, the '17 flood, the '39 flood. On each occasion we stuck it out, and on each occasion we came through. And why? I'll tell you why. We belong here. Our roots go deep. We have our homes, our businesses, our friends. I for one am staying. Who will stay with me?"

Someone shouted from the back: "Me! I'll stay!"

Someone else: "Me too!"

"We'll stick together!"

"We'll stay to the end!"

"God Save the King!"

A shrill voice broke into song: "Land of hope and glory, mother of the free . . ." More voices joined in . . . "Wider still and wider shall thy bounds be set . . ." Most of the congregation now . . . "God who made thee mighty make thee mightier yet. . . ."

The Consul General was waving his hands, "Hear me

A view of Victoria Road, England's show-piece in the ancient Ming city of Tientsin.

out, ladies and gentlemen, hear me out, if you please . . ."

Mrs Tupper brushed him aside. "And what about our martyrs in Canton Road Cemetery? Has our good Consul forgotten those who gave their lives – the English bluejackets, the Sikhs, the Siberians, the American marines? And what about our gallant Volunteers? Did they die in vain? Has our Consul not seen that dying soldier's last plea traced in blood on Peking's legation wall? Was that plea – '*Lest We Forget*' – written in vain?"

"No, never!"

"Never on your life!"

Seats slammed as people rose to their feet. "Three cheers for Mrs Tupper. Hip-hip-hip hooray! Hip-hip-hip hooray!"

Not a sound from the Consul General and his entourage. They had vanished into the wings.

That evening at dinner I asked Tai-tai if she'd heard about Mrs Tupper's harebrained speech.

"What do you mean harebrained? Not at all harebrained. Dear Jenny, she's absolutely right. We've come through every crisis; we'll come through this one. It's unthinkable to leave. What do you suppose we would do in Canada or Australia? We would find their way of life totally alien. We belong here. This is our heritage. This is where we have sunk our roots. Never forget that for three generations we worked our fingers to the bone to make this concession, this lovely corner of England, the show piece that it is. And, if you ask me, the Chinese know they cannot do without us. They'd give anything for us to stay.

156

We've taught them so much. We have so much more to teach them. In Canton Road cemetery your grandfather lies side by side with fellow heroes of the Boxer siege – Victor Jaques and Walter Ward. At Birchcroft Avenue lies your angel infant sister Stephanie. Mr Osgoode has the nerve to suggest that we turn our backs on those sacred plots. Me? I'll never do it. Never! Never! Besides I have a responsibility to my husband and to my three boys, all serving their country. After the war they must have a home to come back to. And you, when you return from India, you too must have a place. This home will always be here, that I can promise you. The family shall be reunited . . . ."

Not all British residents took the view of Mrs Tupper and Tai-tai. A number began leaving. As I stood on the Bund waving good-bye to Mary Hayes, the fascinating beauty with one brown eye, one green, I was overtaken by a sudden urge to be aboard that Jardine coaster. What was to stop me from going down to Thomas Cook's and booking passage on the next ship? Mr Bagshaw told me I'd be going in the spring. Spring might be too late!

I had just arrived at the office one crisp winter morning when Major Ridler, in his officer's field dress – twill jacket, twill jodhpurs, riding boots – blocked my way. "Another emergency. Haven't you heard? Go home and get into your SDs. You should already be with your platoon. I'm heading to HQ myself in ten minutes."

"What's up, sir?"

"Another spot of bother, I'm afraid. Our good friends the Japanese have informed Mr Osgoode that that damned puppet Governor of theirs is hopping mad at our stubborn support of Chiang Kai Shek. He's once again threatening to take over the concession. The Japanese say they're in no position to stop him. An outright lie, of course!"

At HQ, a bustle of activity: armored cars belching blue smoke, men in dungarees loading Lewis gun pans, men from No. 1 and No. 2 Platoons moving out to man strong points.

After a short wait came our turn. Sergeant Murray lined us up for inspection. His chest was puffed like a turkey cock. There was a jubilant ring in his voice: "Good show, boys. I'm proud of the lot of you. Our orders are to defend

London Road Power Station. I know you'll not fail me."

In half an hour we were stowing our kit and assembling our camp cots in the brick guardhouse at the south end of the power station compound. When it came my turn for guard duty, I thanked heaven that I was assigned to the small bridge spanning Weitze Creek. The timekeeper's hut at the edge of the creek would provide shelter from the biting wind. The BMC policeman guarding the bridge had the very same idea. I appreciated his company.

"I'm a native of Hsiao Chang, Hopei Province," he said. "I came to Tientsin in October 1937 after everyone in our family except my older brother and me were butchered by the Japanese. Canadian Missionaries hid us in their school. Later my brother escaped to the mountains to join the guerrillas."

"How did you manage to get to Tientsin?"

"The Canadian missionaries brought me here. One of them introduced me to Inspector Greenslade. That's how I got into the police."

"Now you're guarding bridges. Pretty boring isn't it?"

"Agreed, very boring, but tell me, why is it necessary for you foreign soldiers to be doing the same boring thing?"

"The puppets are threatening the conccssion."

"How can you tell the difference between a puppet and a patriot?"

I shook my head. "I don't know."

"No offense personally, but you should understand that one day we Chinese must take back all of this." He made a sweeping gesture at the surrounding buildings. "It's the sacred duty of every Chinese, be he puppet, Nationalist, Communist, whatever, to regain what is rightfully ours."

"Some Britons agree with you. You can see them leaving by ship every day."

"But I hear many intend to stay."

"Yes, there are some who do."

"In the end they'll all have to go, you included."

An odd event occurred that night. Corporal Mihailoff, my ex-boss, arrived at our guardhouse with two men from No. 2 Platoon. "We've got orders to pick up your ammo."

Chorus of disbelief. "We'll be sitting ducks when the puppets arrive!" . . . "You gotta be crazy!" . . . "What we supposed to do when the shooting starts?"

Nick broke into a cheery grin. "Don't get mad boys. Orders is orders. Hand over your ammo."

Nothing else for it but to dig out the clips from our webbing pouches and toss them onto the card table.

When Sergeant Murray returned from HQ we showered him with questions.

"Okay lads, steady on. I know how you feel. This is the situation. I got it straight from the CO. The powers that be are convinced tonight's the night. Lots of activity going on in the Japanese Concession and Chinese City. Looks like the puppets are finally going to make their move. Our top brass believes that with our puny numbers there's not a hope in hell stopping them. They want no bloodshed. We're going to surrender the concession. It's for the best." The fatigue in his voice made him sound human for once.

Corporal da Silva woke me at three a.m. I squeezed into my boots, wound on my puttees, put on two sweaters, and slipped into my tunic and greatcoat. I slung the strap of my impotent Lee Enfield over my shoulder and stepped out into the raw night.

Volunteer Olshevsky stood waiting for me, motionless as a statue. White vapor escaped from his mouth with every word he uttered. "Very quiet my friend. No sign of puppets. Funny thing, your policeman friend left about midnight. He hasn't returned, and no one's replaced him."

"He probably got frozen," I said, stamping my feet.

"It's cold all right, Dessmont. You're going to be frozen stiff by the time you get relieved."

"How come you're not frozen?"

"Will power, sheer will power. I force myself to ignore the cold. I'm preparing myself for Palestine."

"What are you talking about? Palestine's a hot place."

"Mr Kaufman wrote to say the nights there are just as cold as in Tientsin."

"Hard to believe."

"Well, I believe it. Anyway, I'm off. G'night my friend."

The cold began to sting my nose and ears. With no one to talk to, each minute was an hour, each hour an eternity. I killed time by tramping across the bridge to Elgin Avenue and back. I began keeping count. After twenty turns I'd retreat to the hut where I'd stay until my toes grew numb. Then out I'd go again for another twenty turns. At last a streak of pink showed in the sky. I heard muffled steps. My relief was making his way towards me.

Like one of Captain Scott's polar explorers, he had his head sunk into his upturned greatcoat collar.

"Nothing to report," I said to him. "Haven't seen a living soul let alone a puppet. The policeman's gone."

Bending against the wind, I made my way back to the guardhouse. In the orangey light of a glowing coke stove, Sergeant Murray was holding forth with several men. "This rum's a special treat, boys. Papadopoulis, get me a mug. Ozorio, hand me that there kettle. All right, Volunteer Santos, you're first. This is for you."

"No thanks, Sergeant. Have you got some Coca Cola?"

"Coca Cola? Strike me dead! Sorry I forgot to send for your amah to tuck you into bed last night! Lord, what's the world coming to!"

The door crashed open. Volunteer Baziuk came pounding up to us, out of breath, eyes popping. "Sarzhant, *Nipponski soldat* outside, manny trocks. I tink dey want see you."

"You're crazy as ever, Baziuk. You're suffering from hallucinations."

Chuckles all around. Urik Baziuk always made us chuckle. He had the unique ability of sleeping while standing. He lived in a world all of his own.

"Word of honor, Sarzhant. *Chesneslova*, *Nipponski soldat!*"

"The bleeding Japs," barked Sergeant Murray, "are not allowed in the bleeding concession. Confounded cheek! If it's true what you say, I'm going to kick their yellow arses all the way back to Jap town. If you're telling me a lie, I'm going to kick yours all the way back to the gate for another four hour watch! Now let's go see. And you too," he barked, indicating Ozorio, Papadopoulis, and me.

Through the front gate an astounding sight. All along London Road, bumper to bumper, a line of olive green trucks; and milling around on the pavement, Japanese infantrymen in full battle dress.

A grinning brass-toothed officer saluted us. "Thank you vurr much, please, thank you vurr much. Japan, America, England, have make war. Thank you vurr much, please."

It was December 8 in Tientsin, December 7 at Pearl Harbor.

160

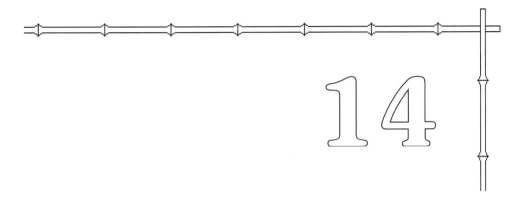

14

"WANGLE" MARU

SERGEANT MURRAY lowered his voice to a hush. "Slip out the back way boys. They've set guards only at the front. Fade into the alleys, get into mufti, double quick time."

In a trance I followed what the others were doing. Olshevsky ditched his webbing pouches. I ditched mine. He went at a fast trot towards the bridge. I stayed on his tail till he vanished into the gloom. To avoid attention I slowed to a walking pace as I made my way along Creek Road and Douglas Road. Suddenly the eerie silence was broken by the clack-clack-clack of someone in hobnailed boots doing the hundred meter sprint. I flattened myself against a doorway, my heart pounding, my lungs seized. Then I saw who it was – Filiminovich of No. 2 Platoon. He spied me and clattered to a halt. His words tumbled out: "War! Nipponskis bombed Pearl Harbor. Sank the whole American fleet. Mass landing at San Francisco. Golden Gate blown up. President Roosevelt in hiding."

Before I could open my mouth, he galloped off with his rifle at the trail, straight for London Road, straight into the enemy cordon.

In twenty minutes I was at my front door. Tai-tai, Jie-jie, Kui Hsiang pulled me in. Fear, relief, tears, everyone jabbering at once. Off came my SDs, puttees, boots. Down they went in a bundle to be buried in the backyard along with Grandmother's collection of ancient swords.

"You'd better get some sleep," Tai-tai said.

Sleep? In my state of nervous apprehension? Like a

moth drawn irresistibly to the flame, I had a suicidal urge to go out and confront the maelstrom. Ancient Yi-jie's caterwauls served only to spur me on as I pushed my bike through the backyard. I pedaled off towards Gordon Hall. Things had to be happening there. They were. A squad of Japanese in olive-green from battle helmet to rubberized boots were setting up a strong point outside Madame Voitenco's Ballet School on Council Road. Another jibber-jabbering squad had formed a cordon between All Saints Church and the American Consulate. On Taku Road I took cover behind a rickshaw as truck after olive-green truck went roaring past.

I ran into Murat and Achmet in Victoria Park.

"Hi, guys. What you think?"

Murat clutched me by the shoulder. "Deska, you got away? When I heard the news this morning I was sure it was kaput for all you Volunteers."

"What did you hear?"

"According to the BBC, the Japanese bombed Pearl Harbor in a massive surprise attack. They sank a lot of battleships."

"Where the heck is Pearl Harbor?"

"What ignorance! It's in Hawaii. It's the biggest American naval base in the Pacific. The Americans are caught up in the war now."

"What about San Francisco? Is it in Japanese hands?"

"The BBC said nothing about San Francisco."

"Was Tientsin mentioned?"

"Not a word. We're just a backwater, after all."

"Then maybe the Japanese will leave us alone."

"Not a hope," said Achmet. "Tolstipiatoff told me they picked up Major Ridler and Chief of Police Lawless and Mendes of Reuters at six o'clock this morning. Took them to American barracks."

"American barracks! What about the marines there?"

"They were taken without a shot fired. They're all prisoners."

"Lucky the East Surreys left Tientsin when they did. Lucky for me I wasn't at Volunteer headquarters when the Japanese arrived, or I too would be in the bag."

"You still could be. They might be out looking for you."

"Come and stay at our place," said Murat. "We claim Turkish nationality. Japan is not at war with Turkey."

"What about my family?"

"Bring the family."

"Thanks. May have to take you up on it."

But no need to take up my friend's generous offer; the Japanese were too drunk with victory to bother with us. And what a flood of victories: Guam, Wake, Hong Kong, the *Repulse* and *Prince of Wales*. Then the unthinkable, the fall of Singapore, pearl of the Empire. The victors erected a huge sign outside Empire Theatre:

"*Ying*" stands for heroic, brave, daring!

SINGAPORE HAS SURRENDERED

All day long martial music blared from loudspeakers strung outside public buildings. So many times did we hear the vainglorious *Imperial Navy Victory March*, we could hum every note of it in our sleep.

Just before the end of February we got the first intimation that our days of freedom were numbered. Word went around that all enemy nationals were to present themselves at the Astor House to register and to pick up an arm band that must henceforth be worn at all times. The arm bands were bright red, and those for Britons imprinted with the Chinese character for England – "*Ying*," a derivation of the word meaning heroic, daring, soldierly; rather ironic for a nation brought to its knees. And even stranger irony for Americans; the "*Mei*" on their red bands representing the word – beautiful. They might have lost their fleet at Pearl Harbor, but in Tientsin at least they could proudly show the world that America was still *America the Beautiful*!

"Dazka! *Shtotokoi?*" Alioshka Bublikoff burst out, grinning clownishly, when he spotted the four-inch-wide strip of red on my sleeve. "You look like one of those guys in Movietone News displaying the Star of David!"

Igor gave him a dirty look. And Achmet. We'd all seen enough of it on the newsreels – chilling scenes of old and young scrubbing pavements while spat upon, kicked, beaten.

But nothing of the kind in Tientsin. And how that must have had the Japanese scratching their heads. Where were the Chinese who had it in for the uppity English and Americans? Could it be they were biding their time, waiting for the moment when they could square the account with *all* Foreign Devils, including, most especially, the Eastern Foreign Devils, the hateful dwarf people from across the Japan Sea?

"Were you at the victory parade?" Alioshka put the question to our little gathering at Victoria Cafe. "If you weren't, you should have been. The Nipponskis put on quite a show. Went on for hours. They must have brought in every regiment from Mukden to Taku. And you should have seen their tanks and field guns. They gonna be hard to beat."

"*I* was there," chimed Maxie Rosentool. "I thought they marched, or rather shuffled, like a bunch of warlord drop-outs – out of line – out of step. Even the Chinese puppets were smarter. And fiercer too, screeching out slogans as they goose-stepped."

"Those puppets are a joke," said Murat. "They'll run at the first shot."

"Or change sides."

"Yes, change sides at the drop of a hat."

"Speaking of dropped hats," interjected the rather dandyish Maxie (on the school stage he was Sir Andrew Aguecheek to my Toby Belch), "brings to mind that other main event, that ceremony in Victoria Park last Saturday when the Chrysanthemum Throne, the guiding light behind the Greater East Asia Co-Prosperity Sphere, deeded to its Chinese satrap full title to the House of Windsor's assets in Tientsin – in other words, handed over the concession, lock, stock, and barrel – waterworks, power station, Gordon Hall, Masonic Lodge, Union Jack Club, All Saints Church, even dear old TGS."

"Wasn't there a dust storm that day? Didn't half the Gobi Desert descend on Tientsin?"

"Quite right," Maxie replied. "Most of the bunting and flags and banners were torn away. Coolies had to be rushed in to support the bamboo dais erected specially for the occasion. But it was an occasion I wouldn't have missed for the world. It was history in the making. There was the park, there was the horde of Chinese bussed in from the native city, there was the brass band – sounding like a circus band – and there on the dais, exposed to the fierce gusts, were the bigwigs, Japanese and Chinese, doing a Charlie Chaplin act, hanging on their wind-blown top hats and flapping coat tails as they bowed and hissed at one another. We all know how much the Chinese love their Charlie Chaplin, yet not a smile showed on the faces around me. In fact stony silence reigned all through the speech given by some top-hatted, white-gaitered swell. And what mummery, what sanctimonious claptrap – heroic Japan bringing an end to Anglo-American exploitation – magnanimous Japan retrieving for China the lands expropriated by the thieving English crown . . ."

"Did he say anything about the Japanese returning their own ill-gotten concession?"

"Not a word."

"You're missing the best part," Aliosha cut in, huffily. "When the speaker at last shut up, there was a roll of drums, a blare of trumpets, and just as the Nipponski bigshot was handing the Kitaiski bigshot a roll of paper tied with pink ribbon . . ."

"I was on the point of coming to that," Maxie sang out. "Just as Fang Chieh, Mayor of Tientsin, began thanking the Japanese for their momentous gift – the original deed the English obliged the Chinese to sign after the Battle of Taku in 1858 – the loudspeaker went suddenly dead. There was some kind of commotion on the dais. I could see policemen scrambling all over it. I saw four of them carting off the limp form of a man in a Western dress suit. It was at that point that the audience began finally to react. First a cheer, then a laugh, then shouts of applause. You'd never believe what happened. A brick, which had somehow got dislodged from the pinnacle of Gordon Hall, came down with a crash on the mayor's head. Everyone thought he was killed, but next day's *Peking Chronicle* rejoiced over Fang Chieh's charmed life. His top hat had saved him. Nevertheless, he was hurt. Concussion. He's in MacKenzie Memorial Hospital."

"Charlie Chaplin couldn't have been funnier."

"Nor could the Japanese bigwigs. They made a laughing stock of themselves."

"They're pretty damned mad. Anyone with an arm band had better stay indoors."

Sound advice. For several weeks I ventured no farther than a block from home. One day, a knock at the front door, and two Japanese soldiers were on the doorstep, grimacing like baboons. They had come to commandeer Doong Ji's '38 Chevvy. They couldn't start it. It had to be towed away. Few days later, another knock. This time they wanted our radio. Dammit! No more BBC. No more

News of "Nessie's" discovery was supposed to tear our hearts out!

Radio Moscow. The only source of news left to us was the Japanese-sponsored *Peking Chronicle*, a ghastly rag for-ever gloating over some Allied defeat on the battlefront or morose happening on the home front. There was that Deanna Durbin story. DEANNA DURBIN SUCCUMBS TO TB! What a shock to learn the world had lost its sweet-heart with the angel smile and silvery voice, the darling of *Three Smart Girls* and *Mad about Music!* Had all that singing been too much for her lungs? And Carmen Miranda too – CARMEN MIRANDA LOSES BOTH LEGS IN CAR ACCIDENT! Poor zany Carmen! No more bizarre fruit-basket hats. No more *Chika-chika-boomchik!* And what about that sensational headline: LOCH NESS MONSTER DISCOVERED! Incredible! Was it a dinosaur? Was it gigantic? Was it taken alive? Maddeningly, the paper didn't say.

"Sheer balderdash," Vice Consul Ogden said to Brian Clarke and me one tiffin time at the Masonic Hall, now given over as a canteen for arm band wearers. "You mustn't believe a word of it. Ludicrous propaganda meant to make one homesick, weaken one's morale. But listen you two, I've got something to tell you that'll really buck you up. I can get you out of Tientsin. You, Desmond, can get to India after all. Britain and Japan have agreed on an exchange of consular staffs and their families. They've also agreed to let some non-diplomats go. I think you young men should get priority."

"What about my mother? My step-father's in Burma. (Doong Ji had gone the previous summer to serve in the British Indian Army.) She'll be left alone. And I've got a younger brother and sister."

"All right. I'll try for the whole family. Hurry to All Saints Church. Mr Bagshaw is there in the rectory taking appli-cations. Get your names down quick as you can. I'll put in a word for you."

Brian had a doctor's appointment or something or the

Des waving
good-bye as
bus takes off
for Tientsin East
— and freedom!

other, but I was out the door in an instant, zipping down Race Course Road. I was far too excited to flinch when I passed through the forbidding Protestant portals of the forbidding Protestant rectory. I gave Mr Bagshaw Tai-tai's name, Tony's, Betty's, mine. I was still burning with excitement when I brought home the good news.

"No thank you!" Tai-tai exclaimed. "Nothing in the world will induce me to leave. The Japanese are not interfering with us, are they? The war will be over before you know it. Everything will be back to normal. But don't worry about us. You go. You won't be satisfied till you get to Calcutta."

My conscience wasn't fully assuaged until I heard that Brian Clarke (like me he was the only adult male in his household) had decided to take up Mr Ogden on his offer.

The supreme moment arrives, the moment I join the exodus of diplomats and the twenty or so non-diplomats and their families in one of the buses parked outside Astor House. A familiar voice reverberates through the bus as I take my seat. "By Jove, Power! So you're coming too! Champion!" Major Ridler beams his hawk face at me.

How did he ever get out of American barracks? Not the time to ask what with all that commotion outside. Well-wishers swarm around the bus, laughing, crying, waving handkerchiefs, shouting good-bye. Japanese fists, heels, rifle butts force a general retreat to the sidewalk. I lose sight of Tai-tai. I poke my head out of the window. I still can't see her. A Chinese breaks through the cordon. It's Kui Hsiang. He rushes up and thrusts a billfold into my hand. The tears in his eyes bring tears to mine. I sink back into the seat and open the billfold. In one flap he has inserted a lucky charm, a print of Chang Tien Shih, Master of Heaven, riding a tiger, wielding a magic sword. In the other flap is a photo I took of Kui a year ago. On the back of it he has penciled a farewell note to me.

I don't smile again till we board the train at Tientsin East. In the second-class carriage the buzz of conversation is punctuated with ripples of laughter. No one gives a thought to the prospect of two stifling days and two stifling nights that lie ahead. Each minute that passes is a minute closer to freedom. But not everyone is rejoicing. On the seat facing Brian Clarke and me, a demented teenage girl sits between two attendants, cockneys, Maritime Customs staff. Gently they restrain her, gently they wrestle her back when she wants inexplicably to bolt from her seat. Her piercing screams jolt us awake in the middle of the night. In the morning she is in a straitjacket, gurgling like a baby. None of us know which way to look.

Major Ridler pays several visits to our compartment, and on each occasion he is accompanied by his daughter Anne, a vivacious girl with sparkling green eyes and peaches and cream complexion. I have hopelessly lost my heart to her by the time we change trains at Nanking. Alas, with total disregard for my happiness the Nipponese put the Ridlers in the carriage ahead; I don't set eyes again on sweet sweet Anne till we reach Shanghai.

At North Station, ugly signs of war: tall concrete buildings pock-marked with jagged shell holes, houses and shops with tops blown off, mounds of brick rubble. The scene of the 1937 battleground acts as a reminder to the Japanese of the high casualties they suffered; they scream, they curse, they herd us into buses at bayonet point.

"Wonder why we're heading away from the Bund?" the man seated beside me remarks. "We're going west when we should be going east."

The bus continues on its errant course. After an age in chaotic traffic it turns into a graceful secluded driveway where it brakes to a stop.

My neighbor nudges me. "This is the Columbia Country Club. It's American, you know."

But the accent of the man who steps aboard the bus is strictly Oxford. "Welcome to Shanghai, ladies and gentlemen. This holding center for repatriates will be your temporary home for a day or two. We'd like you to stick together till we've registered you. Will you please follow me off the bus."

He clears a way through the crowded foyer and shepherds us into a roped off area in the club's library. He checks us off against a roll. He breaks us into groups. I'm in the group of single men who are told to proceed to the bowling alley. But we can forget about bowling; camp cots are strung out head to foot along every lane. We are each assigned a cot.

"G'day cobber!" A man seated on a suitcase in the lane opposite gives me a welcoming smile. "Suppose you heard the *Kamakura Maru* has been delayed."

"No."

"Well it has. We're stuck here for a few more days. Where you from?"

"Tientsin. We just got in by train."

"How did the Japanese treat you?"

"Not too badly. Lot of shouting and pushing and shoving. That's about all."

"You're lucky. We lot from Hankow had a pretty rough time of it. They shot Tony Gorman and Rod Phillips. I thank my lucky stars I've got this far."

My feet suddenly catch his attention. "Stone the crows!

169

those white and brown shoes of yours, they're calf skin aren't they? I've been searching everywhere for a pair like 'em. They look just my size. Wherever did you buy them?"

"Didn't buy them. I had them specially made." I don't tell him any more than that. Don't tell him I cut the ad out of *Esquire* and took it to the shoemaker on Taku Road. And that miracle man came up with a copy so perfect, you would have sworn they were the made-in-Philadelphia originals.

"Soon as I get to Sydney, I'm going to get me a pair of the same. You want a word of advice, cobber? When it's time for kip you 'ide 'em shoes. You want more advice? You make bloody sure you get in the food line before the gong goes. Those bloody missionaries are the greediest sods I've ever set eyes on. Worse than starving pigs, snatch your bloody bread and butter when you're not bloody looking."

In the library that evening a chorus of voices in close harmony give a caressing rendition of *Lead Kindly Light.* I find myself a place at the back. I know the words. I add my voice to the inspiring finale. Hymn follows hymn. *Abide With Me* is interrupted by a heavy-set man, purple around the nose, who maintains his balance by leaning on a harridan, all paint and peroxide. The couple weave their way through the assembly of good Christians. The man stops to address them. His speech is slurred. "I'm lost, mates. I think I took the wrong turn. Can you direct me to me bed? Luba and me are ready for that."

In the morning we line up for the washroom. We line up

for breakfast. Afterwards, we line up for inoculations, for toothbrushes, for Red Cross message forms. Curiously, not much smiling, and none of the light-headed talk you'd expect from those who are about to gain their freedom. Major Ridler isn't long in giving me the reason.

"We're not going. Dirty rotters, they've taken us off the list. They say there's a second ship in a fortnight. They're lying through their teeth. There isn't going to be a second ship. I've got their names. They're going to pay for it after the war."

"Who's *they?*"

"The British Residents Association. Big money's been passed under the table. A number of us from North China have been scratched off the list. Influential Shanghai taipans have our berths."

In the evening the Australian in the next cot next to me shows me his boarding pass. He says he will be leaving at five a.m. When I awake, his cot is empty. He is on his way to freedom. So are my shoes. I line up for breakfast barefooted.

The BRA's dignified gray-haired secretary-treasurer arrives to placate his fellow countrymen. He has an easy time of answering the mild questions put to him by the men of God. The businessmen, old China hands, who know all about dirty tricks, pin him against the wall. An unfortunate mix-up, he pleads. All will be put right. The luxury liner *Teia Maru* will be arriving shortly from Kobe. You'll soon be on your merry way.

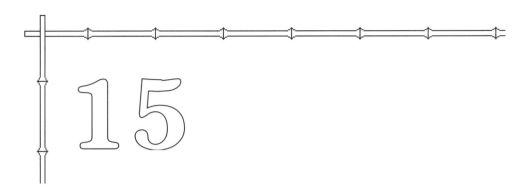

STONE WALLS DO *INDEED* A PRISON MAKE!

A ND we soon *were* on our merry way all right, but not aboard the *Teia Maru.* Nothing so grand. They had a stinking, rusting river tender earmarked for us.

After instructing the bowling alley occupants to be packed and ready, a BRA big cheese, aided and abetted by three lesser cheeses, escorted us onto Japanese trucks. Our roll taken – all present and correct – the trucks roarcd off along Great Western Road, heading for downtown, heading for Holy Trinity Cathedral. What a sight the cathedral yard. If you've ever seen a newsreel of Ellis Island that's what it looked like, a shambles of bodies, kitbags, suitcases, baskets, holdalls, bundles of every sort! Our own disembarkation from the trucks a little too slow for Japanese liking, gendarmes appeared out of the misty rain screaming and yelling. That only added to the confusion. We milled about, not knowing which way to turn. It took a BRA man, obviously a scoutmaster judging by his gentle yet persuasive tone, to get us into line so we could be counted off. Then after a miserable hour in the cold drizzle it was that same scoutmaster who got us on the move. "Right, men, show 'em what we're made of, chests out, chins in. By the left, quick march."

Encumbered by our bags and things, it was no quick march, nor was it a slow one; stragglers getting the prod from Japanese bayonets. The roadway was bare of traffic, but the sidewalks teemed with Chinese all the way down Kiangse Road to Nanking Road to the Bund. It was on that wide esplanade opposite the mighty colonnaded temples

They marched us along the Bund under the mighty temples of finance

of finance that the largest crowd had gathered to witness the White Man's ultimate humiliation. But no insults thrown, no jeers, no catcalls. A sea of silent poker faces saw us onto the waiting tender.

Over on the Pootung side, despite the incoherent goading of our captors, the march degenerated into a spent safari strung out over several hundred yards. And no stopping for a breather, the boot leather of Dai Nippon seeing to that. Stepping around abandoned bags and suitcases, a terrible temptation came over me to lighten my own load. Should I drop the duffel bag so heavy on my shoulder? The suitcase in my left hand? The carryall in my right with its precious contents to see me through the war – the jumbo packet of Quaker Oats, the six tins of Hing Beef, the three of Cross & Blackwell Strawberry Jam? In desperation I drew on that old dodge learned at school when we couldn't run another step in the annual cross-country race – count aloud from one to a twenty, repeat the count, and repeat it again. I was staggering like a drunk and gasping as if it were my last breath, but I made it through the camp gate with all my possessions. A glance at the surroundings, and my heart turned over. For an eighteen-year-old, how could there be anything more sinister than a high brick wall topped with barbed wire, the concrete go-downs, dark and dripping like the stalagmites of a nightmare? "Keep going, damn you," someone cursed from behind. I let him have the choicest bits of my No. 3 Platoon repertoire. We had good reason to curse. The ten-foot walkway along which we were proceeding was ankle deep in raw sewage. I was again at breaking point

– we all were at breaking point. But now from the sidelines gray-faced inmates stepped forward into the putrid mire to take our bags. Our march finally ended in the camp's mess hall, the ground floor of a square brick building that stood at one end of the compound.

I couldn't take my eyes off the squat, bull-necked officer with Sumo wrestler's shoulders who stood on a table facing us. He was literally shaking with rage, the high color of his face accentuating the pale ridged scar that ran diagonally across his cheek. Any moment now he was going to erupt. And he did so even before the last of the stragglers had entered the hall. It took me a moment or two to realize that his garbled tirade was in fact a speech, a speech in English: ". . . This is your Happy Garden so you will be vurr vurr happy here . . . You will thank Imperial Empah of Greater Japan for much kindnesses . . . You bow to guard to show respect for Emp-ror . . . You obey order . . . You must be happy . . . If you are not happy you will be shot to the death! . . ."

Silence – nonplused silence.

The brute's eyes disappeared into their Neanderthal sockets. His face was puce, his scar white as a toad's belly. Where was our appreciation, at the very least a round of polite applause, for the largess the Empire of Greater Japan was heaping upon us? His eruption was sudden and violent. "Dismissu! . . . Dismissu! . . . Go Happy Home! . . . Go Happy Garden!"

As we filed out, one of our own camp officials positioned at the exit handed us each a brass disk stamped with a series of digits.

"Don't lose this. It's your ID. It gives your block and section number. More important, it's your meal token. Without it you'll starve."

"Don't think much of your Commandant's welcome," someone remarked.

"He's not the Commandant, he's the Chief of Police. His name is Konga, but we call him Scarface."

"What a bastard!"

"You're right. Keep out of his way."

"Where's Block Fourteen?" someone called out.

"Over there, the second floor of the building on your left."

I found my block, Block Five, on the ground floor of a two storied go-down. My luck was in. Of the four sections in the block, mine had Ronnie Stewart as leader. I knew

Pootung's gloomy go-downs were even too dank for storing tobacco!

Ronnie from Tientsin, a tough, rugger-playing, public school type, on contract with Jardines, but without the airs and graces of a home-staff swell.

"So you missed the "*Wangle Maru*," he said. "Too bad, Desmond. Can't trust anyone these days, can you? But that's life, and you're going to have to make the best of it. Won't be easy. What they give us to eat here wouldn't keep a bird alive. And, as you can see, they've jammed us like sardines in a go-down so derelict, so riddled with vermin, the British American Tobacco Company had to abandon it years ago as being unfit for storing tobacco. Today's intake, the third, brings our complement to over twelve hundred. And what a motley collection: deckhands, diamond merchants, gamblers, musicians, teachers, missionaries, taipans, and, as you might expect, a full quota of the proverbial 'Old China Hands who've missed too many boats.' Take my advice, keep out of trouble, avoid the guards if you can, don't quarrel, don't pick fights. The crew from the *President Harrison* look a tough lot, but in fact they're well behaved, well disciplined. When this place first opened and conditions seemed totally impossible, it was their indomitable spirit that kept us going. Can't say the same for some of the traders and the holier-than-thou preachers. And watch out for the derelicts the Japanese scraped up from Shanghai's back alleys. Some are funny. And I don't mean funny – ha-ha. You point out to me anyone who gets fresh, and he won't try it again."

I stayed close to Ronnie the rest of that first afternoon. Next day I went out reconnoitering on my own.

175

On our floor, and on the floor above, and on both floors of the go-down adjoining ours, it was what the inside of an ant hill must look like to ants: a crush of fellow creatures forever in each other's way. But whereas the ant, communal to the nth degree, has no concept of self, in our prison society each individual laid claim to a piece of personal real estate, measuring exactly four feet by ten, delineated on the bare floor with white chalk. There'd be an elderly academic lolling on his bunk, poring over some heavy tome, oblivious to the clutch of American Blacks rolling dice on the other side of his chalk line. You'd see a lurid centerfold from some Paris magazine a foot or two away from a priest's crucifix.

From reveille to lights out, the twice-breathed air hummed with talk – food the chief topic, dames a close second. And then there were all those dire predictions – our brutal captors were going to ship us en bloc to Manchuria – they were going to make us work the mines at Tongshan – they were going to machine-gun the lot of us at the first sign of an Allied victory. Not too fanciful if you believed the accounts given by inmates transferred from Hong Kong's Stanley Camp and Manila's Santo Tomas of sick prisoners clubbed in their beds, of wholesale deaths from beriberi and dysentery. So far nothing like that in Pootung. Perhaps the Swiss Consul, directly across the river, had his protective eye on us. If so, it wasn't for long.

Searching one of their own garbage coolies, the guards discovered a note written by an internee. Block by block we were made to line up for identification parade. The coolie pointed no one out. They bound him in a kneeling position on the landing twenty feet from the entrance to the mess hall. For three days and nights the poor wretch underwent torture in full view of the camp. His demented groans was our torture. After his mutilated body was carted off, the Japanese singled out an inmate and shipped him to Bridge House, the dreaded *Kempetai* interrogation center. If he survived – and that was pretty doubtful, he being a newsman, and an American one at that – he would certainly come out a broken man.

I was pretty shaken at the identification parade. To save himself, that coolie could have picked out anyone; he could have picked out *me*. I was soon in for another bad shaking. The self-proclaimed spokesman of the group gathered outside our block's latrine was daring sissies to go take a look at what was inside. Me, a sissy? I went in. I stepped gingerly across a crimson pool spreading slowly over the permanently damp floor. I peered around a partition. I wish I hadn't. A poor fellow who'd decided to end it all had slit his throat from ear to ear.

I couldn't swallow my chunk of bread that evening. It wasn't wasted. Eager hands reached for it. Next morning I was still queasy when I faced my ladle of cracked wheat. What a strange twist for the Americans among us, that cracked wheat. Their Red Cross had rushed it to China as flood relief following the destruction of the Yellow River dikes in 1938. Somehow the Japanese had got their hands on the stockpile and were feeding it to its donors – with additives. In the four years that it had lain in storage, the wheat from the North American prairie had attracted weevils from the Central Chinese plain, a teeming population of weevils. At first I would pick them out and arrange them in a row at the edge of my plate. After a while, as blasé as my dining companions, I spooned down my breakfast just as it came.

At midday we got a ladle of soup and the day's bread ration, an eight ounce black loaf. In the evening, sometimes a ladle of watery buffalo stew, sometimes a two-to three-inch strip of ribbon fish. Too bad if your strip came from the tail end of the ribbon. Nothing but fins and bones.

Hunger drove me to work as a scullion under the sharp eye of "Old Man" Ernie Roberts from the SS *Harrison*. Not only was he a disciplinarian who worked you every minute of the shift, he was a stickler for cleanliness. With a critical eye he would examine every crack, every seam of the large wooden serving tubs for the slightest trace of foreign matter. He never had to complain about mine. Before attacking them with boiling water and a stiff brush, I would run the point of a knife along the seams, often getting myself enough oily flesh for a decent mouthful.

Regretfully, my career as a scullion came to an abrupt end. A dixie of scalding water spilled over my feet. Someone sloshed a handful of wet tea leaves onto the blisters already forming. I was carried to the sick bay on a Baden Powell four-handed seat of interlocked wrists.

So back to a life of hunger and boredom, now exacerbated by a Shanghai winter, the penetrating cold even more penetrating within a go-down – the condensation from damp concrete acting in strict accordance with the first principle of refrigeration. While wearing an extra sweater might give protection in Tientsin's dry climate, not so in moisture-laden Shanghai. Bed was the only place one could stay warm. A lot of the time I'd lie fully dressed under my blanket and overcoat where I'd be treated to a concert by my neighbor, Paddy O'Reilly, ex-RSM Irish Guards, still wheezing, still choking out great gobs of phlegm after having breathed a lungful of chlorine gas at Ypres twenty-six years back.

Oh, if only summer would come! It came all right. After the brief Shanghai spring it came with a vengeance. At roll call we'd all be wiping off rivulets of sweat as the super-heated air from Wuhan, the blast furnace of China, rolled across the Yangtze basin. Even when the sun went down, it remained as stifling as a ship's boiler room, dispiriting everyone, prisoners and guards alike.

My spirits reached their lowest ebb when I heard that the Japanese in Tientsin had rounded up every Briton, American, Hollander, and Belgian they could lay their hands on – men, women, children – and incarcerated them in a camp near Weihsien in central Shantung. How long could proud-hearted Tai-tai endure the life of a coolie? And what about Tony? What about little Betty?

Between Block Five and the wall separating the camp proper from "Happy Garden" (once all shell holes and rubble from the naval bombardment in 1937, now leveled

by inmates under an American engineer's supervision into a playing field where we are allowed during daylight hours), there is a tank of water, a miniature swimming pool, but no swimming, the water dark and fetid. It is part of my morning regimen to sit by the pool for a couple of hours practicing scales and chords on Dickie Reynold's jazz guitar. I try not to be distracted by the circular ripples that break every now and then on the surface scum. I fight a losing battle. With every new ripple I get the same thrill of anticipation I used to get when I spotted the tell-tale signs of knife-fish on the still water of Tientsin Country Club's round pond. Next morning I come armed with one of the bamboo poles that hold up Paddy O'Reilly's mosquito net. And I have a line braided with three lengths of cotton thread, a cork for a float, and a hook fashioned from a pin. For bait I have a well-kneaded lump of black bread. The cork bobs almost immediately, and there is my catch flopping about the concrete walkway. It's a handsome carp, half a pound at least. Needless to say my feat attracts attention. One inmate tells me he's an expert at scaling and boning carp. Another boasts that he has fished every foot of the Wiltshire Avon and if I hand him my rod he'll show how it's really done. Astounding, someone remarks, that there can be fish in an industrial cooling tank. Not so, an old geezer lectures. Back in the twenties, as resident stationary engineer for BAT, he was responsible for stocking the tank with carp fry to control the mosquito population.

I notice I have also attracted the attention of the guard in the watchtower. He is no longer keeping his eye on Happy Garden. He has in fact turned his back on the garden and he is aiming his black pinpoint pupils straight at me. But his look is more of puzzlement than anger. There is probably nothing in his orders about prisoners engaging in the ancient sport of angling. It is when I land my second carp that he starts his hollering. When I ignore him, he draws his Mauser and raps it against its wooden holster. I pick up my catch and beat a hasty retreat.

Next day there is a sign on the wall below the guard tower that says:

"FISHINGS HERE ARE FORBIDDEN."

Forbidden for inmates is what it really means. Sometimes three, sometimes four off-duty guards seat themselves on bamboo stools at the edge of the pool. Their fancy store-bought rods easily reach the middle of the water. Within a fortnight that rarest of piscatorial species, the *carpio pootungnicum,* is extinct.

From atop the water tower we watched the Conte Verde go down.

On September 10 a spine-tingling show in real live Technicolor suddenly and unexpectedly broke the camp out of its cocoon-like existence. It was pure Hollywood from the opening chorus "The *Conte Verde* Is Sinking" to the grand finale "The *Conte Verde* Has Sunk."

A wild dash to the upper floors, a crazy climb to the water tower, and we had ringside seats (if only we had a camera!) of the crack Italian liner, listing crazily, smack in the middle of the Whangpoo. We cheered at the antics of the Japanese marines racing about the dockyard. We cheered when the yellow-brown water lapped across the liner's promenade deck. We cheered loudest when with a sudden motion the proud ship turned on its side and settled on the bottom, leaving only its ugly dull-red bilge exposed above the water line. Someone pointed out the masts of the gunboat *Lepanto* protruding from the water. No more cheers. We were plumb out of cheers.

Italy knocked out of the war! What a boost! Dare we hope the end was in sight? Rumors ran rampant: . . . an American landing at Amoy . . . Chiang Kai Shek's forces sweeping towards Shanghai . . . Japanese civilians in panic, evacuating by the shipload. . . .

No such luck! In a few days we were in deeper dumps than ever. The Japanese made new advances in China, they overran Burma, they were poised for their drive into India. And those weren't rumors, they came straight from Micky Griffiths, camp interpreter, a fellow about my age, who could rattle off in Japanese to beat the band. He had accompanied the guard who escorted a dying inmate to

180

Shanghai's Country Hospital. A Portuguese doctor who listened to Radio Moscow gave the Micky the news.

No good giving in to despair. My escape was to memorize another hundred characters from my *Mandarin Reader* and to practice chord runs on Dickie Reynolds's guitar until I could do them blindfolded.

I am standing with my bad foot on a stool in the Commandant's office. The American Doctor Steinberg has given his little speech about the need for urgent medical attention. Micky has translated the speech into throaty Japanese. A Japanese officer peers through quarter-inch lenses. He stubs his fingertip into the foot's spongy flesh. He sucks air through his teeth. He shakes his head. He hisses out a string of words. Without a moment's hesitation, Micky hisses a string straight back at him. The officer gets red in the face. Before the scene can turn any uglier, Commandant Tsuchiya intervenes. His harangue sounds very much to me like a reprimand, and I don't know if the reprimand is intended for me or for Micky or for the Japanese MO. . . . It's for me.

"No good," Micky says. "Better wait till next Tuesday. This son of a bitch of a Nagaski MO will be off duty. Wakamoto is much easier to deal with."

Doctor Steinberg turns to me: "We'll try soaking it in boracic. Get back to your bunk till we call you."

"I have zinc ointment," says pal Kenny Cance.

"Tiger Balm more better," says pal Tony Garcia.

Thanks to the boracic or the zinc ointment or the Tiger Balm, the swelling goes down. But that's no blessing. I've lost my chance to escape camp, if only for a few days.

I come out of my deep blues when Sandy Kennedy, a Tientsin buddy from way back, but a Shanghailander since '38, tells me I've got a chance, though a mighty slim one, of saying good-bye to Pootung.

"Crazy rumor, Sandy?"

"Go see for yourself. It's on the notice board."

BY ORDER OF COMMANDANT TSUCHIYA, SEVENTY-FIVE MEN ARE TO BE TRANSFERRED TO LUNGHUA CIVIL ASSEMBLY CENTER. THOSE WISHING TO VOLUNTEER ARE ASKED TO REGISTER THEIR NAMES AT THE COMMANDANT'S OFFICE.

"*Those wishing to volunteer*"? Is Tsuchiya nuts? Ask twelve hundred half-starved men jam-packed in a filthy concrete warren if they'd like to move to a university campus in the countryside where a couple of thousand British, American, Dutch, and Belgian men and WOMEN are interned, and how many are going to sign on? Fifteen hundred at the very least, the smart ones putting their names in twice – thrice. Seventy-five out of fifteen hundred? Fat chance my beating those odds! Yet, by all the saints, someone has got to be lucky! . . .

As it turned out, the luck of the draw wasn't the only way to get picked – if you knew Micky Griffiths, that is.

He searched me out. "How'd you like to go to Lunghua? I can get you on the list."

I stared, dumfounded. Ah, but I was no fool, I'd been disappointed before. There was that *Wangle Maru* business. There was also the rumor floating around that the Lunghua transfer was nothing but a ruse, that the Jappos needed seventy-five coolies for the Tongshan Mines, that they wanted them on the sly – no argument, no resistance.

"There's that rumor about Tongshan, Micky . . ."

"Load of crap! For a year the Swiss have complained to the Japanese about the women in Lunghua being over-burdened by physical work. When they requested that the women be moved back to Shanghai, some Japanese whiz came up with the idea of bringing in men from Pootung. That's why the notice. So do you want to go or not? I'm in charge of drawing up the list. I've already typed four names: Hank Behrens, Donald Cance, Kenny Cance,

182

Tony Garcia. Do you want to be number five?"

"Do I want to be number five? Hells bells, Micky, make me number seventy-five, and I'll be your slave for life!"

"Okay, the first five are confirmed. The rest will be drawn from a hat."

Micky Griffiths
my pal for life!

So long Pootung! So long Ronnie Stewart! So long Jimmy Agnew, Dickie Reynolds, Denis O'Shea, Ed Harvey! So long Solomon Delborgo! So long everybody! A stab of regret, but only momentary; once through the forbidding gate and into the bright autumn sunlight, I exulted. I had the feeling somehow this was going to be a beautiful day, a day of wonderful surprises. I wasn't wrong. Soon as the river tender skirted *Conte Verde's* rusting bilge, we could see, parked on the Bund, two buses waiting to pick us up. So, no twelve-mile route march as predicted by our perennial Whining Willies. By golly, we were off on a charabanc outing via Shanghai's western suburbs to the fresh green countryside. And what a rousing welcome from the swelling concourse of internees at Lunghua's main gate! And what wolf whistles they got from us! How could there be so much pulchritude concentrated in one place? And how rich the variety – slim, buxom, tall, petite, fair, dark! Jeepers creepers, they were giving good as they got, those Lunghua belles, their squeals rising to a feline crescendo when Cece Richards, *Harrison's* gentle black Goliath, stepped down from the bus.

"Grand Central Station!" Hank Behrens announced. Easy to catch his meaning – wives, sisters, sweethearts, buddies, all kissing and hugging, all laughter and tears.

We non-Shanghailanders – Hank and his twenty *Harrison* shipmates, and Dick Coppin and myself – were totally out of it. Then someone was pumping my hand, pumping it to beat the band – Brian Clarke, my old schoolmate, my fellow *Wangle Maru* cast-off. Taken ill at the last moment, he'd missed Pootung; now an old Lunghua lag with a bit of Shanghai swank rubbed off on him, he couldn't wait to introduce me to his camp circle: Reggie Euluch, Stonewall Jackson, the Pearson brothers, the Peach sisters. In response, though my heart was skipping beats and my voice inexplicably shrill, I introduced my American companions: Hank Behrens, Gil Monreal, Mike Barrasa, Chief Oke Doke. I was thinking desperately for

183

something heroic to say when Brian – how heartless he'd grown! – dragged me aside. "For God's sake, get moving." he snapped. "You Pootung guys are being quartered in the Assembly Hall. There's time to pick out a choice spot – a corner space on the stage. Come on, we'll show you. Where are your bags? Move quickly you dope. Someone'll beat us to it. What's the matter? Wakey-wakey . . ."

Nothing was the matter. Just plain bedazzlement. How could he stand it, seeing them every day, those Peach sisters – Jill, peachy as Joan Fontaine – Molly, peachy as Olivia de Havilland?

And talk about blasé! Without so much as an "excuse me" to those dream girls, or "I'll see you later, I have a friend to attend to," he and Reggie hurried me to a theater-like building and through a side door and up a short flight of steps, and we were standing on a stage facing an auditorium into which, through the front entrance, new arrivals were pouring in like forty-niners in a gold strike. While I stood by, lost, lightheaded, those two Good Samaritans, Brian and Reggie, went about erecting my cot in a rear corner, thereby consolidating my claim to what surely had to be the choicest spot in the building.

"Tell us, Des," said Brian grinning playfully, "are Chief Oke Doke's brass earrings for real?"

Chuckle-chuckle.

And from Reggie, his eyes popping like a child at a circus: "Is he a real live chief?"

Guffaw-guffaw.

"Are Jill and Molly Peach real live people?" I blurted back at them.

"Why do you ask?"

I closed my eyes and mouthed an emphatic "Wow!"

"Wow? What are you wowing about? Wait till you see their sister Betty. She's the beauty of the family. She'll be in the mess hall in about ten minutes. We'll introduce you. You guys don't eat till second sitting, but we'll sneak you in with us."

"Thanks but no thanks, tomorrow maybe." I'd had about as much excitement as I could take. I needed to get back on even keel, I needed the camaraderie of my Pootung fellows, that band of brothers now crowding the stage, turning it into a gypsy camp with their cots and bags and roped bundles. Tony Garcia had the space next to mine. Donald and Kenny Cance were three rows over, and Mike Levy diagonally opposite. When Section Captain Gerald Someck announced that it was chow time and that we ought to be off to the dining hall, we closed ranks behind him. Wonder of wonders, no hard-bitten ex-police inspector presiding over the doling out; here dainty maidens served our portions. I stared agog, not at the ladle of thick soup in my bowl, but at the slender wrist working the ladle. "Get a move on," someone hollered. "Don't hold up the line." I followed the Cance boys and Tony Garcia to a table where we could feast our eyes on those living breathing nymphs, the likes of which, for close on a year, had existed only in our dreams. We nudged, we kicked each other under the table, we giggled, we talked wild nonsense.

Mike Levy and Bobby Bloomfield called soberly from across the aisle: "How do you fellahs like the soup?" . . . "Don't you think it's great?"

"You bet, way better than what we got at Pootung."

Kenny elbowed me. "And bigger portions. Don't you agree, Des?"

Kenny's nose was an inch from mine. "Don't you agree, Des?" he growled.

"Yes, Kenny, yes," I murmured, absently. I wasn't with him. I was up on a cloud, the same pink cloud that bore me to seventh heaven on that one day of the year, that exhilarating, magical day, when school broke for the summer hols.

The wide-open breathing space of Lunghua Camp.

185

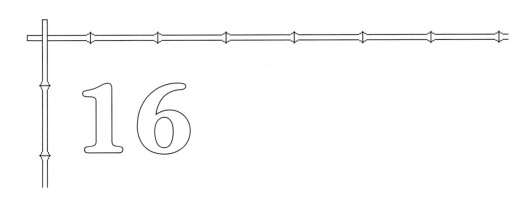

16

. . . AND BARBED WIRE A CAGE

A CHANGE IS AS GOOD AS A HOLIDAY! So Ronnie Stewart remarked when I told him my name was on the Lunghua list. Now, only a week after my transfer, I could cap his words with a thought of my own: YES, ESPECIALLY IF THE CHANGE IS FOR THE BETTER!

No doubt about it, conditions in Lunghua *were* better, a whole lot better. While in Pootung we were hemmed in by prison brick and concrete, here the buildings were spread nicely across a wide campus. I walked the length of a full-size football pitch, and then some, to get to J Block, Brian Clarke's block. And it was a fair walk to the chow lines, and even more of one circumnavigating the "ruins," a row of classroom buildings destroyed by shellfire during the Sino-Japanese battle for Shanghai.

And nothing too hard about the hard labor our captors had brought us in to perform. I was assigned to a Camp Service team whose job it was to gather bricks from the ruins and restore them to usable condition, chipping off mortar with that most efficient of tools – the heavy-bladed, blunt-edged brick mason's cleaver, in common use in China for a thousand years or more. Because of the danger from cave-ins and crumbling walls, the chipping was done off site. In fact, the powers-that-be declared the ruins out of bounds to all except Camp Service work parties. Fat lot of good. All about the place were signs of occupation, hollowed-out love nests, one in particular, it's groundsheet still in place, most inviting as Tony Garcia, Dick Coppin, and I concluded – Dick wanting a smoke,

Lining up for water at "Waterloo."

and Tony and I in no hurry to load the wheelbarrow.

"Okay you lazy bums, at quitting time you can each clean an extra fifty bricks."

That was our shift boss, Fred Bunn, a tough-as-nails tobacco man from North Carolina. Ingrained with the work ethic of Pilgrim America, he never let us forget that a laborer must always be worthy of his hire. (What a fusspot I thought at the time, but in later life I thanked God for the trace of pilgrim ethic that had rubbed off on me when I stood, as I too often found myself, on the razor's edge between survival and disaster.)

We were well into our punishment quota, only twenty bricks to go, when Garcia remarked, teasingly: "Say, Datz, my sister Talma has fran, Belgian girl, name call Poupée who wanna go walk with you."

"You're kidding."

"I no kid. I tell true. I can fix ezak time, ezak place."

"Gus, baby, you're not doing any more bricks. I'm doing yours for you. You're my best friend."

For several concert rehearsals I had accompanied Poupée Bodson on the guitar as she sang with heart-rending wistfulness that French hit of the day, *J'attendrai*. Svelte, dark-haired, alluring, she could melt you with one look. Needless to say, she had no shortage of beaus.

How providential that I could play the guitar. Back in Tientsin that musical whiz Dick McVeigh showed me how to strum chords. In Pootung another Dick, Dick Reynolds, a copper-colored jazz guitarist, taught me the fundamentals. I first got to know him by sidling up to where he sat when Henry Nathan's band, the pick of Shanghai's night clubs, assembled for practice outside Block Five. Dick's powerful eight bar intro, which led the band into the rollicking hit tune *Shine*, totally transfixed me. Thirty – forty – fifty years later, on the rare occasion that I hear that tune played on radio or TV, I am instantly transported back to the compound outside Block Five. And I see myself exchanging smiles with that superlative jazz guitarist, and carrying for him, and standing in line for him, and running to Block Eleven to hand him the pack of cigarettes I earned doing someone's laundry (I didn't smoke). Call it hero worship if you like, but then his trust in me stretched pretty far; he let me take his priceless Gibson down to Block Five for two hours a day, every day. And for every second of those two precious hours, never did I let my fingers rest on the frets, never did I let his observation stray from my mind: *the left hand might look like it do the work, but baby it's the right that wake the soul!*

In Lunghua, no professional jazz musicians; the six-piece dance band was strictly amateur, though the leader, Ikey Abraham, could have turned pro on drums any time he liked. One audition – on a borrowed classical guitar – and hc gavc me the thumbs up. There were bonuses being in the band. Practice time, two afternoons a week, we were excused from regular duties. Better bashing out dance tunes than chipping bricks. No instrument? All it took was camp leader, Mr Bates of Shell Oil, to pass word around, and a nifty acoustic guitar came my way. Replacement strings? No problem. Mr Bates mentioned the need to Commandant Hayashi at one of their morning meetings and a whole slew of spares from high E to low E, arrived from Shanghai. Scores? Same thing. We had our pick of the latest: *Sierra Sue, Green Eyes, South of the Border, Yours, Amapola, In the Mood. . . .*

To ex-Pootungers who'd heard the real thing we must have sounded awful. But then there were those music-starved Lunghua-ites who would come up to us after a dance lavishing praise as though we were Glen Miller on *Hit Parade*. However undeserved, the praise was easy to swallow. I made new friends. Standing in line in the water queue, people I didn't know from Adam would flatter me with a nod and a smile. The guitar was my in. I hobnobbed with Lunghua society. And that was saying something, for Lunghua was largely a British camp, a microcosm of the

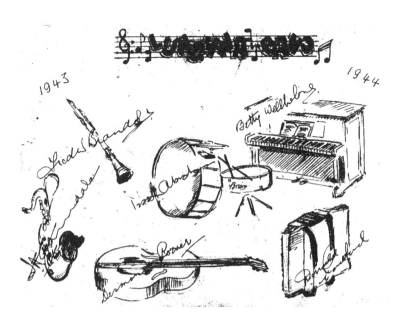

multi-layered colonial world with all layers represented, from the down-at-heel "local" boys to the tetrarchs of Hungjao Road. Ironically, in peacetime, such casual mixing would simply not have been on. Never mind that the Chinese viewed us all as "*jackals from the same hillock*," in the White man's world, strict rules – unspoken and unwritten – ensured that we kept within our own separate spheres.

Kenny's eyes are starry with excitement. "Christmas is coming, the geese are getting fat," he quips impishly.

Donald, his elder brother, is in a more serious mood. "Are you game or not?" he challenges.

I try not to show how scared I am of joining them in their harebrained scheme. It's not geese they are after, but the Commandant's prize roosters, decorative roosters with brilliant plumage and six-foot-long tails. To the Japanese they are show birds, living works of art. To Donald they are edible fowl. What if we're caught? The guards can be pretty brutal as they showed only the other day when Reuben arrived for roll call after the count had been completed and the sergeant scratching his head over the shortage. He let Reuben have it. Wham! Slap! Crunch! Two guys from the *Harrison* had to prop him up during the recount.

189

Remember the Xmas of 1943

"Well, Des, what about it? Got the wind up?"

"Who? Me? Not a bit of it. I'm game." Though I have the shakes, and my stomach feels as if it no longer belongs to me, I force out a weak smile.

"This is how we do it." Donald gives a deft twist to a rolled-up hand towel, demonstrating how very simple is the technique of snapping a chicken's neck.

"And we do it Christmas Eve," he says. "Fewer internees out and about, the Japanese will have their guard down."

"How many of us?"

"Four, absolute max. Three will go in under the wire. They won't have far to go. The coop is only twenty-five feet from the fence. One of us will act as look-out. He will keep watch from inside the wire."

My prayers are *not* answered. Kenny picks the shortest straw. Kenny is look-out.

The night is black. The only sound I hear in the overcharged silence is the sound of my chattering teeth. On our backs we inch our way under the vicious barbs, then we crawl on all fours to the coop. Garcia undoes the latch, and we are inside. Donald strikes a match. The birds are roosting in straight military rows. They glare at us with red agate eyes. Donald reaches, Garcia reaches, I reach. Instant commotion, piercing squawks, flapping wings, floating feathers. I fly after Donald and Garcia. Brave Kenny, with boot pressing down and palm drawing up, widens the gap between the barbed strands. We plunge through. I loosen the grip on my bird's neck. Unaffected by my Girl Guide attempt at strangulation, it goes instantly berserk, nipping, clawing, screeching to high heaven. Donald does it in with a callous two-handed twist. We race to the assembly hall. We shoot up onto the stage.

Christmas morning, hell to pay. The Japanese chief of police has suffered agonizing loss of face. He is going to apprehend the culprits if it's the last thing he ever does. The camp's full complement is paraded on the football pitch. My heart is in my mouth for the entire two hours it takes the guards to rip through every bunk in every block. Donald is unconcerned. Donald knows that search parties always look down, never look up. And the birds, plucked and cleaned, are in pillow cases, way up in the rafters, hauled there by the theater's scene-changing block and tackle. Donald is tickled pink when Mr Bates lets it be known that the perpetrators of the dastardly crime had better come clean if they hope to avoid the dire retribution that eighteen hundred inmates who have lost camp privileges on Christmas Day are raring to mete out. Donald nudges Garcia, he nudges me. "Okay," he says, "let's come clean." He gives us a wink. "When the war is over!" And he bursts into a fit of schoolgirl giggles.

Half an hour after the Japanese abandon their search and we are back in our quarters, Taffy Edwards, ex-inspector of the Shanghai Municipal Police, pays a visit. "Tut, tut, tut, boys, how could you ever think you'd get away with it? It's Christmas you know. A time for giving. I don't want to appear greedy. A single bird will do. I'll keep mum. No names no pack drill."

We present the inspector with the smallest, most miserable of the three birds. The other two we consign to a five gallon gasoline can along with turnips and rice crusts and a can of Delmonte tomatoes. We do our cooking in the most secluded of the ruins' hideaways using a coke-burning chatty "borrowed" from Gerald Someck. Though we let the stew brew for close on two hours, our jaws get a thoroughly good work-out on the ostrich-like sinews of the Nagasaki show birds. But anything's better than the cabbage soup, which is Boxing Day fare for the eighteen hundred honored guests of the Peacock Throne. . . .

It was Christmas Day-plus-five when Commandant Hayashi gave orders for camp privileges to be fully restored. "Boys will be boys," he told Mr Bates. But then how did he square it, we wondered, with his own chief of police? Wasn't his decision tantamount to a slap in the face, and the chief already enduring unendurable loss of face? No two ways about it, Hayashi was playing with fire. According to the rumor mill, he'd already raised hackles in Tokyo by requesting an increase in prisoners' rations, and at a time when the citizenry of Dai Nippon were being asked to make untold sacrifices in a war that had been forced upon them by that ruthless, godless, warmongering monster – Franklin Delano Roosevelt.

Who was he, this Horie Hayashi? What a strange fish! Well, for one thing, no black uniform for him, he was always in civvies, Savile Row suits to be exact. He was a career diplomat who at the outbreak of the Pacific war had been stationed in London where he was accorded Palmerstonian courtesy during his internment. A brief internment, it should be said, for he was one of those exchanged for Britons on the *Kamakura Maru* back in '42. Lucky for him there was no Japanese Residents' Association in London to screw him out of his berth. Lucky for us too. Though some internees swore blindly that there was a shogun-harsh side to him, the majority of us couldn't have wished for anyone more lenient, more statesmanlike to have total control over our destinies.

To the Harrison boys he was a "regular guy," though God knows it doesn't always pay to be such. On New Year's Day (January 1, 1944), I really felt for him. The evening before he had literally crashed our dance, his entrance quite a show in itself, coming in as he did supported by two guards. He indicated he wanted to give a speech. We put down our band instruments. He stood swaying on a table. His words, before turning incoherent, went something like this: "Happy New Year! Everybody is friend forever. You may dance all night today, for I have a secret joy!" He was still babbling when the guards carried him out.

How his thumping hangover must have taken on draconian proportions when he learned – the chief of police probably broke the news – that three inmates had broken out during the night. Two Shanghai boys, Jayjay Roza and Charlie Ozorio, took off with Mary MacDonald, a beauty by any reckoning, an Australian by birth, and a Buddhist by religious persuasion. In possession of that last attribute, the three must already be safe in some holy lamasery. And from that point on, getting to Chungking a cakewalk, what with all those Buddhist sanctuaries dotting the way.

For us in Lunghua, no sanctuary, nowhere to hide. You could feel it in your bones, you could almost smell it, the tension in the air, the electrical tension that precedes a summer storm. But the storm never hit. Before Hayashi and his police chief could agree on suitable punishment for the camp, the escapees were apprehended by the Imperial Japanese Gendarmerie, and in downtown Shanghai of all places. Chilling to think what those captives must be going through. The Japanese played for keeps. They were sure to call out their firing squad. Of the three who made the gallant attempt, I knew Charlie best. Only a fortnight back we'd played on the same soccer team. And now he was held in a condemned cell waiting to be shot. I anguished over him. I couldn't dismiss his boyish face from my mind. I consulted with our section leader Gerald Someck. And a good thing too; he was full of understanding – a sage. "You're going to have to learn that life is not always a bed of roses," he offered. "When distressed, you must put your mind to other things."

On my day off, a bleak January day as I recall, I was working my way through a rather difficult passage in *Aldrich's Written Chinese, Book II*, when Gerald Someck stepped over to my cot. Inexplicably, at that very instant, an eerie sense of *déjà vu* came over me. Even though I anticipated every word he was going to say, icy shivers shot through me when he said them:

"The Commandant wants to see you in his office."

"What for?" I blurted out.

"Something about you getting a transfer."

"To Bridge House, the Kempetai Interrogation Center?"

"Bridge House? Why do you say that? What have you been up to?"

My heart was pounding to beat the band. I lowered my eyes. "Nothing, Mr Someck, just curious, that's all."

"You'd better get to the office on the double. Don't keep the man waiting. Bates says he's beside himself over something."

"Is it about his chickens?"

"How in the world should I know? Now get on your feet. Hop to it."

I was utterly drained. I could scarcely take another step when the guard showed me into the Commandant's office.

But far from being "beside himself," Mr Horie Hayashi was all toothy smiles. "You are Desmond Power? Glad to see you." He stuck out a bony hand. "Your mother has been confined in Weihsien Civil Assembly Center. You are aware of that?"

"Yes. Didi Sayle who arrived from there last week gave me a message from her."

"She is well, I trust."

"Thank you. According to the message, she is all right."

"Of course she is all right. Weihsien is a much better place than here. It's half way between Tsinanfu and the

summer resort of Tsingtao. The climate is much better than Shanghai's, the food more abundant."

He knitted his brow. He stared at me with his doe-like eyes. "How would you like to be sent there?"

"Sent there?" My mind raced. Weihsien was five hundred miles to the north. Why would the Japanese go to the trouble? Was this a trick?

"I need time to think, sir."

"Time to think? You should jump at the chance. You've been a rather naughty boy, haven't you?"

He had me cold. He knew about the chickens. He was playing games with me.

"In times like these, families should be together. It's wrong to be separated. I'm not going to take no for an answer. Have your things packed and ready by nine o'clock tomorrow morning. My assistant, Mr Binsho, will take you to North Station where you will join a group of Italians who are being transported to Weihsien. Mr Binsho will accompany the party on the train journey north."

Thoughts whirled crazily through my mind. The Commandant was indeed playing games, earnest games, but not with me, with the chief of police. Was he not arranging for me to escape the man's clutches? But then what about those other chicken thieves, the Cance brothers and Garcia? The cat was out of the bag. I'd better go warn them, pronto.

	Name		Sex, Age, Nationality			Former Occupation
1256	PORTER	Muriel	F	47	B	-
7	"	John	M	49	B	Cloth Dyer
8	POSKIT	Edward	M	62	B	Sec, SSPCA
~~9~~	~~POWER~~	~~Desmond~~	~~M~~	~~20~~	~~B~~	~~Clerk~~
1260	PRATT	Donald	M	35	B	Accountant
1	"	Ethel	F	31	B	-
2	"	Joan	F	10	B	-
3	"	Virginia	F	4	B	-
4	"	Christopher	M	73	B	Manager
5	"	Jessy	F	71	B	-
6	PRICE	Frederick	M	62	B	Missionary
7	"	May Annie	F	43	B	"
8	"	Elizabeth	F	49	B	"
9	PRIESTLEY	Cecilia	F	55	B	-
1270	PRINCE	Harry	M	39	B	Police Officer
1	"	Elizabeth	F	36	B	-
2	PROUD	Henry	M	48	B	Engineer
3	"	Winnifred	F	38	B	-
4	"	Norma Ann	F	12	B	-
5	PUDDLE	Harold	M	47	B	Director - B.A.T
6	PURCELL	Richard	M	54	B	Merchant
7	"	Antoinette	F	42	B	-
8	PURCHAS	Stella	F	40	B	Teacher
9	PYM	Madeline	F	63	B	-
1280	QUINALL	Ahhendre	F	36	B	-
1	RADFORD	Stephen	M	48	B	Works Manager
2	"	Margaret	M	47	B	-
3	"	Stephen D.	M	19	B	-
4	RAFEN	May F.	F	69	B	-
5	RAMSAY	Anne	F	42	B	-
6	"	Edith	F	56	B	Manageress
7	"	Noel	M	67	B	Sales Rep
8	RANCK	Grace	F	47	B	-
9	"	John	M	14	B	-
1290	RANSON	Frederick	M	41	B	Surgeon
1	"	Emily	F	45	B	Nurse
2	RASEY	Rose	F	47	B	Missionary
3	RAPPAPORT	Lilly	F	40	B	Secretary
4	RAYDEN	Charles	M	43	B	Sec'y Race Club
5	"	Irene	F	39	B	-
6	READ	Robert	M	51	B	Accountant
7	"	Joan	F	46	B	-
8	"	Robert J	M	11	B	-
9	"	Moira	F	71	B	-
1300	"	George	M	24	B	Accountant
1	"	Elfreida	F	23	B	Stenographer
2	"	Philip	M	45	B	Merchant
3	"	Bernard	M	56	B	Med. Researcher
4	"	Charles	M	26	B	Office Sec'y
5	"	Polinbina	F	48	B	Music Teacher
6	REEVES	William	M	49	B	Shipbroker
7	"	Lucy	F	43	B	-
8	"	Mary	F	82	B	-
9	RENARD	Marcel	M	43	Bel.	Banker
1310	"	Maria	F	33	Bel.	-
1	RICHARDS	Cecil	M	40	Amer	Crew SS Harrison

Removed to Weishien 31-1-44

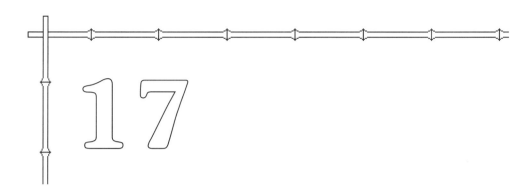

COURTYARD OF THE HAPPY WAY

U NDER THE AUSPICES of His Most Divine Majesty, Emperor Hirohito, I embarked on my grand tour of ancient Cathay seated alongside Mr Vice Commandant Binsho in the rear seat of an olive-green, consular-issue, 1939 Chevvy. Mine host saw to it that the driver took a bit of a side trip so I could see for myself the very spot where the three New Year's Eve escapees had been apprehended. "Very foolish of them," Mr Binsho remarked. "Most exceedingly foolish. The military wanted them shot out of hand, but the good Horie Hayashi San intervened. He managed to have them transferred to the civil authorities. They are now in Ward Road Jail."

Most elevating that news, not that I needed elevating, the trip going like clockwork – the train on time, the group of Italians I was to travel with already there on the platform at Shanghai North when we arrived. I stared, rudely. How could I help it? Except for the one or two with red, swollen eyes you never would have dreamt they were on their way to a prison camp, the men suave in homburgs and fine worsted, the women chic in mink and white fox, both genders reeking with perfume. The scene reminiscent of those old Orient Express films, the players anxious for the train to go and for the mystery and romance to begin. But that's as far as the similarities went. When the Japanese gave the order to board, the Italians refused to comply. And the fiercer the Japanese ranted and flashed their bayonets, the more the Italians circled about, gesticulating, beseeching the heavens. But the bayonets finally prevailed, and the whole contingent, letting off steam like a triumphant chorus from some grand opera, paraded up the iron steps and into the hard-seat carriage.

One of the group, a middle-aged man with silver and black hair, meticulously brushed, asked with a show of Victorian propriety if he might occupy the seat next to mine. He introduced himself as Signor Giovanni Piscatelli, founder of Shanghai's celebrated Marco Polo Gallery. His English was as fluent as a Cambridge don's. Easy to see why; he gave it constant practice. "Have you ever been to Peking?" he asked. And then immediately: "Have you seen the Temple of Heaven? Breathtaking, not a nail in its construction. Did you know that? And did you know that Hsi An was once Chang An, China's ancient capital? And that if you visit the place as I have done you will be rewarded by the sight of a magnificent bell tower. I know about bell towers. Do you want to learn about bell towers?" Before I had a chance to consider his offer, he was jerking his chin to draw my attention to the passengers on our left. Then with head inclined and mouth shielded by a hand, he uttered, guardedly: "Tragic case that Signora Depretis. Her husband was executed by firing squad. He paid the price for scuttling his ship. And he was only following Badoglio's orders . . ."

Involuntarily, I glanced over to the left. Only one signora in view, but oh, what a signora – raven-haired, sultry, mysterious . . . Merle Oberon in person, or perhaps Hedy Lamarr . . .

That brief spell of being allowed my own thoughts came to an abrupt end when the irrepressible art dealer caught hold of my hand and gave it an unpleasant squeeze. "No, not that one," he whispered. "That one is Signorina Mazzini, a Sardinian from Cagliari. I mean the fair one, the tall one from Rome. Where is she? She must have left her seat. By the way, I have to tell you that I have traveled this line before. I know every yard of it. I know Nanking. I know Kaifeng. I have climbed Tai Shan, China's sacred mountain. I know that mountain as Confucius knew that mountain. I know Shantung Province. I have been to Weihaiwei, Tsingtao, Chefoo, and, of course, Weihsien, which, in case you are unaware, happens to be our destination. I wish to enlighten you with the fact that Weihsien is renowned for its hand-painted New Year pictures. Did you know that China's finest calligrapher,

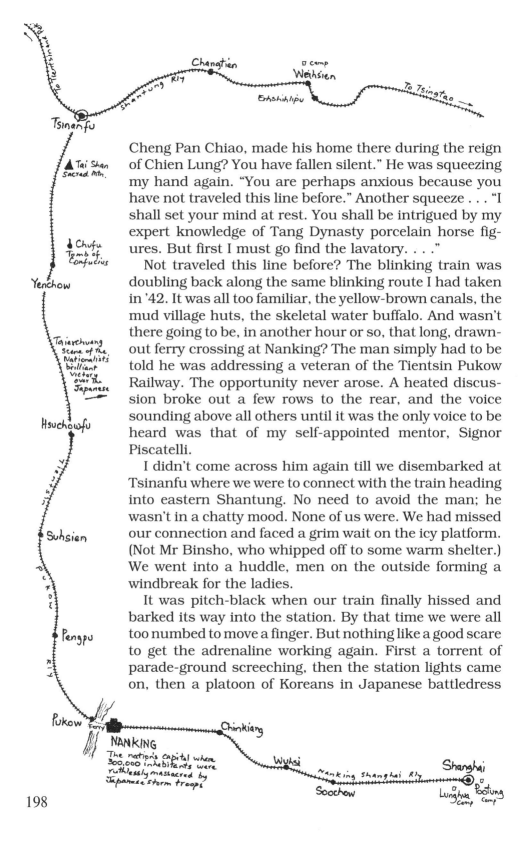

Cheng Pan Chiao, made his home there during the reign of Chien Lung? You have fallen silent." He was squeezing my hand again. "You are perhaps anxious because you have not traveled this line before." Another squeeze . . . "I shall set your mind at rest. You shall be intrigued by my expert knowledge of Tang Dynasty porcelain horse figures. But first I must go find the lavatory. . . ."

Not traveled this line before? The blinking train was doubling back along the same blinking route I had taken in '42. It was all too familiar, the yellow-brown canals, the mud village huts, the skeletal water buffalo. And wasn't there going to be, in another hour or so, that long, drawn-out ferry crossing at Nanking? The man simply had to be told he was addressing a veteran of the Tientsin Pukow Railway. The opportunity never arose. A heated discussion broke out a few rows to the rear, and the voice sounding above all others until it was the only voice to be heard was that of my self-appointed mentor, Signor Piscatelli.

I didn't come across him again till we disembarked at Tsinanfu where we were to connect with the train heading into eastern Shantung. No need to avoid the man; he wasn't in a chatty mood. None of us were. We had missed our connection and faced a grim wait on the icy platform. (Not Mr Binsho, who whipped off to some warm shelter.) We went into a huddle, men on the outside forming a windbreak for the ladies.

It was pitch-black when our train finally hissed and barked its way into the station. By that time we were all too numbed to move a finger. But nothing like a good scare to get the adrenaline working again. First a torrent of parade-ground screeching, then the station lights came on, then a platoon of Koreans in Japanese battledress charged onto the platform and into one of the carriages. They began yelling at the Chinese passengers to get off. Not a Chinese budged. The Koreans set upon them with shovel handles. Despite crunching blows and spurting blood, the Chinese held their ground. At the height of the fray, Mr Binsho arrived with a squad of Japanese regulars. No contest; they cleared the carriage at bayonet point. It was ours now, blood stains and all.

Never mind the foul air of the packed compartment, I luxuriated in its warmth. From the seat directly opposite, the Sardinian beauty whom I'd seen far too little of since crossing the Yangtze (she seemed always to be under the protection of two, sometimes three Romeos), fixed me in a stony stare. Me? Why me? I was never to know. Call it timidity, call it cold feet, call it what you like, I dropped my eyes and stared at my hands. It was while I was intertwining my fingers, twisting them, stretching them, wondering whether it was safe to sneak a glance, that the man next to me leaned his green-tinged, eau de Cologne-smelling forehead right against mine and with a voice from the tomb let out: "Will the Japanese treat us the way they treated those poor *Cinesi* at the last stop?"

"Yes, if you break the rules."

"Did they beat you?"

"They beat me many times, but never could they break my spirit." That was an outright lie of course, but then wouldn't the audience, especially the Sardinian signorina, hold me forever in awesome respect?

Moments later I sat even taller in my seat. That was when the Valentino with the oiled-down hair and toreador's sideburns snapped open a briefcase, drew out a glistening bottle of Vat 69, and tapped it with his immaculately polished fingernails. Did I think he could sneak it in, he wanted to know. I was front and center stage, and I made the most of it. With narrowed eyes I drew a finger slowly across my throat. What a rumpus that set off! What wailing! What yammering! But it all simmered down when the one who was forever crossing himself forced open the window and tossed the bottle out into the darkness.

The swaying carriage drummed a lullaby, consoling the weepers and silencing the whisperers. We dozed off, heads on borrowed shoulders. I was adrift a million miles away in some other sphere when a sudden violent furor jolted me back to earth. It was a guard at the carriage door

199

screeching furiously at us to get off the train. I had to call on my very last ounce of will to force my cramped joints to obey. But once down on the platform, a few whiffs of the chilled champagne air, and I was revived. While the others milled about, slapping their sides, muttering oaths, I edged towards the perimeter wire fence, drawn there by a scene straight out of the Celestial Empire – a massive city wall, a towering rampart gate, awesome yet serene in the pink early morning light. This must be Weihsien then, the ancient county seat of Wei, renowned through history (according to Mr Piscatelli) for its calligraphers, its painters . . . A sudden hard shove put a stop to my musing. Another shove and I realized I was in the path of puppet militiamen, swaggering, cursing, hawking, spitting.

"Look, the Eastern Devils have roped in more of the Western Devils."

"They're going to finish them off."

"Should have done so long ago."

"The Westerners refuse to board the trucks."

"Give them a jab with the bayonet."

"Let the Easterners handle it. It's their problem."

"Just listen to the fuss the Western Devils are making."

Several of the more fiery Italians were protesting loudly about the filthy state of the trucks. One of them grabbed hold of me. "Interpret," he yelled into my face. "Tell them they must clean out the horse dung." Me tell them? And set myself up for a beating? I shook my head. Undeterred, they stood their ground until the kicking started, and the slapping, and the rifle butts to the small of the back. We all clambered aboard – obligingly. In our truck, standing room only. When it shot forward, it was only the flimsy tailgate that prevented us from collapsing like a house of cards. With every lurch on the rutted road we clung wildly to each other for balance. (Where oh where was my black-eyed Sardinian?) Out in open country the ride somewhat smoother, but no less daunting. In every direction grave mounds of countless generations studded the sullen landscape, a perfect setting for the Day of Last Judgement. . . .

The truck made a wide swing, then headed straight for a stand of wintry trees. Moments later, a collection of buildings, some Western design, some Chinese, began to show through the screen of leafless branches. We pulled up before a grand ceremonial gateway. Foot-high Chinese

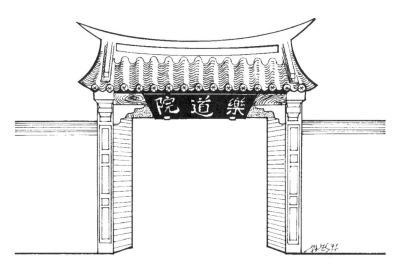

Within this portal lies the "Courtyard of the Happy Way"

characters emblazoned on the high arch spelled out the words: *LE DAO YUAN – Courtyard of the Happy Way.* If it's such a happy place, I reflected, then why the electrified barbed wire strung all along the wall? Why the watchtowers? And why all that angry Japanese shouting to get us down from the trucks?

As we proceeded single file under the arch and into the camp, my heart suddenly leapt to my throat. There in the front row of a cluster of internees stood Tai-tai. I stared unbelievingly. A shabby smock hung from her shoulders. Her dark auburn hair, now streaked with gray, was tied in a bun. Her cheekbones protruded, but her eyes still shone with that fierce look of determination I knew so well.

The instant she spotted me, she let out a verbal volley: "Lovely to see you . . . but you're all skin and bones . . . never mind, we'll fatten you up in time for your birthday . . ."

Birthday? I had completely forgotten that my birthday, my twenty-first, was only a fortnight off.

Tangy wood smoke permeates the 10 x 10 hut Tai-tai shares with my half-sister Betty. Our ecstatic reunion over, Tai-tai attends to the kettle singing on the sooty brick stove, the centerpiece of her worldly goods. I am saddened for her. What a comedown – no cook, no boy, no coolie. But I am also happy for her. She has possession of a hut. (What fireworks for all concerned had she been

201

stuck in one of those twenty-bed dormitories!) Though there is hardly room to turn, visitors pile in: Half-brother Tony, Gerry Lucker (his late mother and Tai-tai were classmates at the Tsingtao Convent), Vincy Murray, Bessie and Lucy Attree, their parents Tommy and Anna. A loaf of date bread appears, and biscuits and tea. Just like old times. Everyone is speaking at once, paying no attention to the knocking on the door until it turns persistent. Mr Binsho stands at the entrance, bowing little Japanese bows.

"Pardon my intrusion, Mrs Power, I have come to pass on the compliments of Mr Horie Hayashi, Commandant of Lunghua Civil Assembly Center."

Stupefied silence. But what else to expect from Weihsienites totally unfamiliar with Hayashi's eccentric ways?

Tai-tai rises to the occasion. "Sorry, you took me by surprise. You see, I haven't been called Mrs Power for so long. I've been Mrs Lambert for twenty years. Do come in. Have a chair."

"No, no, thank you very much, Madame. I will not impose myself. I just want to make sure that your son is in safe hands. Those are the orders of my superior in Lunghua."

"He looks well." Tai-tai announces, shooting me a fond glance. "Your superior is most generous for delivering him to me. Please convey to him my heartfelt thanks. Tell him I shall never forget his act of human decency."

"Yes, Mr Hayashi is indeed a humanist, and in more ways than you suspect. For instance, Madame, he removed your son from gross moral danger."

I stare uncomprehendingly at Mr Binsho and then at Tai-tai. Her eyes are wide with astonishment.

"Your son has been exceedingly naughty."

"Naughty?"

"Yes, you see, Madame, we had occasion to observe him, arm in arm with a young lady, entering a forbidden area of demolished buildings, obviously with indecent intent."

There is nowhere I can hide my burning face.

My first roll call in Weihsien, so different from those Shanghai camps. In Pootung they counted us off in a murky go-down, in Lunghua on a dilapidated stage, here they had us form up in a court bordered on two sides by elegant ivy-clad classroom buildings in the style of 1890's America, and on the other two by venerable plantings of azalea and lilac. In the court's right-hand corner stood a *tingzi*, a summer pavilion, as picturesque as you'd ever see in ancient Soochow. All around me faces glowed pink, eyes shone. Hayashi was right. The air sweet and unpolluted, Weihsien had to be healthier by far than Lunghua. And to think I had resisted Hayashi's offer to move me to this place!

Assigned to the job of stoker at Kitchen Two (the kitchen that catered to some nine hundred internees from the Tientsin area), I was quick to catch the uplifting spirit that prevailed on the shift. No grousing, no scrimshanking. The shift boss, Major Evenden, and his assistant, Major Sowton, both of the Salvation Army, led by example, never balking at the dirtiest task. It was they who sifted through the half-rotting sinews and entrails of the day's meat supply, slicing off whatever edible pieces they could find for the communal pot. At clean-up time it was they who rolled up their sleeves and reached for the scrubbing brushes to tackle the *guos*, the giant cauldrons in which all the food was boiled. They seldom found fault, but neither did they lavish praise. Therefore it took only a smile, a single word of approval after a hard day's work, and we were off to the washhouse glowing. Everyone on shift vied for that approval. When feeding fires, I put on quite a show, clanging my shovel against the cast-iron doors. I smashed clinkers with a foundryman's ferocity. But then I had an additional motive for gaining Major Evenden's attention – his daughter, the radiant Eleanor, was in camp.

As it so happened, I did indeed gain the Major's attention, but not in the way I had intended. I did it with a breach of conduct that even after fifty years has me squirming whenever it comes to mind.

Because all of our water – drinking water, toilet water, laundry water – had to be pumped by hand from a well, a bucket was an inmate's most prized possession. On my second day in Weihsien I found that Tai-tai of all people had no bucket. For two years she'd managed with an enamel washbasin, but managed awkwardly, slopping half the contents before getting it back to her hut. And the

4.45 a.m.
Clinkers drawn,
fire roaring, and
No. 1 Guo "singing",
which ought to
please the cooks
when they arrive.

situation so easily remedied. I reported for work at 3:30 a.m. when the kitchen was bathed in morgue-like silence (the cooks didn't arrive on shift till 6:00), and where in a neat row stood four buckets of gleaming zinc, all for the taking. As far as I was concerned, it was perks, fair and square. At 4:00 a.m. I deposited a bucket outside Tai-tai's door. At 8:00 a.m., after the sour bread-porridge had been served up and Number One *Guo* was ready to be cleaned and refilled for the day's soup, Major Evenden asked: "Desmond, did you happen to see anyone come in to borrow one of our buckets?" At 8:15 Major Sowton asked the same question. And the same again a little later from cook's helper, Gavin Chapman.

"No, Major Evenden, I did not" . . . "No, Major Sowton, I did not" . . . "No, Gavin I did not." And that, strictly speaking, was gospel. Other than those on shift, not a soul came in that I saw.

End of the matter? Regrettably, not. The said bucket sprang a leak, and Tai-tai took it to the official tinsmith (her long-time friend George Cox) to have it fixed. And George, noticing the symbol K2 tooled into its base, mentioned to Charles Peacock how curious it was that Kitchen Two was lending out buckets. Mr Peacock mentioned it in passing to my old TGS science master, Mr Foxlee, within earshot of ex-BMC Chief of Police Lawless, head of the camp's Discipline Committee. When word got

Soup line-up at
No. 2 Kitchen
–
Woe betide the
stoker who can't
bring the *guo*
to the boil !

out that an investigation was under way, Tai-tai crashed the Discipline Office and delivered such a tongue-lashing, the poor beleaguered police chief thought twice about laying charges. As for me, I would far rather have undergone the stiffest punishment meted out by the Discipline Office than face up to Major Evenden. But no avoiding it. I hung my head. I made my Act of Contrition. "Major, I am deeply ashamed. It won't happen again, I promise you. You see, my mother, not having a bucket, I . . ."

"Think no more of it, young fellah. We all make mistakes. Heaven knows I've made enough in my time. Now look to Number Two *Guo*. The fire's too high. Bank it down a bit."

He did not know, he could not possibly know, how deeply he touched me, how for the first time in my twenty-one years I felt what it was like to have a father.

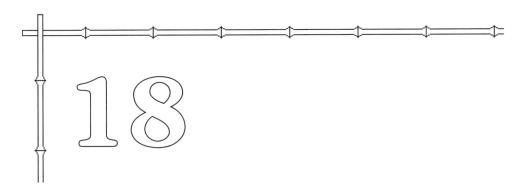

THE GAME IS UP

WASN'T IT TOLSTOY who said something to the effect that it is the endless variety of men's minds which prevents a truth from ever presenting itself identically to two persons? Whoever said it, sonovagun, how true!

Ask Denis O'Shea what's the first thing that strikes him when he thinks back to Pootung, and he'll tell you it's the specter of hunger. Embedded in his memory is the line of gaunt figures waiting for the day's ladle of soupy-thin cracked wheat. Put that same question to me, and I'll tell you that Pootung spells overcrowding. Even now I can see the musty go-downs jam-packed with rough, raw Joseph Conrad characters.

And what Tommy Rudland remembers first and foremost about Lunghua may not necessarily be what springs to my mind – that most wondrous concentration of goddesses ever to smite a mortal's eye.

And I'll be more than a little surprised if band leader Earl West's immediate impression of Weihsien is the one I have – a unique mixing of the spiritual and the worldly, of the highbrow and lowbrow, in that microcosm of the foreign presence in China.

And a unique mixing it surely was. In scouring Mongolia, Manchuria, and China's northern provinces for "dangerous" enemy aliens, the Japanese dragged up a veritable cornucopia of churchmen, academics, doctors, lawyers, engineers, bankers, traders, shopkeepers, clerks, entertainers, vagrants, even a felon or two on the "wanted" list of half the nations of Europe.

What a rare opportunity for religionists of every persuasion to debate the existence of free will, for archeologists to speculate on Han funeralware, for classicists to expound on the *Book of Songs,* the *Book of Rites*, the *Analects of Confucius*. And what a chance to argue their hearts out, those taipans and bankers and traders, over the pros and cons of re-introducing the silver standard, of manipulating the currency exchange rate.

The enforced togetherness in the over-crowded pen brought about an unheard of degree of fraternizing between those perennial rivals, the seekers of souls and the seekers of profit, though it has to be said there still remained under the surface a festering concern that one side was undercutting the other's God-given rights in China.

"The Game is Up" was the theme of the guest speaker (a missionary doctor with a Harvard PhD) at one of the regular Friday night businessmen's discussion groups I attended. From the start he had the group on edge. At the conclusion he had them bristling. "First thing you people ought to do when the war comes to an end is sell out and head back to the States, the UK, Australia, Canada. It's not too late to start life anew."

"Doctor, you've been stuck too long at Yenching University. You know nothing of the business world. Don't you realize the treaty ports will simply collapse without us? The Chinese don't have the foggiest idea how to run our businesses. Tientsin and Shanghai will go the way of Hankow. Have you been to Hankow? Have you seen how the place has gone to the dogs?"

"By your colonial standards that might well be the case. But if that's what the Chinese want, that's what they're going to get. You'll simply have to face the fact that they now call the shots. The unequal treaties have been abolished. The British Concession in Tientsin and the International Settlement in Shanghai have been handed back to their rightful owners."

"You are obviously referring to that silly masquerade when the Japanese authorities presented our concession's title deeds to those scalawag puppets."

"Not at all. I am referring to the joint abrogation of our special rights in China by Roosevelt and Churchill. Ask your own camp leader Ted McLaren. He knows all about the agreement signed last year. He got the details from the Swiss representative Egger on his last visit."

"I can't believe it," snorted the pudding-faced Yorkshireman, Albert Pym. "I built up my wool packing business by the sweat of my brow. The equipment, the stock, the warehouses, they're all mine. As for the land, I hold title to the crown lease which the BMC is obliged to honor. Besides, just before Pearl Harbor, our Consul General insisted that we stay to protect Britain's assets. He never would have done so had the intention been to sell out."

"Your Consul led you down the garden path, and I'll warrant it's not the first time that that has happened."

The normally reserved Jock Mackay of Mackay Imports broke out of his shell. "With all due respect, Doctor, you don't know Tientsin. Tientsin is not your academic Peking. From the turn of the century Tientsin's concessions have been the driving force behind North China's robust international trade. The Chinese don't have a clue how to run things. They can't do without us."

"They most certainly *can* do without you. They can do without your Jardines, your Sasoons, your machinery, your opium. Every last one of you will have to pull up stakes. But it's not the end of the world. After all, you've had a good innings – all milk and honey. Why, even here in this camp you're a lot better off than most Chinese."

"And a lot happier, I suppose you are going to say, than we ever were at the Country Club . . ."

"You may not know it, but you really are. I'll wager you've never been so contented, so fulfilled. You all yearn to be free. You talk of nothing much else. Yet, ironically, once outside this place you are going to miss it. You are going to experience a strange let-down, a vague disquiet. You will feel as if you've lost something vital. You will grope for that something. You won't find it because you won't know what you're looking for. So I'll tell you right here and now what that something is. It is the deep-rooted instinct latent in all human beings – the instinct of the tribe, working for the common good, standing shoulder to shoulder in the face of danger. It is the flame that ignites brothers-in-arms, that inspires pilgrims. It breathed life into the early Christian communes. It is the driving force behind the modern-day kibbutz. But alas, dear friends, alas, we never seem to realize that it has touched us until we have moved on to other things. So I earnestly encourage you to savor this moment. Make the most of it. You may never experience it again in your lifetime . . ."

"Next you'll be telling us it's a privilege to be locked up here."

"Yes, that's exactly my point!"

Shouts of derision, hoots of laughter. And I was one of the hooters.

But then, boy oh boy, didn't it hit home, the professor's message, when peace eventually came, and we were thrust into the dog-eat-dog world? Why had it eluded us during our imprisonment? The signs were all there. Even though we should have experienced that soul-destroying scourge of prison life, the slow-slow creep of time – nothing of the kind. The opposite in fact. The months simply flashed by.

Nevertheless, those months were not without their moments of excitement. There was an escape. Laurance Tipton (British) and Arthur Hummel (American) went over the wall one dark and moonless night. And didn't that send our Nagasaki jailers into hysterics! Then, completely out of the blue, Brian Clarke arrived in camp, transferred as I was from Lunghua. He brought news of a second Lunghua escape which, unlike the one on New Year's Eve 1944, was successful – the five men involved getting clean away to Kunming in free China. The fact that I knew four of the five added spice to the news. One was Reggie Euluch, Brian's buddy, who helped settle me in when I arrived from Pootung, two were fellow Pootung transferees – Tommy Huxley and Mike Levy, and the fourth, Roy Scott, crossed paths with me at the Columbia Country Club following the *Kamakura Maru* fiasco. Only Lewis Murray-Kidd, the escape leader, was a total stranger.

Why the flurry of escapes? For one thing, the food situation was going from bad to worse. In Weihsien our rations were so reduced that camp leader McLaren picked out six of the skinniest inmates and had them parade bare-chested before the Commandant. I was one of the six. Mr McLaren gave an impassioned speech. He pointed at our corrugated ribcages, our jutting cheek bones. He quoted the Geneva Convention. The Commandant's response was equally impassioned. "You people are luckier than you think. You are better off than the citizens of our home islands. You have more to eat than our soldiers in the field. Even so, I have managed to postpone a reduction of your vegetable marrow allocation. But I won't be able to do that again. You must expect cuts. And you won't be the only ones affected. I've already told my chief of police that the guards' rations are to be reduced. It's a bad time for everybody. You must remember there's a war on. And as long as the war continues, I can do no more for you."

But he did do more, a lot more – for us Limies, that is. I am referring here to the episode that kicked off with a breath-taking spectacle, a biblical caravan (if you can visualize Shantung mules as the camels of Araby) trundling through the ceremonial gateway and up the incline towards the main road, heavily laden with cardboard cartons, stamped triumphantly with the universal symbol of the Red Cross.

Camp interpreter Al Voyce, who was present when the Commandant inspected three of the cartons, got himself all tongue-tied describing their fabulous contents: Klim, Spam, Hershey Bars, cheese-spread, coffee, sugar. And clothing too: shirts, pants, sweaters, field jackets, boots. But it was all too good to be true for those of us who did not hail from the *Sweet Land of Liberty*. We were dealt a gut-wrenching blow by a group of Americans (missionaries predominantly) who raised a great big stink with the Commandant. They demanded that he hand over the cartons to Americans only. They stated that it was both illegal and immoral to do otherwise because stamped on the outside of each and every carton were the words: GIFT OF THE AMERICAN RED CROSS.

For a week the cartons remained stacked in the church while the Commandant pondered the issue. In the end his Buddhist principles prevailed over the claimants' Christian ones. He saw to it that those considered alien by the American Red Cross (as the claimants had led him to believe), alien Britons, alien Hollanders, alien Belgians, all got a share of the prize. And he didn't omit the alien Italians, the elegant set I traveled with from Shanghai, who, for reasons best known to Tokyo, were walled off together with their Peking, Tientsin, and Tsingtao compatriots in a camp of their own, a camp within a camp so to speak. (Though I was never more than 150 yards from them the whole time I was in Weihsien, not once did I catch sight of my travel companions, not Signor Piscatelli, not

Signorina Mazzini, my dusky Sardinian Cleopatra.)

What grand parties we had, decked out in our spanking new khaki finery, savoring the long-forgotten aroma of coffee, gorging on Spam and cheese and chocolate! What a bonanza for us! What a bitter pill for the Japanese who were more and more feeling the pinch! For weeks their invincible army had been at the point of crushing British resistance at the gateway to India and snatching up for their own Emperor the vast sub-continent, the jewel in the British crown. But something must have gone awry in their plans. *Peking Chronicle's* repeated headline: "IRON RING AROUND IMPHAL" went from the front to the middle to the back page before disappearing altogether. A little while later there was brief mention of such and such Imperial Japanese division putting up a gallant last ditch stand against overwhelming odds near Mandalay. Mandalay! They must have been chased right back across Burma. And then there were those *Domei News* reports openly admitting the immense devastation and loss of life caused by the non-stop fire bombing of Tokyo by massed B29s. Where were all those Japanese victories that only half a year ago had been our daily fare? The scant few reported were so spiced with statistics as to border on the ridiculous. There was that front page piece (the American landing at Okinawa was squished into three lines on page 5) about Japanese invincibility which went something like this: "*In a brilliant frontal attack, shock troops of the Seventeenth Field Regiment, Watanabe Brigade, smashed through Chinese defenses at Changsha, killing 1,827 and capturing 2,132, together with 76 machine guns, 3,002 rifles, 129,837 rounds of ammunition, 126 bicycles, 31 trucks, 59 mule carts, and 116 wheelbarrows. Japanese casualties: 3 killed, 14 wounded – 5 seriously, 9 walking cases. . . .*"

Good for a laugh? Yes, if we could but for a moment forget our captors' ruthless side, which we could not. We were, after all, hostages held at their mercy. It didn't take much to put two and two together: the ten-foot ditch that had been dug outside the southeast wall, and Field Marshall Terauchi's public threat that the moment the Americans attempted a landing on Honshiu all Allied prisoners were to be butchered. But it was curtains anyway if a stray Yankee thousand-pound bomb landed smack on the Imperial Palace. Fortunately, nothing of the kind – no landing, no errant bomb. What did occur though was entirely unforeseen – our captors' iron hard discipline began coming apart at the seams. At first it titillated us, the crazy night-time drinking bouts sounding in their compound. Not so funny when the weird yells and demented chants turned into blood-curdling screams followed by volleys of shots as they turned on each other. And it got downright dangerous when their gunfights spilled over onto our side of the wire. Block monitors went from dormitory to dormitory warning everyone to stay indoors after lights out.

"What if I have to have a pee?" Vincy Murray asked our block monitor, the flamboyant academic, Doctor Lucius Porter.

"Try to hold on till morning."

"What if I can't?"

"Then use a tin can like I do."

Even during daylight hours we had to be on the alert. *Saki*, we were told, had delayed action; some of the guards might still be sozzled. One certainly was. He mislaid his Mauser, and a young mother found her four-year-old playing with it outside her hut – it was loaded and cocked. No good Mr McLaren protesting to the Commandant. The man had lost what little influence he had over his chief of police, and the chief was fast losing control of his men. Where they had been operating the black market strictly on the q.t. (after snaffling it from our own racketeers), a guard would approach us openly now, offering eggs or *baigar* (local firewater), in exchange for a watch, a ring, gold teeth. But there'd be trouble if another guard happened by. They'd start hollering at each other as only the Japanese can holler. When they reached for their holsters, it was time to cut and run. They weren't playing games; they could have taught Capone's hit men a thing or two. One morning the camp was presented with the horrific spectacle of a corpse draped over the electrified barbed wire. The peasant, poor soul, had apparently arrived late with his delivery of eggs; there had been a change of guard, and the replacement, a man from a rival black-market gang, flipped on the switch.

It was clear to one and all that we were living through the most dangerous period of our internment. The affable, worldly-wise American, Gerald Detring Lucker, summed it up best when he said: "We are in a race against time.

The longer it takes the warring Japanese to come to terms with the warring Allies, the more certain our chances of running afoul of the warring guards. And there's not a damned thing we can do about it except sit tight and hope for the best."

Viewed from the ten-foot ditch:
the electrified barbed wire,
the southeast guard tower,
and section of the hospital wing.

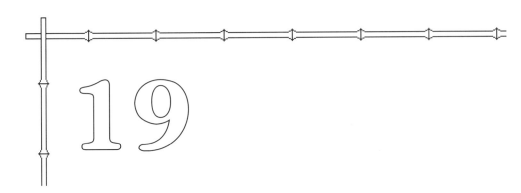

19

"TSAO NI MAMA, BU-SHING-DI!"

IT IS NOW AUGUST 1945, the third August of our internment, and the stress is beginning to tell. A lot of people are getting on edge, some are close to cracking, one for sure has already cracked. He or she is an ax-wielding maniac who has taken to decapitating cats, those forlorn strays that on wandering in through the wire were instantly clutched to the bosom of our incorrigible cat lovers. (Yes, cat lovers persisted in our midst as they persist in every society under the sun.) And then there is the strange case of lay preacher, Garth Jergens, a long-armed orangutan of a man, who gulps down his lamp-oil issue the moment he receives it, who at full moon climbs the tallest tree so he can fill the high heavens with blood-curdling wolf calls. And what about that shocking exposé of the gang-bang orgies conducted on a Caligulan scale in the den of a depraved gypsy woman, the players under her direction comprising her own two adolescent daughters and a clutch of twelve- and thirteen-year-olds, several of them the sons of taipans. Wow!

I pride myself on keeping mostly on even keel. After all, I'm a veteran of three camps. Come to think of it, I've been under three different commandants. Not many can claim that. I say "*mostly on even keel*" because from time to time I do suffer the odd lapse, just like that Canadian missionary I'd heard tell of who lapsed into "cabin fever" when by a trick of fate he was marooned for a whole year in the northern tundra. And fate plays tricks on me too, for what else but fate has me standing on the balcony of our second-floor dormitory when the roll-call bell sounds? And why, when I would normally be taking my place in line, do I stay put, gazing idly down at the men and women of Block 24 being shepherded to their mustering point by that portly, blustery nincompoop, Sergeant Bu-shing-di?

He is called Bu-shing-di because he is forever yelling *bu shing* this and *bu shing* that. (*Bu shing* being his throaty attempt at the Chinese vernacular for "no can do" and the *di* ending similar to the "er" in such English words as "fighter," "singer," etc.) It's been about a year now since that pompous sergeant, affronted by his sobriquet, took it up as a grievance with the Commandant. And to oblige him, the Commandant posted an order on the camp notice board stating: "*It is forbidden to call Sergeant Bu-shing-di, Sergeant Bu-shing-di. Henceforth everyone must, under pain of punishment, address Sergeant Bu-shing-di as Sergeant Sato!*"

But back to my moment of madness. Before I can stop myself, I am shouting out for the whole world to hear that most profane of street argot profanities: "*Wo tsao ni mama!*" (I copulate with your mother) Bu-shing-di stops dead. He cocks his head, puzzled. He can't make out the source of the outcry. Still under some terrible demonic influence, I raise my voice even louder: "*Bu-shing-di, wo tsao ni mama!*" (In naming him, I am implying that he is the result of my copulation.) He spots me. He springs for the building entrance. Instantly myself again, I make a mad dash for the stairwell where we line up, one inmate to a stair. And just in time, for Bu-shing-di is already half-way up the stairs, ranting like a mad bull. Close on his heels, interpreter Al Voyce is sweet-talking him. It has no effect. The enraged beast comes to a ponderous halt and puts a throttle hold on the first person within reach, a youth, the ward of that gentlest of gentlemen, the Reverend Simms-Lee of the Anglican Church. I don't need the gauntlet of eyes to tell me what I must do. My nodding head and foolish smile ought to assure Brian Clarke, Speed Murray, Doug Finlay, Art Kerridge, John Simmonds, and all the rest that I know what I must do, and that I'm going to do it. But first a gulp of air to combat the icy constriction in my breast. That buys me time to reconsider. Surely there must be some other way. There has to be. But there is no other way. So this is it? Game over! As if detached from myself, I step forward. Between hasty

Out on the balcony of Block 23 Room 9 "X" marks the spot where Des shouted down at Sergeant Bu-shing-di

gasps I force out in a thin falsetto: "*Shi wo, shi wo.*" (I am the one, I am the one.) The brutish grip on my shirt-front lifts me off my feet and thrusts me back and forth like a rat in a terrier's jaw. The stairwell spins. The block monitor's pleas sound vaguely in the distance. Then the blows begin, but they are not the nose-crunching, lip-splitting blows of the Japanese, which everyone knows can crack a millstone when delivered with the edge of the hand, rather they are motherly pats to the cheek, and each pat accompanied by a peevish chide mouthed in Mandarin – the tones all wrong: "*Huai haizi, bu shing, bu shing.*" (Naughty boy, no can do, no can do.)

Afterwards, Brian Clarke corners me. He shakes his head. "You were damned lucky to get away with it."

He never said a truer word. Talk about luck! How lucky for me it didn't happen six months earlier when the Japanese were still cock-a-hoop. It would have been a different story then, and I wouldn't be here to tell it.

Easy to see why our captors were no longer cock-a-hoop; they were losing on all fronts. We knew that from reading between the lines of the *Peking Chronicle*. And when that paper stopped coming in, we still kept abreast of world events simply by scanning the Japanese dailies, many of us capable of interpreting the root Chinese of their *Kanji* script. But came the inevitable day when no amount of grubbing about the guards' dustbins would

216

land us an *Asahi Shimbun*. We existed in a vacuum, an ideal breeding ground for rumors. There was that electrifying report of Russia declaring war on Japan and the mighty Red Army sweeping through Manchuria. The pessimists pooh-poohed it. Not so our block's prize optimist who was quick to point out that the Commandant himself had begun calling Stalin some very naughty names. But then our hopes were dashed when one of the more dependable guards told Bobby Grandon that Russia had indeed launched an all out attack, but not against the Japanese – they were crushing the British and American armies in Germany. Several days later we were up again in the clouds when the well-regarded Father De Jaegher told George Cox that he knew for certain the war *was* over. It took the rebuttal of Dr Mortimer Brown, the celebrated author of *The Taoist Influence In Shinto Thought*, to bring us back to earth. "Wishful thinking," he declared at a gathering in Kitchen One. "We're stuck here for another two years at least. Lieutenant Tominaga, a Berkeley grad – and Berkeley men, as everyone knows, are totally above lying – has just advised me of the stunning victory won by the Imperial Japanese Navy in the seas near Okinawa. They sent two US battleships and three fleet carriers to the bottom. And that's not all. The *Kamikaze*, the divine wind that saved Japan so miraculously in the thirteenth century, has dealt the US fleet such a devastating blow that Subic Bay is now a graveyard of American ships. Admiral Nimitz has gone stark raving mad . . . General MacArthur has been relieved of command . . . President Truman is suing for terms. . . ."

The cold certainty of Dr Brown's statement sent our spirits plummeting. We were down in the deepest dumps when word spread that Mr McLaren was going to make an earth-shaking announcement in Kitchen Two quadrangle. He arrived with John Stewart, number one at British American Tobacco, and Sandy Cameron of Hongkong Bank. Three taipans! The earth-shaking news they were about to disclose couldn't be any more official.

"Ladies and Gentlemen," announced the good Mr McLaren. "We have reason to believe the war is over. We ask you to remain calm, to carry on as usual. We'll keep you informed of developments. No questions, please. No questions. . . ."

So what was so earth-shaking about that? We'd heard

that rumor a dozen times or more. And carry on as usual? For how long? When the day ended, then another, and yet another, and still the same routine, lining up for roll call, for a watery meal, for the toilet, black despair engulfed the camp. . . .

"What do you think is happening, sir? What should we believe?" I asked Doctor Robinson who was treating me for boils.

"Take it from me, laddie, the war *is* over. The Commandant will have to come out with it any moment now."

The USAAF beat the Commandant to it. On August 17th 1945, at exactly nine o'clock in the morning, an almighty blast just about shook our dormitory building off its foundations. We gazed goggle-eyed at one another: "What the heck was that?" . . . "Train crash?" . . . "Earthquake?" . . . "Bomb?"

"Shut up," Brian Clarke snapped. "Listen."

Cupping my ears as he was doing, I picked up the drone of airplane engines, now faint, now dying away, now coming on palpably. The others heard the same. We scrambled outside. We searched the sky.

Vincy Murray broke into a high-pitched squeal: "Look, there, over there."

"Where?"

"Can't you see? Over by the hills."

Then I spotted it, way out on the horizon, the silhouette of a plane, its bulky shape much like one of those transpacific clippers we used to see on pre-war Movietone News. Now it was hovering, now it was turning, ever so slowly, until its nose was pointed at the camp. And Jiminy Crickets, it was coming straight towards us, low, almost at tree-top level, and the nearer it came, the more incredible its size, the more deafening its engines, until with a stunning shock wave, it wooshed overhead. In that split second of ear-popping concussion I caught sight of a pink hand waving in a gun turret.

Waving hand! Must tell the others. Too late. They were charging helter-skelter for the ball field. When I caught up with them everyone was pointing up at the plane sailing gracefully towards us. About a quarter of a mile away it began ejecting bundle-like objects from its belly, and in a trice the objects blossomed into parachutes. "Let's go," someone yelled out, and that was enough to start a frantic stampede for the gate. What about the guards? No

レンゴウグンノホリョヘ

ALLIED PRISONERS

The JAPANESE Government has surrendered. You will be evacuated by ALLIED NATIONS forces as soon as possible.

Until that time your present supplies will be augmented by air-drop of U.S. food, clothing and medicines. The first drop of these items will arrive within one (1) or two (2) hours.

Clothing will be dropped in standard packs for units of 50 or 500 men. Bundle markings, contents and allowances per man are as follows:

BUNDLE MARKINGS				BUNDLE MARKINGS			
50 MAN PACK	500 MAN PACK	CONTENTS	ALLOWANCES PER MAN	50 MAN PACK	500 MAN PACK	CONTENTS	ALLOWANCES PER MAN
A	3	Drawers	2	B	10	Laces, shoe	1
A	1-2	Undershirt	2	A	11	Kit, sewing	1
B	22	Socks (pr)	2	C	31	Soap, toilet	1
A	4-6	Shirt	1	C	4-6	Razor	1
A	7-9	Trousers	1	C	4-6	Blades, razor	10
C	23-30	Jacket, field	1	C	10	Brush, tooth	1
A	10	Belt, web, waist	1	B	31	Paste, tooth	1
A	11	Capt, H.B.T.	1	C	10	Comb	1
B	12-21	Shoes (pr)	1	B	32	Shaving cream	1
A	1-2	Handkerchiefs	3	C	12-21	Powder (insecticide)	1
C	32-34	Towel	1				

There will be instructions with the food and medicine for their use and distribution.

C A U T I O N

DO NOT OVEREAT OR OVERMEDICATE   FOLLOW DIRECTIONS

INSTRUCTIONS FOR FEEDING 100 MEN

To feed 100 men for the first three (3) days, the following blocks (individual bundles dropped) will be assembled:

3 Blocks No. 1
(Each Contains)

2 Cases, Soup, Can
1 Cases Fruit Juice
1 Case Accessory Pack

1 Block No. 5
(Each Contains)

1 Case Soup, Dehd
1 Case Veg Puree
1 Case Bouillon
1 Case Hosp Supplies
1 Case Vitamin Tablets

1 Block No. 3
(Each Contains)

1 Case Candy
1 Case Gum
1 Case Cigarettes
1 Case Matches

guards, they'd evaporated. I charged through the gateway and quickly gained on stragglers wandering aimlessly along the mud road. No aimless wandering for me. I had a pretty good idea where those chutes came down. They must be there to the right, in that field of mature seven-foot-high *gaoliang*. I swerved off the road and thrashed my way through the close-growing inch-thick stalks. Not a sign of life. I burst out of the *gaoliang* and into a stand of millet. Still nothing. I ploughed on. Then I saw it, there on a path beside a grave mound, a length of green and brown fabric lying in folds. I inched towards it.

"Hands up! Freeze!"

I froze.

From behind the mound rose a figure straight out of *Flash Gordon* – exotic spaceman's helmet – gaudy one-piece space suit. Even the miniature carbine he had trained at my middle was an instrument of death from some other planet. The only give-away that he might be a mere earthling was the strips of common sticking plaster attaching his spectacles to his nose and temple.

"Don't shoot," I choked out, "I'm British. I'm from an internment camp nearby . . ."

"Ammurrka has got a gigantic bomb . . ." was all I caught of the burst of words he fired at me. Like an imbecile, I shrugged my shoulders and shook my head.

He repeated in a flat monotone: "Ammurrka has got a gigantic bomb . . . super bomb . . . dropped two and killed ourselves half-million gooks . . ."

And still those words, for me the very first of the new post-war era, refused to sink in.

We were standing gazing warily at each other when two men from the camp came plunging through the waist-high millet. They threw themselves on the Martian, they hugged him, they slapped his back, they kissed him. Tears were streaming down one man's cheeks. "You saved us, you saved us, we were all about to die." (What a fib!) "Is the war really over?" the other gasped out between sobs.

"Ammurrka has won the war," the deadpan para-trooper was back to his monologue. "Ammurrka has got the biggest goll-darndest bomb in the world . . . super bomb . . . Hiroshima and Nagasaki zapped . . . killed ourselves a half-million Japs . . . MacArthur is sitting on Hirohito's throne calling the shots . . ."

It took a second Martian to switch him off. This one, borne shoulder-high by adulating internees, fired a salvo of unintelligible jargon at us. And our Martian countered with a salvo of his own. Was this strange lingo the lingo of the Brave New World? If so, we were going to have a lot of learning to do. But not right now. Right now, our hero reverted to standard John Wayne English. "Okay buddies, we gonna head for your camp. Give us a hand with the chute."

Two idolizing inmates jumped instantly into action, gathering and bundling up the tangles of cord and heavy green and brown fabric.

In triumphant procession we passed under the ceremonial arch and into the *Courtyard of the Happy Way*. The main road was a bedlam of people screeching and bellowing and dancing the madman's jig. Someone grabbed my arm. "The war's over! We've won!" Someone else pounded my back. "The Americans have invented a wonderful new bomb. They dropped ten on Japan. Wiped out five million Jappos!"

"Not five million, eight million," a jubilant beetroot-faced man cried out. "Tokyo, Nagasaki, Yokohama, Hiroshima, all turned to ash. Bloody marvelous! Absolutely marvelous!"

Everyone was pushing and shoving towards the Commandant's courtyard. I squeezed my way in. Mr McLaren was standing on a table, waving his hands, calling for silence. All he got for his trouble was a chorus of rude epithets. But when a Martian officer got up on the table there was instant silence.

"I am Major Staiger of the OSS. I can confirm to you that the Government of Japan has agreed to Allied surrender terms. What I can't tell you though is how the Japanese army in the field is going to react. It's possible they may refuse to obey Emperor Hirohito's order to lay down their arms. The Japanese garrison in Weihsien might turn on us. To calm your fears I want you to know that I have sent a message to their commanding officer advising him that we're here on a humanitarian mission. After witnessing the horrors of the prison camps in Europe, we were expecting the worst here. It's a great relief, let me tell you, to find you alive and kicking. Now, I'm sure your first and foremost desire is to get out of this place. I'm afraid that might take some days, maybe a week, to arrange the necessary transportation, but you can rest assured we'll do our best to speed you out. In the meantime, I've radioed for more supplies, and for more support personnel. I must ask you now to exercise patience. You've stuck it out for the best part of three years; you ought to be able to manage a few more days. For your own safety I'm going to insist that you stay strictly within the walls of this camp. I'm going to ask your senior representative to organize a security team to police the exits. Also, the Japanese guards will retain their arms; I've given orders that they continue guarding this place as before. . . ."

Someone in the crowd let out a boo. It didn't faze the major. He just went right on: "I'm afraid we've no alternative. There's a lot of fighting going on in the countryside

221

On the camp's Main Road, the ceremonial gate visible in the background, a smiling Bessie Attlee with a now unlimited portion from No. 2 kitchen.

around us. The Chinese are locked in a bitter civil war. No one is to leave this place. That's an order, and it's for your own good. Now, if you don't mind, we've had nothing to eat since dawn. We'd like to share lunch with you."

Mr McLaren raised his hand to squelch the shouts of laughter. Then, smothering his own smile, he said to the major: "You're welcome to come along to Number Two Kitchen, though you might not find it quite up to the Ritz."

Accepting the invitation was the biggest mistake of the major's heroic mission. He and his men came down with an unrelenting dose of the trots.

Just as the OSS hero had promised, more Americans arrived next day, but not by parachute; they came in a C47 transport that landed at the Japanese fighter airstrip at Erhshihlipu five miles to the south. In bustled a rotund army major, his "re-orientation" team at his heels.

"First thing we gonna do," he announced, "is re-orientate you folks. Can see you need it real bad, so gonna do it real good. Everyone to the church hall, sharp at three, to learn about the new United Nations, its charter, its establishment in San Francisco last April."

The business-like re-orientation team set to work stringing cables, and in jig time had powerful loudspeakers installed on all the main buildings. At six next morning we got our first taste of reveille. But no bugle call; we were jolted awake by a powerful baritone rendering of *Oh What a Beautiful Mornin'*. It seemed our friendly disk jockey couldn't give us enough of that rousing song. He played it again. And then again. And he squeezed it in between *People Will Say We're in Love* and *Kansas City* and *Surrey with the Fringe on Top*. Occasionally, he relented and put on other hit tunes denied us during our lost years: *Sentimental Journey*, *As Time Goes By*, and so on. But then he was back to his favorite, now the camp's theme song, *Beautiful Mornin'*.

Complaints hit Mr McLaren thick and fast, some demanding the volume be turned down, some that it start after breakfast, and some that there be a total ban on that "ghastly racket." I was not one of the complainants. I never tired of that music then, and I never tire of it now.

Buzzing here, there, and everywhere, the tubby orientation major was forever demanding our attention. His voice would come over the loudspeaker: "Now hear this – hear this – hear this – all prisoners (meaning his prisoners) are to present themselves at 1:00 p.m. in the church hall to see a film on the surrender of Germany."

Next day, he was at it again. "Prisoners are to attend a film sharp at seven this evening to view the atrocities committed by our German and Japanese enemy."

He meant it when he said "sharp at seven." When I arrived at 7:05, he was well into his school-marmish introduction: ". . . You people seem to bear no ill will toward your enemy. You demonstrate a curious 'couldn't care less' attitude. But I suppose that can be forgiven. You are obviously unaware of the inhuman crimes that have been perpetrated. Well, we'll put that right. You are going to be orientated. You are going to observe in living color what the Japs did in the Philippines, what the Krauts did in Poland . . ."

And what we observed was ghastly beyond imagination. If it dazed even those of us who were more or less sound of mind, what did it do to the ones teetering on the brink of mental breakdown? Impossible to believe that the major could be so insensitive. Could the war have warped his mind, turned him as callous as the very monsters the shining knights in armor of the Great Democracy had so gallantly set out to put down?

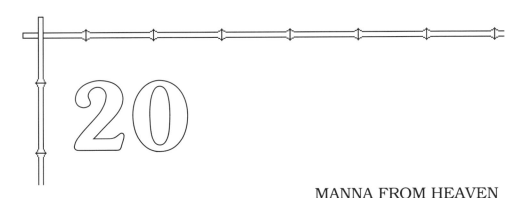

MANNA FROM HEAVEN

SEPTEMBER came and went, and there we were still holed-up in the gray mission compound. To keep our spirits bolstered, the re-orientation team had Block 35 converted into an information center complete with the latest issues of *Time, Life, Look, Readers Digest, Field & Stream, Saturday Evening Post* as well as a flashy array of the new fandangled pocket books. Bolster our spirits? Quite the reverse. It galled us to read about the opening session of the United Nations at San Francisco, about Britain's Prime Minister Clement Atlee promising independence for India (what had happened to Winston?), about the new wonder drug – penicillin, about the new craze – the Bobby Soxers. Left stranded on the sidelines as the world rolled merrily along its way, liberation was fast losing its relish for us. We'd had enough of lecturing, and were tiring of Spam, and were getting pretty blasé about the planes that came over everyday, the C47s, the B24s, the B25s, even a diminutive L5 which put on a spectacular aerial display entirely for our benefit. But maybe not so blasé about the B29s. They were incredible. First sign of them was the deep rumble of distant thunder, and the rumble all the time increasing in resonance until with a deafening eruption they broke into view. And we thought the B24s huge! How could such a colossus of seventy tons deadweight defy the natural laws of gravity? The lead behemoth would swing open its bomb bays, signaling the rest to follow suit, then in the blink of an eye the sky was a galaxy of variegated chutes. Alarmingly,

some chutes failed. Wired in tandem, fifty-five gallon drums, trailing tangles of red and white silk, came crashing down, spewing deadly missiles from the war factories of Dole and Heinz and Maxwell House. In one furious blitz on the camp hospital, ten-pound cans smashed into the wall immediately above a row of cots, splattering the patients with 67 varieties of soup and stew. Miraculously, no deaths, no injuries.

Just as on liberation day, the gates were flung open and out we dashed into the countryside. We had to be quick about it. Local peasants were already there gathering up the manna from heaven. Twenty feet from where Aubrey Grandon and I were stuffing ourselves with Hershey Bars from a smashed carton, bronze-faced natives were sucking soup and pineapple juice from punctured cans. One old geezer was squeezing Barbasol shaving cream into his mouth when Aubrey called out that the stuff was not for eating. The old man's lips spread in a frothy grin. Then he was laughing. Then we were all busting ourselves, we and the natives. It was carnival time.

A very pink, very sweaty, very out-of-sorts GI came trotting up to our little fiesta. He bellowed at the Chinese: "Who the hell do you gooks think you are? That's our chow. Beat it. Go on, scram." The Chinese stared without expression. The GI drew his Colt and pointed it threateningly. Still the Chinese held their ground. The GI said to Aubrey, "Tell deeze sonzabitches to get lost." Aubrey converted the order into a polite request. One of the

B 29 targeting
Block 23

Chinese replied: "Tell the soldier of the foreign invasion army that this is *our* land, not his. Tell him that for the last three years the Eastern Ocean Devils confiscated our seed grain to feed you Western Ocean Devils. Tell him that in sustaining you, we were brought to ruin."

And did Aubrey tell that to the foreign invasion soldier? Not a chance. The soldier himself was doing all the telling with his: "gonna shoot you sonzabitch gooks if you doan get yer ass outtahere pronto. . . ."

The peasants did pick up and leave, and as they sauntered away, I noticed that one was armed with an ancient fowling piece. By itself, no match for the American Colt, but a million fowling pieces, ten million, a hundred million? . . .

That there were two sides to the American character bewildered me no end. I brooded over it. How could they be so overwhelming in their warmth and generosity, yet without qualm run roughshod over the hapless peasants? Even more dismaying than the incident at the airdrop was the way their officers were openly embracing the infamous General Nieh, the puppet commander, who only a month back had collaborated with the Japanese in their rape and pillage of central Shantung. "Embrace"? Yes, not too strong a word if you were witness to what I was.

Soon after their arrival in camp, the Americans called for Chinese-speaking inmates to volunteer as interpreters. I was one of the first to do so, but it was Roy Tchoo who got the plum assignments, and well he should; his Peking Mandarin was Mandarin at its purest. *He* was the one who headed out to the hills with the rescue party to bring in the US Navy pilot shot down while strafing Tsingtao. *He* was the one to sit at the American commander's side during the negotiations with Weihsien's city fathers. But then I was not totally left out. I was Roy's assistant for the big show the Americans put on for General Nieh.

The strutting re-orientation major's first act as master of ceremonies for that occasion was to unceremoniously turf out several internees who happened to be using the center at the time. He then had his men set up a coffee urn, and lay out platters of Spam and cheese sandwiches, and inviting displays of Hershey bars, Wrigley's gum, and Camel and Chesterfield cigarettes.

226

勝利紀念

一九四五年九月二日攝於中國山東省濰縣樂道院

Our guests were late. We twiddled our thumbs for close on an hour before they paraded in. What a bunch of cutthroats the general and his entourage! Not a glimmer of a smile among the lot. You'd never want to bump into them on a dark night.

They scooped up the cigarettes. They left the food and candy untouched. They stared tight-lipped at the major as he launched into his welcoming speech, which Roy repeated in Chinese, three, four sentences at a time. The speech dwelt on the solidarity of the Sino-American alliance. It lavished praise on Generalissimo Chiang Kai Shek and his hierarchy of loyal generals of which the name Nieh was put at the very top. It concluded with the grand pronouncement that America and China would march forward together, their eternal friendship cemented by General Nieh's unswerving faith in freedom, justice, and democracy . . . .

While Roy was apologizing for the lack of real China tea, a US sergeant pinned blankets over the windows. The film projector began to click and whirr. Some of the newsreels were black and white, some Technicolor, all concerned

Seated,
Left to right:

Ron Chapman
Ted McLaren
Miles Halton
Wilfred Pryor
Maj. Staiger
Unknown
Col. Weinberg
Capt. Kranik
Ernie Schmidt
Jock Allen
Bill Howard
Percy Whiting
Unknown
Unknown

227

American firepower: battleships, carriers, tanks, artillery. We saw carpet bombing, dive bombing, incendiary bombing. We saw battles galore: Saipan, Manila, Okinawa, Bastogne, Falaise. And we saw mountains of dead – dead Japanese, dead Germans, and, surprisingly, dead Russians. The sight of Russian dead brought the General and his thugs to life. They clapped heartily. They cheered "*Hao! Hao!*"

The major preened. He beamed a toothy smile at Roy. "Thanks for your help, buddy. We really impressed them, and they never even got to see Hiroshima. Looks like Uncle Sam has won himself a fine ally."

Then he rounded on me as if it were my fault the guests hadn't touched the food. "Why don't the gooks eat? You get them to eat, Buster. That's your job, goddammit."

I presented a tray to one of the Chinese. Shaking his head coldly, he muttered: "None of you Americans are touching the food. What fools do you take us for?" The man next to him added: "You eat it. You poison yourself." As I retreated, I heard one of them say: "If I had my way, it would not only be the Americans we'd get rid of, but all the Foreign Devils, the whole stinking lot of them, before they once again spread like vermin across our land."

As it turned out, the man had his way all right, and almost the very next afternoon, but not with the "whole stinking lot." A group of six hundred internees, about half the population of Weihsien's Foreign Devils, left by train for the port of Tsingtao. After that, no more trains. The line was cut, bridges downed, stations set afire. China's factional war had flared up across the land. All night long we heard the din of battle, but then at sunrise the shooting stopped, and there they were, out in the fields, droves of peasants bent over sickles, working the harvest just as countless generations of their forebears had done before them. With such scenes of pastoral tranquillity it seemed peace had returned. If that were only so. Came dusk there'd be a desultory shot, then another, then two in succession, then a fusillade, then machine gun bursts, then the loud thud of grenades and mortar bombs; and you wondered how a single peasant could survive the carnage. Yet at daybreak they were back again, whole families, reaping and gathering. I could vouch for that. I saw it with my own eyes when as interpreter I rode out each morning in the truck with a squad of GIs to the abandoned Japanese airstrip at Erhshihlipu. Pretty eerie out there in the wide open waiting for the day's supply plane. Though the strip was guarded by a contingent of General Nieh's troops, we never really felt safe. Who would with that slovenly, scrofulous lot armed with antiquated single-action rifles and strings of grenades dangling perilously from waist belts?

They were sneaky too. You'd tell their sergeant it was forbidden to go near a plane, and he'd be shouting and screaming at his men, threatening them with the firing squad if they strayed close. Yet the minute you turned your back, he himself would be sneaking aboard to see what he could snaffle.

Not only was it the Chinese who got up to mischief. A GI made a playful grab for a puppet's rifle. The puppet hung on for dear life. The GI turned to me: "Tell this crazy gook he can fire off my carbine if he'll let me take a coupla shots with his funny old museum piece." The puppet sergeant intervened. "*Bu shing, bu shing.* Firing of rifles is forbidden. Even when under attack we are not allowed to pull the trigger until given the order. But if he likes, the honorable foreign soldier can toss a grenade or two." And when I translated that for the American, his eyes popped wide. "Does he think I'm nuts? I wouldn't ask my worst enemy to yank the string on one of those rusty old chunks of iron!"

On my first outing to the airfield I puffed with importance. Wasn't I at last doing my bit in the war? Second time out, I felt less heroic. It soon began to pall, those long hours of idleness on the sun-scorched mud flat. The GIs had but two subjects of conversation. When they had talked themselves out about the gals they had left behind, their Marie-Lous, their Suzy-Anns, their Josie-Belles, they were vehemently defending their home towns and home states. Nothing could compare with St Louis, Missouri . . . the only place to live was Sacramento, California . . . El Paso, Texas was number one. . . . I dreaded the question, but it always came: "Say bud, where you from?" Confess to Tientsin, Hopei and they'd gape as if I were some freak brought up in a punk-smelling mud hut. Why bother telling them about Kiesslings and Empire Theatre when I knew in my heart of hearts that Tientsin would

229

Tientsin was proud of its Empire Theater, seen here on the left, with D'Arc's Hotel directly behind the oncoming rickshaw.

soon exist for me only in my dreams?

But no need to take all that Yankee guff. I could always walk away from their truck and button-hole some puppet soldier. Easier said than done. The conscripts shied away from my city Mandarin. And the sergeant? Why he was off on an English speaking jag. Poor wretch, it nearly did him in, his English. To show off his newly learned vocabulary, he pointed a wagging finger at a dark-skinned GI while he laughingly mouthed the words: "Black Face!" How could he possibly know that in joining together those two innocent words from his English Primer he had loaded them with deadly venom.

An hour before sundown the puppet soldiers would begin to agitate. In twos and threes they would abandon their posts and head towards us, first those guarding the far end of the strip, then the point men, then even the idlers grubbing about the wrecked Japanese aircraft. Time to go, they'd say, gazing longingly at Weihsien's protective city wall. Soon the first shots would sound, heralding the evening battle. Didn't the Americans realize that out in the open they'd be sitting ducks?

Of course the Americans realized it. It set them off. "Why don't the Sixth Marines in Tsingtao fly in and kick hell out of the sonovbitch Commies for once and for all?"

"Not a hope. Them marines got too much on their hands."

"Yeah, all them Russian babes in port."

"Then we might as well say good-bye to this landing strip."

"Might as well. These useless gooks will run at the first shot."

With every passing day the deterioration of General

Nieh's guard contingent was plainer to see. Its depleted ranks were now mostly made up of youths barely able to shoulder the weight of their rifles.

"What happened to your sergeant?" I asked one of them when for several days running that scarecrow in uniform failed to show.

"He's deserted."

Deserted! Polite way of saying he'd gone over to the Reds.

There came the day when our morning excursion to Erhshihlipu was put on hold. And when the truck stayed parked for a second day, then a third, a fourth, a fifth, we had to assume the worst – the Reds had overrun the strip. Numbing thought. It was the third week of October and the tenth since World War II had come to an official end. You began hearing people say they were better off under the Japanese; at least then they lived in the hope of being free as birds the minute the war was over. Now, no such hope. Someone ventured the opinion that this other war now entrapping the camp was the Chinese version of the *Hundred Years' War*. Hard to argue against that. Hadn't the Nationalists and Communists been slugging it out since 1927? And weren't they still in round one, for goodness sakes? "We're stuck here till doomsday" was the common refrain in Kitchen One and Kitchen Two. Faint hearts! How could anyone lose faith in the sublime ability of Americans to move mountains when so inclined?

It was Tai-tai who broke the news. "They're going to fly out the whole camp tomorrow."

"What! Seven or eight hundred in a single day? Impossible!"

"Peter Orlick got word to Betty, and he ought to know."

Orlick, a signals corporal in the OSS, one of the original team that liberated the camp, was romantically involved with my half-sister Betty. Now stationed in Peking, the hub of the American military presence in North China, his teletype machine must be burning hot with signals concerning plans for our evacuation.

When I passed on the news at the workers' meal table in Kitchen Two Annex (Yes, we continued working right to the end), it started off the armchair generals. ". . . If the Yanks don't have control of Erhshihlipu, how they gonna land their planes?" . . . "Who said they can't take over the place?" . . . "The Communist 8th Route Army said . . ."

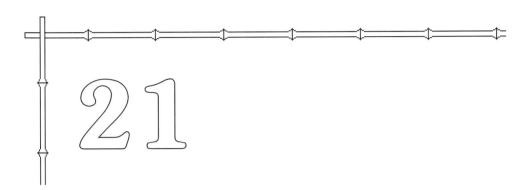

. . . RIGHT BACK WHERE I STARTED FROM

A S IT TURNED OUT, for one momentous day in October, October 22, 1945, to be precise, Erhshihlipu was in American hands. That was the day they airlifted us out, the whole camp, the whole kit and caboodle. How could one not marvel at the Yankee efficiency that made it possible – the masterly organization, the clockwork scheduling. You saw C46s and 47s circling above, you saw them swooping down one by one to synchronize their landing with the arrival of the trucks from camp.

When it came our turn to board a plane, two crewmen helped Tai-tai up the metal steps, then ushered in Tony, then Betty, then me. We sat buckled into canvas drop seats attached to the bare-metal side of the aircraft. Buckled in opposite us were a man and a woman and their two boys. The man called out: "I say, don't we get parachutes?" And the passing crewman, taking it as a joke, gave him a big horse laugh. No parachutes! My lungs seized. I exchanged sheepish grins with the woman and the two boys.

One engine exploded into life, then the other. For a half-minute, maybe more, the fuselage shuddered violently; then both engines slowed to a pulsating rumble. Something must have gone wrong. Through the small oval window I could see a wing flap jerking up and down in a futile attempt to lift the plane off the ground.

"Why don't we go, Daddy? Is the airplane broken, Daddy?" Both boys and the mother stared wide-eyed at the father. So did I. And all the father did was mouth a

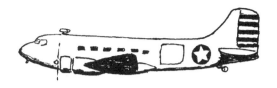

Sailing home
courtesy the
USAAF

silent prayer.

At last, at last, we lumbered forward, bumpety-bump, on the corrugated mud surface. Suddenly the engines erupted madly. The fuselage drummed, my skull drummed, my teeth drummed, my every joint drummed. Now the ground was zipping by, the forward movement digging the canvas strap hard into my side. It was when the deafening roars reduced to a steady rhythmic drone that I experienced that same uneasy flutter I used to get in the pit of my stomach each time the school's playground swing swung to its highest point.

When I finally convinced myself that shifting my weight wasn't going to dip the plane out of balance, I twisted around to peer through the window. It was toy-land below, everything in miniature – trees, winding creeks, mud huts. And how tranquil it all looked. Hard to believe the country was engulfed in bitter conflict.

A thick mist cut off my view. We must have flown into a cloud. If a cloud is only vapor (according to TGS science master Mr Foxlee), why then was the plane bouncing so out of control? You'd think the crew would all be strapped in their places, saying their prayers. But not a bit of it. A baby-faced crewman wearing a baseball cap came lurching through the cabin handing out boxes of K rations. A violent series of dips and yaws, and he shouted over the roar of the engines: "Doncher worry, folks, everything's normal." Is a condemned man consoled by the warder's last words? What might be normal to a flier was a nightmare to a landlubber. And there was still another hour of nightmare to endure.

On constant alert for the minutest change in the crescendo of sounds reverberating through the cabin – each new sound spelling doom – a sudden mournful whine from the engines froze my breath. Worse still, my insides seemed to be floating in defiance of the laws of gravity. Through the pinging, drumming window I could see mud roofs, a dirty brown river, junks with tattered sails, all looming larger by the second. An almighty jolt, a moment of terror, then bewilderment, then heart-warming relief, as the engines gave one last triumphant roar, and we were rolling smoothly along the runway. Tai-tai stopped saying her rosary. Opposite me the man and wife, no longer stony-faced, were chattering away like magpies.

The impish crewman swung open the cabin door. "All ashore for Sing-Sing," he announced.

"Tientsin," the woman opposite corrected him, cheerfully.

"Ting-Sing, Sing-Sing, all-a-same-a-me, Ma'am."

Bursts of hearty laughter from all sides.

On terra firma, a chaos of trucks, jeeps, men in khaki. Where were we? It was nothing like the Tientsin I knew. Trust the Yanks to land us in the wrong place! Then I spotted Konsty Ovchinnikoff. I had to look twice. Last time I saw him he was in British Volunteer uniform. Now he was in a GI field jacket, GI cap, GI pants. His eyes caught mine. He rushed over. He embraced me. He kissed my cheeks *à la Russe*. "You made it, thank God, you made it." He turned to Tai-tai. "Welcome home, Mrs Lambert, what terrible privations you must have suffered. It is wonderful to see you all again."

"Thank you Constantine. It feels good to be home, and even better to be met by dear friends."

"Where the heck are we, Konsty?" I asked.

"How could you forget? You're at the old Japanese airfield in the Russian Concession. Come on, I'm a guide for the Third Amphibious Corps. I'm supposed to get you to your bus."

Soon as we crossed International Bridge, I gained my bearings. There were those old familiar landmarks – Imperial Hotel, Hongkong & Shanghai Bank, Moyler Powell, Gordon Hall, Victoria Park. But something *was* different, very different. Suddenly it hit me. The traffic! All those green Yankee trucks, cars, ducks, jeeps – why, they were driving on the wrong side of the road, the right-hand side, scattering rickshaws and mule carts unable or unwilling to do likewise.

We pulled up at Astor House. While squeezing our way through the sidewalk crowd, someone flung his arms around Tai-tai. Mr. O'Connor. The O'Connors, Irish Free

State citizens, had escaped internment. The hugging and kissing and foolishness over, Tai-tai pulled me aside. "Desmond, here's the house key, here's the rickshaw fare. Go and see what state our home is in. Then come over to the O'Connors. We'll be staying there."

The O'Connors? Not me. There was Murat to look up, and all my other cohorts. When I reached 35 Sydney Road I found a notice pasted over the front door latch. It was printed in both English and Chinese:

ENTRY PROHIBITED
EXCEPT BY AUTHORITY OF
GENERAL WEDEMEYER,
COMMANDER U.S. FORCES,
CHINA THEATER.

"It's my home, I don't need authority," I muttered as I broke the seal and tried the key. The door swung open. What a mess! Garbage littered the hallway. In the drawing room, not a stick of furniture. Carpets, drapes, everything gone. My heels made a hollow echoing sound as I went from room to room. This was going to break Tai-tai's heart. Upstairs I found the only item the Japanese had left – a canvas camp cot. The thieving swines must have taken off in such a hurry they hadn't time to dismantle it. Well, at least I could kip down for the night.

Mid-morning, Alioshka Bublikoff arrived, then Karl Dietrich, then Murat Apakaieff. Murat had a bottle of Tiger Brand Vodka with him. We swigged it from the neck. In minutes I was floating. "Let's go eat," someone said. And half an hour later we were at our old haunt, the dumpling diner on Taku Road.

"Too bad about Bobka Vladimiroff."

"What do you mean?" I asked Aliosha.

"Disappeared, shot, so everyone believes."

"Also Igor, Mischa, Alex, Gorgor," Murat chipped in.

"Igor Kapoostin?"

"Yes, Igor Kapoostin. Executed by the Japanese."

A vicious stab cut through my haze of alcohol.

Karl broke the silence. "Did you hear Eric Lange died of TB."

"TB? Impossible! He was an athlete, a champion rower."

"Hard to believe, but it's true."

"Also hard to believe about Roger. He went down with

his troopship."

"Roger Fleuriet?"

"Yes, Roger Fleuriet. He was with the Free French."

"Is it true Aliosha Marinellis was killed in Weihsien?" Murat asked.

"Yes, it's true," I said.

"How did it happen? Was he shot?"

"No, he fell from a tree. As punishment for some minor offense he was sent up to cut branches. He slipped and fell."

"I always liked Marinellis."

"Yes, a great guy."

"Also Eric Liddell. We heard he was killed too."

"He wasn't killed. He died of a brain tumor."

"Many were the times I saw him run at the TAAA track meets in the Min Yuan."

"In camp he still raced," I said. "I saw him race Aubrey Grandon in the fifty-yard dash. Aub won by a foot."

"How could that be? Aub is no Olympic runner."

"Aub is twenty-six, Mr Liddell was in his forties."

We finished the meal in silence.

That afternoon, Achmet, who worked at a PX, told me the Americans had an office in the German Concession where returned prisoners could get bedding and provisions. I borrowed Karl's bike and went to check. Icily, the American officer explained that the supplies were meant for Americans only. I gulped with embarrassment. I bit my lip. Then I heard him saying, "What you waiting for, kid. Fill out this form. For home address, you write: 242 Elm Street, Billings, Montana." He called out to a sergeant to help me load up a rickshaw with fluffy wool blankets, a sack of flour, cans of sugar, coffee, milk powder.

"Too bad about your furniture," Karl Dietrich said. "Couldn't have been more than two weeks ago, Johnny Husisian told me he saw the Japanese family that occupied your house taking off in mule carts with all your stuff. They must have been heading for the place near the Chinese City where the Japanese military and civilians are being concentrated before being shipped home by the Yanks. Your Japanese might still be there. Why don't you go find out?"

"How am I ever going to identify them?"

"The police will do that. They'll have a list for sure."

236   "Which police?"

Nationalist flags fly from every building

"There's only one police now, the Kuomintang police. Do you remember Jefferson Wu from school? He's a big shot now in the mayor's office. You should go and see him."

Murat and I rode out on bikes to the Chinese City. On the way we were nearly finished off by crazy Yanks careering their trucks and jeeps down the wrong side, first on Davenport Road then on Rue du Chaylard. But no Yanks in the Japanese Concession, the place was deserted, shops boarded up, windows shuttered. It was there that I saw my first Nationalist regulars – coal scuttle helmets, German gray battledress. They jabbered fiercely at us in Kuang Hsi dialect. We retreated. We conferred. We decided to take the roundabout route via the Italian Concession and Austrian Bridge. Only once were we held up when a cheering throng on Via Roma thought we were American marines. In the Chinese City, Nationalist flags were everywhere, the largest over the administration building. Murat sweet-talked the sentries at the gate. Inside he greased palms, and within seconds a policeman was escorting us past a long line-up straight to Jefferson Wu's office. I recognized him immediately – slim, pasty-faced, wearing that permanent half-smile you see on Chinese opera masks. He rose from his desk and came forward with outstretched hand.

"Desmond Power! Welcome back. Glad to see you survived. Your family's well, I trust?"

"They're fine, Jefferson, thanks very much."

"Isn't it most gratifying, the defeat of Japan? Our Generalissimo always said he would defeat them in the

237

Ah Chin
with Yi-jie
(now blind)

end. He deliberately let them win the earlier battles, drew them in, then he gave them the *coup de grâce*. In a month or two, there won't be one left on our soil."

"They haven't all gone yet?"

"No, not yet."

"That's what I've come to see you about. Is there any way you can help me locate the Japanese who occupied our home while we were interned? They looted the place."

"Sorry, not possible. We face the huge task of reconstruction. Factories, go-downs, machine shops, all stripped bare. Those places are more important to us than residential property. Besides, yours is not the only one. Did you not see all those people in the hallway? They're all in the same boat as you. And, to be candid, we must deal with Chinese losses before others. Also, it might surprise you to know that the Americans have laid it down that the Japanese must not be molested, even those who committed atrocities. As for your possessions, the Americans have given carte blanche to the Japanese to take away with them whatever they like. So if you have a complaint, lay it with the Americans, not with us."

He shook my hand. He smiled his rueful half-smile. "Good-bye, Desmond. Peaceful journey to your native country."

"What native country?" I pondered as we cycled away.

At the O'Connors I broke the news to Tai-tai about her home being stripped bare. She had already heard. She amazed me with her coolness.

"Mr Husisian told me about it," she said. "I wept at first, all the treasures my mother left me, gone – the ivory inlaid eight-leaf screen, the beautiful blackwood sideboard, the nests of tables, the carpets, the bronze buddha, the ivories, the Ching porcelain. But at least we have our lives. We must thank God for that. We can always make a fresh start. The O'Connors, the Makaroffs, the da Silvas, the Von Brunows, they've all lent us things to get us going. Ah Chin came to see me. He wants to come back to work for us. Yi-jie can't. She's too old, poor thing. She's gone totally blind . . ."

Yi-jie blind! I took a deep swallow to smother my shock.

". . . Ah Chin will be cook. I've given him money to buy provisions. You go back and stay in the house. Doctor Pertzel wants me in hospital for a few days, nothing serious, just a checkup. Tony and Betty will be living with the O'Connors for the time being."

Ah Chin was all over me when I got home, jabbering excitedly, smelling of strong drink. I waited for him to calm down then I asked after Jie-jie his wife, our Number Two amah. His brow wrinkled in a frown. He stumbled over his words: "She's changed. She's become independent. She says she will never work again as a servant."

"*Meiyou fazi*," was all I could think of saying.

"*Meiyou fazi*," he parroted as he reached for his bottle of *maotai* on the window sill.

He held it out to me. I shook my head.

"Do you want me to cook you some food then? You must be hungry."

"No thanks, I've already eaten."

"Then I'll be going. I'll be back in the morning. What time do you want breakfast?"

"Don't really care. Eight o'clock will be fine."

"By the way," he mumbled. "Kui Hsiang came looking for you this afternoon."

"Kui Hsiang? Is Kui Hsiang back?"

"Yes, he was here. While we were waiting for you he helped me move in the furniture Tai-tai's friends had sent over. He couldn't stay. He said he'd try to find you again tomorrow."

"Tomorrow!" My heart leapt to my mouth.

At breakfast next morning, Kui Hsiang stands suddenly before me. I jump to my feet. We clasp hands.

"You never got to India?" is the first thing he says.

"No."

"What happened?"

"Skullduggery by our own people."

"The dwarf devils got you?"

"Yes."

"You survived in good health?"

"Yes, thanks to your lucky charm."

"Lucky charm?"

"Don't you remember? Here it is." I open my billfold and show him the print of Chang Tien Shih, Master of Heaven, riding a tiger, wielding a magic sword.

He nods gently. His luminous brown eyes search mine. "Did you have a hard time?"

"Not that hard, not the last eighteen months anyway. It

Chang Tien Shih
"Master of Heaven"
my talisman all
through internment

was toughest in Pootung, the first camp. How about you? Did you manage to find work during the occupation?"

"I scraped out a living. It wasn't easy. I had to go underground."

"Underground, why?"

"I was engaged in anti-puppet activities. Our cell executed six collaborationists before the provincial police got on our tail."

"The Kuomintang has taken over. You will be safe now."

"On the contrary. Several of the most blatant collaborators now have high positions in the Kuomintang. But our time will come. The war of liberation is gathering momentum. Much of Hopei, Shantung, and Shansi has already been freed. The large cities will take longer. In Tientsin and Peking we have not only to oust the Kuomintang, we have the Americans to deal with. Though their present administration supports Chiang blindly, we are aware that a significant segment of US public opinion is against their intervening in our affairs. And that, I believe, will force their President to order the Marines to withdraw."

He grips me by the shoulder. "Enough of politics. I came only to see if you were all right, and to say good-bye. May your journey from here be peaceful."

Me? My journey from here? I cannot believe what I am hearing. I am so flustered, so tongue-tied, that all I can do is beam an embarrassed smile. My friend and mentor is lumping me in with those long-time demons of his, the blood-suckers, the opium traffickers, the plunderers of Chinese souls, all of whom, as he has so often declared, must be sent packing.

Before I can come up with a suitable response he is gone, slipping out with hardly a rustle, and I am left gazing wistfully at the contents of the billfold. When I turn over the photo of him, the penciled inscription on the back jumps out at me.

"To Desmond, my dear friend,
I shall never forget our parting this 11th. day of August, 1942."
Hsiu Kui Hsiang"

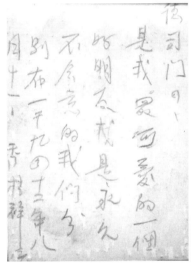

Those sentiments he expressed in 1942 came straight from the heart. Now, nothing of the kind. He is too preoccupied with the stirring events engulfing the land, events in which I have no part to play. I might be China born, three generations of my family have lived here, yet to him, indeed to every living Chinese, I am and always will be – *a Foreign Devil.*

241

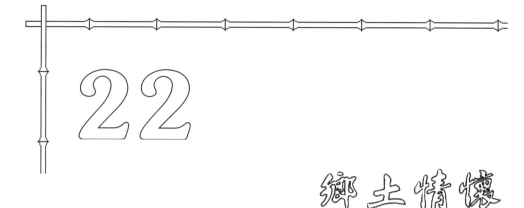

22

郷土情懷

FAREWELL, CHERISHED LAND OF MY BIRTH

KUI HSIANG was right on track about the Americans pulling out. They made it official; they were ending their occupation, scotching for once and for all the spate of rumors about a new concession coming into being, an American one, complete with garrison, law courts, clubs, schools. For days their decision was all the talk at Tientsin Club, once strictly exclusive, now thrown open with fees waived to all ex-internees. So there I was at the bulletin board, shoulder to shoulder with the elite, reading the latest Reuters and United Press despatches; or at the communal lunch table in the glittering dining room, breaking bread with taipans.

It wasn't the happiest of times for legitimate club members. Faces grew bleaker by the day. One lunch I was seated beside "Moo-jiang Smitty," Weihsien's jovial carpenter, now no longer jovial, no longer a carpenter, and no longer "Smitty." He had reverted to Archibald Alistair Smith, Esq, Managing Director, Snelgrove Smith & Co, Tientsin's largest wool packing plant. I don't remember his face being beetroot in Weihsien; it was certainly that now. Purple even. All through lunch he fussed and fumed: "Did not the Foreign Office specifically ask us to stay behind to protect British interests? And what was our reward for staying? Eh? Three years in a filthy prison camp! And little did we realize while we languished there what 10 Downing Street had in store for us . . ."

A fellow taipan, taking his place at the table, interjected: "What's your beef today, Archie?"

With eyes aflame and chaps quivering, Mr Archibald Alistair Smith aimed an accusatory finger at the man. "The bloody Anglo-Chinese Agreement of 1943, that's what! The snuffing out of our livelihoods with the stroke of a pen."

"Hold on to your hat, Archie. The agreement can always be renegotiated. Can't you see the deadlier, more immediate problem we face?" That came from George Wallis, camp baker in Weihsien, now waiting to be called back to his desk at Tientsin's prestigious Fairchild & Co.

"You've lost your marbles George. No problem can be deadlier. That infamous agreement of which I speak calls for Britain to relinquish the concession's assets accumulated over the years by municipal taxes paid by you and by me, and not by the bloody Court of St James. And what about the Crown Lessees Fund which everybody and his uncle knows was created by the BMC to compensate us when our sub-leases run out in 1964? The powers-that-be have gone and signed it over to the bloody Kuomintang. And now those buggers have declared the leases null and void. They've ruined us, Georgie me boy, ruined us utterly!"

"Not me, Archie, not me. I'm not one bit affected by that monkey business. I don't own an inch of property. But I'm personally ruined all the same. Galloping inflation has done me in." He waved a bank note through the air. "This here thousand dollar note is nothing but small change. What you could buy for ten thousand yesterday will cost you a lakh by the end of the week. My total savings at Chartered Bank wouldn't cover a rickshaw ride to Morling's Corner!"

"All the more fool, George, for keeping your savings in local currency."

"How was I to know? . . ."

While the two hammered away, I reflected on my own little encounter with runaway inflation. It began with a notice appearing on the club's bulletin board advising Britons of cash grants being handed out at the consulate. All one had to do was show one's passport. Literally, money for the taking. At the consulate, after a two-hour wait in line, a clerk handed me a form on which I had to fill in name, age, occupation, the names of three references, and the proposed method of repayment. Twenty minutes later, with the princely sum of one hundred

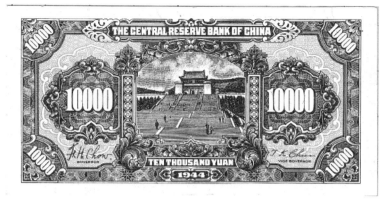

thousand dollars bundled under my arm, I hailed a rickshaw. As we progressed past Chase Bank, someone on the front steps called out my name. It was Jimmy Winslow of all people! We were more than passing acquaintances. In Weihsien we were teammates on Kitchen Two softball team.

"Well, well, if it isn't Des Power, our lefty first baseman! What you up to these days?"

"Nothing much. I'm getting itchy feet."

"I'm skeedaddling myself soon as my replacement arrives. Say, you used to work for a stock broker didn't you?"

"That's right, Doney & Company, but their doors are locked tight. My boss, Major Ridler, who was interned in Lunghua, is on a ship bound for England. Mr Gilmore, his partner, is too old and infirm to re-start the business."

"How are you managing to survive?"

"I just got a hundred-thousand-dollar grant from the British Government."

"Local currency?"

"Yep."

"Chicken feed! Play money! We're dishing it out to all comers. You can have as much as you can carry. Follow me."

I followed him through the bank's marble foyer and into a strong room at the back. It was stacked to the ceiling with crisp ten-thousand-dollar bank notes.

"The Japanese left the stuff. It'll be worthless in no time. Take what you want. You don't have to sign for a penny of it."

After loading the rickshaw to the gunnels, I called out:

"Say, Jimmy, do you know you've made me a millionaire?"

He threw his head back, laughing. "Play money, my friend. Only good for Monopoly."

Thirty-five Sydney Road came to life the moment Tai-tai stepped through the front entrance. It was like old times to hear her voice ringing through the house, supervising the cleaners, painters, plumbers. We certainly needed plumbers. Two of Tientsin's ablest took a whole day to clear the pipes clogged with human hair, Japanese hair! It took all of a week for the smell of new paint to give way to that old familiar mingling of kitchen odors and furniture polish. And once again, mahjong tiles click-clacked in the drawing room. Who else at the mahjong table but that ebullient foursome: Ilse Von Brunow, Ruby Hawkins, Philo Cox, and Gracie Lambert?

For days I waited to catch Tai-tai alone; I had to tell her what needed to be said.

"You should be thinking of selling out."

"Selling out! Have you lost your senses? Why should I sell out?"

"The US Marines will soon be leaving. The Chinese are going to send us packing the minute that happens."

"Don't you believe a word of it. A captain in the Third Amphibious Corps told Mrs O'Connor they are going to leave a regiment behind to protect American and British interests."

"I heard that at Tientsin Club. I heard also that the American Consul has categorically denied it. Why do you think those families are leaving, the Travers-Smiths, the Cooks, the Marshalls?"

"They are going on home leave, that's all. Pierre Travers-Smith told me he has every intention of returning in May to renovate his Peitaiho bungalow. Hongkong & Shanghai Bank is open for business. Also Chartered Bank. Tientsin Grammar School is enrolling students for the spring term. Everything will be back to normal, just you wait and see."

"Joe Grandon thinks the Chinese will have us out by the end of 1947 at the latest."

"Stuff and nonsense. Joe Grandon doesn't know what he's talking about. Someone should advise him that the British army has re-occupied Hong Kong, that they'll soon be sending a battalion up here as they've always done. Ilse

Von Brunow told me the Russians are in Port Arthur and Dairen. It's just like old times. I'm going to start looking for linen and furniture. Jim, Pat, Brian, and Jocelyn have all, by the grace of God, survived the war. I'm going to get the home readied for their return."

"Are you so sure they want to come back?"

"Of course they want to come back. They belong here. You belong here."

"Don't you think they've had enough of war? Why would they want to get mixed up in China's war?"

"Chiang Kai Shek and Mao Tse Tung will make peace just as Wu Pei Fu and Chang Tso Lin used to do every Chinese New Year."

"Chiang and Mao are no warlords. Whoever wins will kick us out."

"Never on your life!"

"I won't stay. I'm going."

"Go then. You always were a loner, a wanderer. The sooner you get that silly roving bug out of your system the better. You'll be back. I know you will. I'll keep your room ready for you."

I rode Karl's bike to the consulate. The pink-cheeked man at the counter, probably fresh out of Hong Kong, listened to my request, scanned my passport, picked up the phone, spoke a few words, then wrote out a travel warrant. And as he did so, he mumbled, disinterestedly: "There's an American LST leaving from the Bund tomorrow morning at seven sharp. It'll take you to *HMS Alacrity* anchored at Taku. The *Alacrity* is on its way to Shanghai. You can get a berth to the UK from there."

Tomorrow! At seven sharp! The full impact of what I was doing hit me square between the eyes. I never dreamt that one quick phone call could decide something so momentous, so final. Lightheadedly, I forced out the words:

"And where on the Bund will I find the LST?"

"Behind the Astor House Hotel."

I am up at first light. At the front door Tai-tai shows no emotion. "See you in Peitaiho next summer," are her parting words. No rickshaw in sight, I pick up my battered suitcase and start off on foot. The raw Mongolian wind cuts through me like a knife. I spy an unoccupied rickshaw at the curb bordering Small Park, but no sign of the

coolie. Treading my way past D'Arc's Hotel, I take a fond last look at the mellowed brick façade, the pride and joy of my grandparents back at the turn of the century. Along Meadows Road the wind whips up half a gale. I sink my neck into my overcoat collar. And I stay hunched like a tortoise even as I pay my respects to Gordon Hall, to Victoria Park, to the Cenotaph. Three blasts from a ship's horn, and I break into a run. No need to panic; the dark-gray LST is as frozen in place as the Astor House itself. My teeth are chattering, my ears and cheeks blue by the time I mount the gangplank and show my papers. An officer directs me to a mess at the stern where a dozen passengers sit huddled on benches. A fuzzy-faced sailor hands me a doughnut and a steaming mug of coffee. Is there no end to American generosity?

A metallic voice from a crackling loudspeaker, then three blasts from a horn, and the vessel casts off, cutting through the surface ice along the river's edge. Reaching the center channel, she swings her bow and heads downstream for Taku. In no time the brick and concrete skyline gives way to desolate mud flats. I am only vaguely aware of the throbbing engines, the officers' commands, the crew's responses, the chitter-chatter of fellow passengers. My mind is on Tai-tai, Tony, Betty, Kui Hsiang, Yi-jie, Aliosha, Murat, Achmet. One consolation, I have surmounted what I dread most – the onrush of childish tears.

"We're at Taku," someone says. I go outside to look. Nothing much has changed, the same scattering of mud huts, the same derelict wharf; and seawards, the same collection of junks, lighters, tugs, tramps.

"There's one of the old forts." A white-haired passenger indicates an earthen mound shaped like an upturned

247

basin. "In early days we used to romp freely over those slopes. Later we were chased off by silly Chinese, shouting 'Foreign Devils out, Foreign Devils out'."

I gaze at the primitive earthworks. I marvel at the tenacity of the medieval Manchu warriors who confounded the pride of the Royal Navy, who repulsed Lord Elgin's Anglo-French storm-troopers, and who, when taken from behind, fought to the last man on that fateful day in history eighty-eight years back when the ancient Ming city of Tientsin fell to the foreign invader.

The LST is hardly out of the silted river mouth when she runs head-on into the fresh chop of the Po Hai Gulf. The wind whistles a mournful dirge. Spray stings my face. "Hold tight," a sailor calls out. I grab onto the rail with both hands. Smack! Bang! Wallop! We are tossed about like a matchbox in a torrent. Surely we can't take much more. Surely the Yankee skipper will turn back into the estuary. But nothing of the kind. He braves it out, and the farther we head into the gulf the angrier the sea, some waves shooting us up so high the propellers clatter in empty air before we come crashing down in a gut-wrenching free fall. "Whoop Whoop Whoop" goes a ship's siren. It's the *Alacrity*, alongside, doing the *danse macabre*, leaping and plunging hopelessly out of sync with the LST. Hoarse shouts and flashing lights. Lines coil through the air. In the split second that the two hulls cross, a passenger is hurled from American to English hands. When my turn comes, a brute of an English tar takes one look at my GI field jacket and hollers: "Blimey, a bloody Yank, toss the bugger back!" I claw frantically at his duffel coat. I cry out: "British! I'm British!" His steel-blue eyes penetrate mine. Then he barks: "Orl right, tyke the blighter below!"

A nauseating amalgam of diesel fumes, engine grease, and wet paint turns my stomach. Sickly green-tinged light plays on the constant comings and goings of crew members worming their way through the clutter of mess tables, lockers, hammocks, stanchions. I am cramped in a tiny space with four Jack Tars sipping lip-scalding unsweetened tea. The pitching and yawing, the sudden weightlessness followed by irresistible pulls of gravity send alarming spasms of queasiness through me. My mouth fills with watery saliva. The tars' eyes are on me, waiting for my comedy act – the helpless convulsing and spewing up of my breakfast. I purposely let the enamel mug scald the tips of my fingers. I take enormous breaths. I grit my teeth. The sternest of the four keeps his eyes peeled on me while he addresses a messmate: " 'ookey, as you was syeing, them putrid bodies you found in the 'old, was they six dyes or seven dyes dead? Didn't you sye the stench myde the old man puke over the side? . . ."

I do the sailors out of their fun. "When do we get some grub?" I ask.

"You've bin a matelot before," the one called 'ookey snorts huffily.

I shrug my shoulders. "When do we weigh anchor?"

"We've already done so. We're moving. Can't you feel the motion?"

"I think I'll go up and take one last look."

"Careful of your step, me old China."

I grab onto a rail on the sheltered side of the deck. A signal light is blinking in the darkness. A sailor on watch turns to me. "It's a Yank wishing us a happy new year and best of luck for 1946."

My eyes sweep towards the land, my land, my motherland, my *zu guo*, as the Chinese say. One by one the orangey lights on the shoreline fade into the black void. I think I see a glimmer, faint and solitary. I strain my eyes to hold it. But it too is gone. The dark and brooding night has consumed it, just as it has consumed some vital essence deep down in the innermost part of me.

POSTSCRIPT

October 1994

A year after *HMS Alacrity* bore me away from Taku Bar, I was with the family (except for Doong Ji, still on active service in India) in a photographer's shop in Brighton, England, having our picture taken. It was the last occasion we were all together before going our separate ways. This is that picture.

Tai-tai, seated on the right, is giving only the pretense of a smile. Easy to imagine what is going through her mind. She is bound and determined to return "home" to China – with us in tow. Alas, for her, that was never to be. She spent her remaining years in England, all thirty-six of them, lamenting her exile from her beloved Tientsin.

Immediately behind Tai-tai stands Patrick, a Squadron Leader in the RAF. As a radar specialist he was among the lucky few to be evacuated from Singapore before its fall. It was his only close call of the war. Afterwards, he lived variously in Malaya, the Bahamas, the US, and Canada. It was not until 1976 that the luck of the Irish failed him. Soon after arriving in Edmonton, Alberta, where he had decided to settle, he was felled by lung cancer.

Next to Pat is Brian. When war broke out he interrupted his studies at London University to serve with the Royal Irish Fusiliers. He saw action in the North African campaign. He was wounded in Sicily. After Germany's surrender he adopted England as his mother country. He makes his home in London.

Jocelyn stands at the center as well he should, for it was he who threw open his home to Tai-tai on her arrival from China, just as it was he who who organized the family gathering and photo session in Brighton. Having signed on in the Royal Navy as a boy in 1936, he was an old salt by the time war broke out. He saw action in every theater, mostly in cruisers. He was aboard *HMS Swiftsure*, the first RN vessel to enter Hong Kong at the time of Japan's capitulation. Granted compassionate leave in February 1946, he made his way from Sydney to Tientsin to convince Tai-tai she must quit China. After the war, like Brian, he chose to settle in England, first in London, then in Ross-on-Wye. Now thirty-five years later he has moved to Spain, which he first saw close-hand while serving in *HMS Shropshire* during the Spanish Civil War.

Agnes is seated in front of Jocelyn. Though half-blind, she is flashing the brightest smile of all. Why not? She is surrounded by her grandchildren, all of whom have come through fire and brimstone, privation and hunger, just as she herself had done forty-seven years back during the Boxer siege of the Peking legations.

On the left is Betty, smiling the confident smile of someone whose mind is firmly set on a career. She is a dancer. She is going on the stage. She sees herself rising above the mini-stardom she enjoyed in Tientsin's Russian ballet. And she achieves her goal with flying colors. Now retired in Blackpool, she can look back with pride on her tours of the Continent, Japan, Australia, the Middle East, but more especially, on her appearance before Queen Elizabeth and the Duke of Edinburgh in the Royal Command Performance of 1960, when, as the exotic dancer *Zari*, she shared equal billing with Liberace, Nat King Cole, Sammy Davis Jr, Vera Lynn.

Tony is directly behind Betty. After the rigors of Weihsien, the rigors of austerity Britain were inducement enough for him to emigrate. Though the five years "Down Under" were good to him, he headed back (with a wife and son) to the land of his fathers. His present address is Leamington Spa, Warwickshire.

I am the one between Tony and Jocelyn with the vague half-smile revealing my restlessness. How right Tai-tai's determination that I am a born wanderer. In the years ahead I will be pulling up stakes in three continents before planting them finally on the treed slopes of Vancouver BC. I think I can safely say "finally" because that's where Deborah, my wife of forty years, and I have brought up our two daughters and two sons. But is Tientsin really out of my system? I took Deborah there in 1984. I showed her our home on 20 Edinburgh Road and the one on 35 Sydney Road. I showed her the Min Yuan, Tientsin Grammar School (I couldn't find St Louis College), D'Arc's Hotel, Astor House, Victoria Park, but alas, not that grand old citadel, the Gordon Hall; it crashed in ruins during the disastrous earthquake of 1976. But the *tingzi* still stands, the old *tingzi*. No kids playing kick-the-can mind you, just an old geezer seated on a balustrade, living out his memories. I was tempted, but didn't have the gumption to ask in my rusty Mandarin if he'd ever been pestered by little Foreign Devils shouting Tiger! Tiger!

June 1984, by now an "old" Foreign Devil, Desmond poses with Deborah in the indestructible tingzi in Victoria Park (renamed the Peoples' Park).

INDEX

(Omitted from the following index are the
invented names for those who have
become uncertain of lost in memory.)

SOURCES OF ILLUSTRATIONS

Grateful appreciation is extended to the following who so generously made available their photos and drawings:

Ron Davie, Vancouver BC, 175, 183

Brother "Kenny" Doheny, Hong Kong, 14

Angela (Splingaerd-Cox) Elliott, Vancouver BC, 100

Rolfie Gartner, Anstead QLD, 95

Samuel Harvey, Hong Kong, 179

Douglas Haywood LVO MA, Abbots Bromley Staffs, 44

Frederick Istl, Toronto ON, 92

Keystone Press Agency Inc/Time-Life, New York NY, 32

The late Alistair William Laidlaw, 69

Alex Liu, Exmouth Western Australia, 15

Lucy (Attree) Lucker, El Paso TX, 3, 81, 147, 227

Jiim "Speed" Murray, Ross-on-Wye Hereford, 216

George Nathing, Eleebana NSW, 15

Denis O'Shea, Richmond BC, 173

John Phipps, New Westminster BC, 244

Christina (Veresmith) Pirozek, London, England, 121, 254

The late Boris Romanovsky, 127

John Seddon, West Vancouver BC, 176, 180, 182

Alan Taylor, West Vancouver BC, 125, 230, 247

Willie Ward, Seattle WA, 16, 64

Jean Weight, Calgary AB, 185, 187

Charlie Wolter, Glide OR, 118,119

Commissioned by the author for this book or given him during internment:

Jeremy Power, North Vancouver BC, 8, 20, 23, 30,66, 67, 111, 112, 113, 141, 166, 204, 205

Sun Shu Jun, Vancouver BC, i, 82, 83, 148

James Wang, West Vancouver BC, vi, 31, 163, 201, 237, 242

Isaac Abraham in Lunghua Camp, 189

Donald Cance in Lunghua Camp, 190, 191, 194

Roy Tchou in Weihsien Camp, 209, 213, 219,222, 225, 226

From the author's private collection :

viii,4, 5, 6, 10, 11, 16, 18, 19, 26, 29, 33, 34, 38, 42, 43, 46, 49, 54, 56, 59,60, 63, 71,72, 73, 74, 77, 84, 85, 86, 87, 88, 93, 96, 103, 106, 109,114, 117, 122, 128, 129, 131,135, 136,138, 139, 150,152, 167,169,170, 194, 198, 233, 238, 241, 250, 252

Other illustrations in general circulation:

From the ancient tablet on the Great Wall at Shanhaikuan, 61

From an ancient Chinese painting, 240

China Times, 12, 40, 47

North China Daily Mail, 25, 27,137, 149

North China Star, 51, 53, 55, 99, 144, 153

School Grammarian, 17, 22, 24

Tientsin Press, 90, 91, 156

Chinese Clipart, Milpitas CA 2, 9, 21

About the author and his books

He was born in Tientsin, Hopei Province, during the hour of the
Rat on the eve of Lunar New Year 4620 (1923AD), or, to be more
precise, as the clock was striking midnight, ushering out the
Year of the Dog and heralding the Boar. Most propitious being
half-canine half-swine, according to one oracle. Not so, countered another.With his Earthly Branches mixed, he might turn
out as a lotus in a crosscurrent, stressed, blooming late, if at all.

And the latter prediction was close. As a "late-bloomer"he didn't
launch into his career in computers until he was thirty. He didn't
start writing until after his retirement. It was not until 1990 that
he published his first book – the whimsical novel *Merry-Go-
Round* for which he used the pseudonym Robin Maxwell. But he
reverted to his real name Desmond Power for his personal
account of life in China's treaty ports – *Little Foreign Devil*. His
next book will be *Flambard's Canadian Capers*, which is about
the misadventures of a computer consultant harassed by the
foibles, vanities, and affectations of the captains of industry. And
ready in final draft are two works: *Rogue Manchu - Rogue Irish,*
a novel whose underlying theme is the challenge of inter-racial
marriage, and *The Courtyard of the Happy Way* trilogy, set in the
war-torn Siberia of the 1920s, the foreign enclaves of Shanghai
and Tientsin, and the London/Hong Kong base of one of the
world's greatest banking empires.